AF324214

Texas Spirit

by Anne Hargrove

Anne Hargrove

front page:
Kenny Spence, Sam Horton, Pancho Schmidt, Robert Spence, and
George Driskill prepare for a ride.

Stillpoint-by-the Sea Books
P.O. Box 90016
San Antonio, Texas 78209

Copyright (c) 2005 by Anne Hargrove

All rights reserved. No portion of this book may be used or repro-
duced in any manner without written permission of the author,
except in the case of brief quotations embodied in critical articles
and reviews. For permission, write Stillpoint-by-the-Sea Books,
P.O. Box 90016, San Antonio, Texas 78209

ISBN 1-890498-18-1

Artwork and layout by Ann Pressly

Printed in the United States of America

For additional copies:
Stillpoint-by-the Sea Books
P.O. Box 90016
San Antonio, Texas 78209

Introduction

Taylor and Murray Burns.Utopia, 1949

During the course of our telephone conversations these days brother Taylor usually remarks, "Be glad you lived when you did." Lately I have given much consideration to that piece of wisdom, and I am not only glad I lived when I did but also where I did and within the family God gave us. Growing up in the Texas Hill country during the forties and fifties is a blessing only a few of us have received.

I know there are many of you who love it as much as I do, and cherish the memories we made there while becoming adults. In Utopia in the fifties we were free, unencumbered by worldly cares as we swam in the Sabinal; I rode my mare to the arena daily to practice the barrels; Murray and Taylor fished in the streams and hunted whatever was in season. We learned to love nature, how to hunt, ride, fish, have fun, make friends, work, and worship God.

Our parents raised us with a light hand, and we were given free rein to use our common sense as to most of our activities. Our Mother never cried, "Watch out for snakes," instead she would call "Have a nice time."

Later I married Mac Woodley and moved to the Woodley Ranch at Yucca Switch, Texas west of Sabinal. On a ranch something different and unexpected happens almost daily, so you need to have an open mind, a first aid kit, be able to shift gears in 10 seconds, and keep a shotgun loaded. Also being a seamstress, cook, bookkeeper, cleaning lady, gardener, plumber, chauffer, caretaker to the help, and Mother to orphan animals comes in handy at times. A quality one needs to cultivate is not to panic.

Annalee wrote a column of Hill Country Housewife discussing the coming and goings of Canyonites for forty years. After our Dad became ill, I would fill in for her at times, later when she retired I began to pen a column for the Uvalde Leader News concerning the happenings in our part of Texas.

Circumstances and marriage to Joe Hargrove have continued to provide me with much ranch life material, and we now reside at Rancho de Paloma outside of Crystal City, Texas.

Several friends have asked if I was going to compile my columns into a book, and when I realized how quickly the years are slipping by, it seemed time to get the project off hold. I thank the Uvalde Leader news for permission to reprint the columns. And a special thanks to my talented friend, Judy Cavendar for her calligraphy contribution, Texas Spirit.

Contents

2001

2002

2005

What I Love About Texas

Great Grandmother Mary Susan Simons Fisher

Listening to "Country Classics" the other afternoon, the Tom T. Hall song, "I love, coffee in a cup, little yellow ducks, and I love you, too." set me to thinking, so sat down to list a few reasons why I love Texas. Then a friend e-mailed me a message discussing all the great advantages of living in Texas, which prompted continuation of my list. Am sure you can jot down your own, and if you do, send me a copy.

So here goes: Utopia, the Sabinal river at Fisher Camp, Bob Willis music, the Utopia Rodeo, the Lost Maples, Willie Nelson's music, especially when his sister Bobbie is accompanying him on the piano, the Uvalde County Junior Livestock Show, the Blanco River, Yucca Switch, Texas, Concan, Garner Park (I may request my ashes be scattered over the dance floor, just kidding), Del Rio, the Utopia store, Mason, Jones Cemetery, Utopia Arts & Crafts Show, the drive from Utopia to Bandera, the Bownds-Burns baseball field, Rio Frio (where Henry & Annalee taught school together and fell in love), Sabinal Methodist, St. Patrick's Catholic Church, the Alamo, green water hole at Montell, Sabinal Memorial Library, George Strait's music, cattle roundups, dove season, a norther blowing in after a soaking 3 inch rain, J. Frank Dobie stories, George Bush, Alpine, Sul Ross University, La Fogata Restaurant, South Texas brush country, Audie Murphy, Fredericksburg, the ocean front at Corpus Christi, Canadian geese in the winter cornfields, brush country bucks, the high bridge over the Pecos River, supper around a campfire with friends after a successful day's hunt, fields of bluebonnets, live oak trees, the Nueces River, cedar elms, the State Fair, Fort Worth, Cowtown (once we had a bumper sticker stating: Foat Wurth, I Luv Yew), baby Angora goats, fawns, the San Antonio Riverwalk, Laredo, Marathon, Marfa, the Fort Worth stockyards, Fort Davis, Double D Clothes, lantana in bloom, rib-eye steaks - cooked medium rare, Tyler and its rose garden, First Mondays at Canton, the Carnegie library at Ballinger, Larry McMurtry's bookstores at Archer City, Beefmaster cattle, Quarter horses, winecups, chili rellenos, Medina's Apple Festival, the story of Pecos Bill, Resistol hats and the men that wear 'em, Ray Price's music, Mi Tierra restaurant, the St. Anthony Hotel, Blue Mountain Wine, Wildseed Flower Farm, Border collies, Fort Clark, Patsy Cline's Music, the drive from Vanderpool to Medina, Schreiner's Department Store, Laity Lodge & H-E-B camp, tiger-striped cows, M. D. Anderson Hospital, shopping at D&D Ranch headquarters, the Argyle, San Jose Mission, longhorn cattle, dining in the old hotel in Catarina, the town of Columbus, Round Top, Houston's Jones Hall, the Blanco County Courthouse, the Houston Quilt Show, shopping at Creations in Kerrville (quilters understand), Utopia Methodist, Carrizo Springs library, chili con carne (my recipe), the drive from Utopia through Vanderpool, out on top to the Divide, then on down highway 35 along the Guadalupe to Ingram and Kerrville, shopping at the Peach Tree in Fredericksburg, Castroville, Crystal City Methodist, the Knippa Coop, yuccas blooming in the spring, Davy Crockett, Alamo Village, Burns-Bownd house, Dale Evans, mariachi music, the town of Goliad, La Bahia mission, the Welder Wildlife preserve, the King Ranch, retama in bloom, Spanish kid goats, the saga of the Alamo, children in boots and wranglers, Knippa Trading Company, the winery at Del Rio, George W Bush, the Gage Hotel, the book and movie "Giant," Marvin Hunter's museum, the Fisher Family reunion, Lucchese boots, Utopia Memorial Library, Dan's Meat Market at Castroville, Barbeque at the City Meat Market, Luling, the Stagecoach Inn, any farmer's market, cantaloupes from Pecos, hunting season in the brush country, barbequed cabrito, fishing at Falcon lake, white wing hunting in the Rio Grande Valley, eating migas in Zapata, chili pequins, D'Hanis, my kin folks, the Landmark Inn, Laura Bush, the Texas Food & Wine Festi-

Jamie Burns and show heifer, Fort Bend County

val, La Paloma Ranch, Knippa Emmanuel Lutheran Church, Alto Frio, the Majestic theater, Nolan Ryan, the State Capitol, the National Wildflower Center, floatin' on the Frio, bobwhites, Sam Houston, Bob Morehouse's photographs of the Pitchfork Ranch, the Amon Carter Museum, Montell Episcopal Church, West Texas Feedlots, Tilden, Cowboy Smith from Abilene, Ben's Western Wear, the Y.O. Ranch and Hotel, Watt Matthews, Albany, red and blue heelers, Hattie Stillwell, turkey gobblers struttin' in the spring, Colonel William Barrett Travis, Sabinal Methodist, Daughters of the Republic of Texas, Vega's in Laredo, children at youth rodeos, pinto beans, Comfort, Willie Shoemaker, Crystal City Library, the windswept oak trees at Rockport, King's Inn restaurant, the drive from Marathon to Alpine onto Fort Davis to Marfa, parties catered by Don Strange and Rosemary, Aggieland, the Stagecoach Inn, mountain laurel in bloom, Ima Hogg's home, La Loma Ranch, Mission San Jose, gray horses, Jim Bob Altizer, Phil Lyons, Fred Whitfield, baby lambs playing in the spring, watermelons, rattlesnakes, Crider's rodeo and dance pavilion, armadillos, hawks circling high on a fresh norther, white cotton fields, fire rings, Retama Park, golden waving fields of wheat in the Panhandle, buffel grass, Julio's chips, cactus wrens, Night in Old San Antonio, Sea World, La Moca Ranch, cardinals, King Ranch chicken, John Connelly, shopping at Neiman-Marcus in downtown Dallas, Gonzales, Ted and Frances Harper, new Uvalde Memorial Library, pico de gallo, vermillion flycatchers, cattle grazing on green oat fields, the Southwest Craft Center, whitetailed deer, fried shrimp, country bands with a fiddle player, Indian paintbrush, our family, Henry & Annalee, the legacy of our great-great grandfather, O.A. Fisher who came to Texas in 1840 as a Methodist circuit rider, and his wife, Rebecca, whose portrait hangs in the Capitol, our great grandfather Orceneth Fisher who came to the Sabinal canyon as a Methodist circuit rider, his wife, Mary Susan Simons, who continued to raise her 11 children after their father's untimely death, my husbands, Mac Woodley and Joe Hargrove, both Texas cattlemen, and the can do spirit of the Texas people.

2001

Inevitable Change

Rancho De La Loma, 1988

The one force in our lives always in motion is change. We all struggle to resist its power, cry over its circumstances, and clench our fists against its sway which sweeps us along in its tides.

Over the past few years, change has reached out and grasped our family through illnesses, deaths, taxes, and business transactions. In real life there are no true insurance policies. At times one felt as if we were riding a small raft down a raging, out-of-control river, clinging on for dear life.

Learned this life's lesson during those years, NEVER SAY NEVER.

Had always stated, "Will never sell this house we built on the ranch."

But two years living solo behind a locked gate taught me the true meaning of loneliness. Plus how little one person can maintain, where there had been three or four to keep the place in order.

So when opportunity knocked, the decision was made, and I began to pack my books. Never did I realize there were so many, plus years of periodicals to boot.

At first just set aside a few to pass on to the Utopia library, soon a few became hundreds and at the end even 23 cooking books went the Utopia route.

My right hand advisor and friend, Beth Pringle, guided me on the proper principles of packing; collect as many boxes as possible, choose your most valued possessions first, wrap them in newspaper, mark boxes as to contents. All this procedure worked well for two weeks, then it was abandoned for grab and snatch.

It had been 30 years since we'd moved across Hwy. 90, from Yucca Switch, Texas, to La Loma. We had the new home, but precious few possessions to fill it, so one or two horse trailer loads were sufficient. I can still see Nacho and Jose loading my pots of petunias for the journey.

So how did we accumulate all these thousands of things we needed to move now? And how would we ever accomplish the task?

Every night a small (large?) cloud floated over my head proclaiming, "This is NOT possible."

But friend Caroline, veteran of many military moves, assured me it WAS possible.

Decided to begin by packing the dishes, gave the blue Staffordshire plates to Caroline (lover of blue), hung onto the Talavera ones from Madeline's in Piedras, and sent the flowered ones to Sis in Frisco. Still many, many dishes seemed to hop and jump from every nook and cranny.

And the new abode needed painting and carpet change, so packing was slowed considerably by many trips back and forth to Sabinal.

First load Will, Cuco, and Ben placed in the horse trailer, same one as 30 years ago. Would the Spanish cabinet, which had stood in Jane Mac's living room for years, fit into its appointed place?

But where would the huge china cabinet (constructed by Enrique of Laredo) go? Dallas and the Jamie Woodley home provided the answer.

What about the piano, which Annalee played for family gatherings, and the queen's chair which Allie Burns Noon had named? Again, Dallas, and the Noon residence provided a proper place.

Literally thousands of paid (hopefully) bills and old bank statements stared me in the eye. These were the hardest to deal with, for here was paper evidence of the daily fabric of our lives, which we struggled to pay and to provide for employees and family. The dumpster was filled to over flowing with 'em.

What does one do with 43 "Gimme" caps and 20 jackets with HI-PRO embroidered on the front? Being a child of Depression parents, I was taught never to part with items that might be used someday. But as time and the move progressed it became easier to let go.

We progressed from the horse trailer to a covered truck with a lift - in went the brown sofa, Mac's easy chair, Biggie Wentworth's pie safe.

It became necessary to deposit one truckload in Utopia as there was no room to house Burns' wicker sofa, ordered from Sears in bygone days. Couldn't part with that piece of our lives.

One accident slowed activity when Cuco caught his thumb in the tommy lift. Paula Gilleland and PA Ben Dure graciously aided us through the crisis at the Sabinal Clinic.

Oscar Contreras and crew painted, nailed and hammered fast and furiously at the new abode. Cuco, Will, and Ben constructed a sturdy yard fence.

At night I pondered, "How will Paloma (Mac's German wire-haired pointer) ever adjust to town life?"

Boxes began to be loaded in the truck – how to dispose of 17 sacks of sculpting clay? Where to store the drafting table Murray had presented Mac?

Could the brown sofa be maneuvered through the new front door? Keep or toss 10 baskets of interesting rocks collected on the ranch? Do the birdhouses go or stay? STAY as there were birds in them that could not be displaced.

I went out of the flower pot business when many disintegrated as we lifted them. Be sure to hang on to Harold Reily's World War II sword. Should my purple A&I Lantana dress go to hospice?

Both boys arrived to help close out paper work and assist with last minute details. One evening we sat outdoors and recalled a few of the many events which had taken place on the hill.

Next we carefully placed the last pieces of Mac's sculpture in TM's Tahoe and drove away. Kept in mind Mary Tom Harper Hefte's advice, "Be grateful to God for what lies behind; be grateful to Him for what lies ahead."

Discover the Alluring Comfort

Several months ago I found myself in the Hill Country, with time on my hands. "Why not explore Comfort?" I questioned.

It was within easy driving distance and I was interested to know if Jamie Maverick still maintained a shop there for her whimsical and colorful wood carvings.

Soon I was turning off the Interstate, slowly finding my way to Comfort's main street. My last visit there had been years ago, perhaps when our son T.M. III stood by young George Driskill as he took Karen for his sweet bride.

Main Street spoke a lovely, easy-going, bygone melody to my mind; only a few cars, no hustle, no fast food establishments, no noise. Only Peter Ingenhuett's Mercantile store, turn of the century frame houses, small shops, pecan trees, and flower beds behind iron fences comprised the town center. I was wandering along the

The Wentworth sisters - Mariella Maulden, Lola Arnim, Annalee Burns, Georgie Smith, Lucille Matthews

sidewalk when a voice welled up inside and told me, "Hey, this feels like the 1950s, the Hill Country, neighbors, family, friends, home."

Sure enough, my intuitions were correct when I ambled into the Antiques Mall, not truly shopping, but re-living the past as I gazed at Franciscan apple pottery (our best dishes, growing up); and cross-stitched table cloths while Guy Lombardo's band smoothly crooned, "Blue Moon, you saw me crying alone, without a dream in my heart." One of Annalee's favorites.

There I found Aunt Georgie's bright colored aluminum tumblers–red, yellow, purple, bright blue, plus the pitcher to match. From these glasses the Wentworth clan, sisters, husbands, children, had drunk thousands of gallons of sugary iced tea to wash down 7-UP pound cake. As we visited upon the cool, green carpet grass, stories of ancestors and neighbors were related to the Sabinal group from the Utopia sisters. Oh, just to be able to relive one of those summer afternoons with all of those beloved aunts and uncles present.

In a group of china serving pieces sat a Belleek pitcher, similar to the one I transported back to Auntie Mauldin from Shannon, Ireland, after my first journey across the Atlantic. She always displayed it in a prominent place, but never used it for coffee cream.

These women who came through the Depression saved their best dishes, never using them often. Besides Auntie knew without a doubt she was never going to travel to Ireland, so how could she ever replace the pitcher if it happened to get broken?

Deep into the aisles I spotted a cross-stitched sampler, stating, "A Friend Loves at All Times." Was it the exact sentiment as the one which hung on Aunt Lucille's wall? The design was similar, but time had bluffed my memory as to the verse. Naturally, Lucille had stitched it herself, probably during long, lonely nights while Jack sailed the high seas during World War II. "Perilous times," as Lola would remark.

Perched atop a wire frame hat stand was an elegant, pheasant feathered Lilly Daché number such as Bess Burns would don for Hartford Insurance agency meetings. With the outfit she wore her green platform pumps. While Bess was at the office, Burns would look the other way as I played "Dress Up" in the pumps.

So much to remember, so many items speaking loudly of the manner in which we lived our lives in Utopia and Sabinal, and what we wore on our occasional forays out to Uvalde, Kerrville, San Antonio, and Corpus.

Made a mental note to question Faye Kelly concerning the history of the Ingenhuett Mercantile, built in 1867. The grocery hardware establishment still remains in family ownership, and took me back to the times when we charged at Red and White and Boyce and Davenport. No, we three children did not charge; Henry saw to that.

My first remembrances of Faye Ingenhuett were seeing her barrel-race during the Utopia 1950s rodeos.

Made myself a promise to return and reside at the Comfort Common, a Bed and Breakfast establishment. The building was designed by Alfred Giles, and built in the 1880 for Peter Ingenhuett as a hotel. One could stroll through the gift shop, and out upon a wide verandah and courtyard. The toughest decision would be choosing between the Algelt, Karger, or Meyer (each room is named) accommodations.

Purchased a small sign in the Commons Gift Shop. It states "Because Nice Matters," and will hang in our Bownds house, Utopia. Reason being, June Fisher, Annalee, Gladys Jones, Lucille, Thelma Porter, Auntie Mauldin, Janie Tubbs, Grace Fisher, and Biggie Wentworth are but a few of the Utopia women who taught me nice does matter.

Driving home, I felt warmed by Comfort's serenity and other decade charm. How rare are these places in the year 2000. But fear seized my heart as to how long this unique town would withstand the onslaught of over-development and the rapid growth which is enveloping the Hill Country. Will they be able to juggle the dilemma of growth without noise, ugliness, and pollution? Who can say? Who will referee?

But if you seek a day or two's respite in which to meditate upon the years of your childhood, choose Comfort. You'll find much there to jog your memory.

Old Windmills

Perhaps it was sheer envy over Sophie Falkenburg's windmill, given to her by son Dean (Mother's Day?), which prompted my decision. Or could it have been memories of the old, red wooden mill and water tank which stood behind our home in Utopia?

Maybe, both of these images mixed in my mind, along with recalling the many, many times we'd be driving through the Hiler ranch, stop, check the windmills, and Mac would remark, "Don't let me forget to call Joe, and tell him the rod is broken at number 12." Joe being our faithful windmill man, Joe Villasana. Just to prove my memory is sharp our mill man before Joe was Sam Heine. Do any of you remember Sam?

Anyway, driving by Uvalco, it occurred to me that a windmill would be the perfect gift for Annalee and our Utopia home. Knowing Murray was in residence at Burns-Bownds house, he and son-in-law Kevin could transport the contraption home. Then Mother and those at "Home" would be able to discern the direction of the prevailing winds, always an issue of importance to our Dad and our Grandmother Burns. The real windmill had been removed before our move to Bownds house, so it would feel right to have a semblance of one on the place.

Shuffling old papers I came upon a check which Edna Burns wrote on September 7, 1940, to P. M. Boyce for the sum of $14.98. She signed it Mrs. B. T. Burns and in the corner noted for "work on mill."

Friends tell me how much they loved hearing the steady throb and clang of a windmill near the house or in the pens during their childhood. There is something most comforting about these machines which brought the lifeline of water to the farms and ranches of Texas.

For the past 30 years, I have gazed out of my kitchen windows upon an Aeromoter as it pumped water into the steel tanks below our house. One of the reasons I love the things is because of the life-giving liquid they provide to all creatures during the dry, dry, times in our country. During the terrible summer of 2000, roadrunners, turkey, coyotes, rabbits, dove, snakes, deer, all manner of wildlife survived due to water pumped by mills.

Searching for some names of the different types of mills, a friend provided information found on the Internet. At Big Country, located in Fairbury, Neb., and also at Hesperia, Calif., you would be able to find new, used, vintage, or obsolete parts for the following makes of windmills: Dempster (we had many of this brand), Aeromoter (and also this one), Monitor, Challenge, Flint-Walling, Eclipse, Diamond, Parish-Kenwood, or Western.

Saw two huge Eclipse mills at the Hill Country Hyatt, which uses windmills as their logo. Varying sizes and types of mills are located in and around the hotel as decorations and focal points. The Texas countryside is quickly moving away from the need of these machines which have dotted the landscape for over a century.

Having windmills on my mind, there was one prominent in the background, when John Grady Cole returned to a "shortgrass" ranch near San Angelo after his sojourn south of the Rio Grande. John Grady is the prime character in the movie, "All The Pretty Horses." Having read Cormac McCarthy's novel relating the adventures of two West Texas boys in Mexico, I was anxious to see if the movie held true to the novel. Indeed, it did, and those of us from the Southwest can easily relate to the apt portrayal of our landscape, people, the log pens, the mindset, during the early 1900s. McCarthy had to have lived a period of time in West Texas to be able to write such accurate descriptions of life along the Texas-Mexican border.

How very kind and generous of Mary and Francie Doughty to endow the new West Main Library Fund with such a grand donation. But Mary has always been a lady with a generosity of spirit. Whenever you would be visiting with Ross Doughty, he would greatly enjoy relating stories of his boyhood youth in Uvalde. Uvalde was the home of Ross' heart. Our Dad and Ross attended Schreiner Institute together, along with Jack Woodley. Also, Ross Jr. and I attended Texas A&I (now A&M) University in Kingsville, at the same time. Young Ross loved to dance. Gracias, and God Bless to both Mary and Francie.

Sad to learn of the loss of Smitty Schmidt to our Sabinal community. My memories of this kind, friendly man, are seeing him ride down Center Street with his Boston Terrier close to the wheel. Mable and her family have lost two members in a very short time span to the most dreaded of diseases– deepest sympathy to all of them.

The Knippa community lost George Knippa, a long-time area farmer. George was active in the community and in his church. His daughters were dear, close friends to our sister-in-law, the late, Mary Jo Burns, and the ties of youth are not forgotten. Our condolences, and best to the Knippa family.

Hill Country Drive

Recently my naturalist friend, Quentin, and I were able to find time for a visit after all the busyness and bustle of the holidays. A student of native plants, Quentin loves to travel the back roads of Texas, searching out the very few areas relatively untouched by progress, if one cares to call it that.

With Forty-Two, Quentin's Fox Terrier keeping us company, we headed for Hwy. 83 and the Frio River canyons. First stop was the Real County Library to inspect the handsome building and attractive native planting there. Several years ago (two perhaps?), Annalee and I attended the official dedication of the library and listened to Elmer Kelton's fitting address.

When I reintroduced myself to Elmer, he gave me an exact account of the article he had written for the Livestock Weekly when Mac sold some steers for the grand price of 60 cents. Uncle Cecil Arnim's comment on the story, "Well, Mac, you better enjoy prosperity while you can; we'll never live to see any 60 cent cattle again."

Leaving Leakey we took the west prong of the Frio route, which I had not traveled since childhood. Past the Prade Ranch, as we climbed higher, the clouds descended and mingled with the blue-gray hills.

So wonderful to enjoy a stretch of country without litter, billboards, or traffic; just a few goat sheds, some sheep, and the sparkling river to add to the panorama.

The Lone Star and Old Glory were flying as we passed the Leinweber gate. Recalled what an elegant couple Mr. and Mrs. Ernest Leinweber always were at

Jamie, T.M.,III, and T.M. Woodley, Jr. in front of Yucca Feedyard, 1973

Hill Country social functions. Mr. Ernest, without fail, wore a suit, tie and highly polished boots.

Arriving in Rocksprings, we hoped to dine at the restaurant in the hotel, but were out of luck, as they are closed on Sundays, open every other day of the week. After peeking in the tastefully renovated building of the American Angora Goat Breeders Association, which is now an artist's studio, we took a long look at an ancient, large house, awaiting repairs.

Later a brisk walk around the town-square got our circulation going again. The People's State Bank is being given a white rock facelift and the small square stand unmarred by flashing signs or vulgar modern advertising. A perfect example of old-time Texas town planning, the commerce buildings are all neatly laid out around the courthouse.

Heading out Hwy. 674, I saw the sign on the Lowell Hankins ranch. Thought of Mac's story about what a red-letter day in his life it was when he had saved enough to invest in a Hankins Cutting Horse from the Poco Bueno lineage. Am not certain if the famous "King" Quarter Horse stud was owned by Jess or Lowell or perhaps jointly owned between the two. Whichever, the names of King and Hankins are linked together forever in Quarter Horse history.

The drive along the West Nueces is spectacular; the clear, cleanness of the river makes it live up to the name The Land of One Hundred Thousand Springs.

Passing the PH. Coates gate, I wondered if Wynell still lives on the ranch. Have not had an opportunity to visit with her for several years. Whenever I felt fainthearted about going it solo on the ranch, I'd think of Wynell and my Grandmother Burns.

Arriving in Brackettville, Quentin and I decided upon a tour of Fort Clark where she once kept a small condominium. There the restaurants were also closed but we vowed to return and reside at the motel located in "Patton House" on the Fort sometime soon.

Since food was scarce during our travels, HEB was a welcome sight and we purchased grilled lemon pepper chicken and wonderful bread for a proper dinner at La Loma.

Relaxing after our trip, we discussed the possibility of growing Burr Oaks in Edwards County, related to Quentin seeing a magnificent Burr Oak growing on the Cauthorn ranch near Juno. But, we decided it had flourished due to being properly watered and protected.

Quentin promised to root some coral beans for me and hopefully soon we'll head out to the Chisos Mountain Basin on another adventure.

Research Center Aids Farmers and Ranchers

So delighted to read of the award conferred upon the Forage Ryegrass Research Team and presented on January 9, by Dr. Edward A. Hiler, Vice Chancellor and Dean of Agriculture and Life Sciences. The team received The Vice Chancellor's Award for Excellence for a research team, one of the top honors bestowed upon employees of the Texas A&M University System Agriculture Program.

Team members included our comrade and long-time partner in rye grass projects, Dr. Hagen Lippke, associate professor in the animal science department at Uvalde. During the decade of the nineties, Hagan and Mac spent many hours and much study in the analysis of grazing conditions, effects of fertilizer and weight gains in cattle.

We first ventured into the planting of rye grass when we lost a large number of fat steers to bloat on wheat pastures. One fall season we had an exceptionally outstanding set of yellow charbray steers. I persuaded Mac to move them onto the west Albright pasture by our house so we could enjoy seeing them graze nearby. That plan turned into tragedy during a wet, lush March; almost every morning, we would arise to spot one or more (always, the most outstanding individuals) bloated and dead. It was enough to make even Mac want to quit the cattle business and seek a livelihood selling Fuller brushes.

Of his many talents, public speaking was not one about which Mac felt comfortable. He was asked to present the following talk in Tyler, Texas. When I arrived I found him in a tizzy and imbibing in a double amount of Copenhagen. However, he presented the following story of our ventures into rye grass quite nicely.

"I want to thank Dr. Lloyd Nelson for asking me to participate in this program as I am anxious to do what ever possible to show my appreciation to him and everyone in developing these new varieties of rye grass.

"Several years ago I began hearing about growers producing 200 bushels of wheat per acre in England – so we traveled over there several times to find out how they did it. Because I became good friends with a British wheat farmer, the Royal Agricultural Society invited me to participate in a panel similar to this one, of International Wheat Growers. They can't understand how we survive growing just 30 bushels an acre. Just before my time to talk, I said to my friend, 'Oliver, should I tell them a quick, funny story?' He responded, 'Woodley, there's no way you can tell a quick story.'

"Well, I was reading this speech to my wife and guess what she said! "You're reading too fast." I hope you will bear with me as I talk too slow or read too fast. They always say you get what you pay for and you all are not paying me anything!

"Now a short background as to why I personally love rye grass. My Father always planted oats for cattle grazing and we did that for many years. Oats would do well in a wet year, until about January when it got cold, then they'd quit growing. We would face an enormous problem holding cattle until the oats started growing again, about the last of February. Then if our hope of a wet spring did materialize, the rust would take over and ruin the other half of the season. In the seventies, the Mexico wheats and triticale seed became available and I decided to try them. The second year our triticale was beautiful beyond belief. During Christmas week, the temperature dropped to fifteen degrees and killed it – roots and all.

"Next I got interested in planting beardless wheat, which is very cold tolerant, and grew well. But to succeed with it, we also needed to own a rendering plant. The fatter and more beautiful the steers, the quicker they died. Each year with beardless wheat, we experienced a 5 percent death loss of our steers, and paid over 20 dollars a head for bloat guard. I was almost ready to give up on winter grazing and go back to row crops.

Dr. Lev Gayle and Mac Woodley, Woodley Ranch

"Now my story becomes more interesting. Dr. Lev Gayle of the Diagnostic Lab at A&M and I became good friends. We worked together trying to prove a magnesium deficiency was involved in the bloat problem. At about the same time, Dr. Bill Holloway was appointed the Director of the Uvalde A&M Research Center, and together they began to apply their time and talent to the bloat problem, which was widespread in our area.

"I furnished the steers and the irrigated wheat pasture for their experiments. One thing I learned, if you are dealing with Aggies, the more of them you have involved, the better off you are. They will 'GIG' each other to achieve results. I remember not so many years ago, if you weren't real good friends with the oldest Aggies in town, you couldn't even get in to see the county agent.

"After our second year's experiment on beardless wheat, Dr. Lippke said, "I would like to have rye grass instead of wheat on my experimental acres next year. I do not feel we can control the bloat on the wheat and expect an economic return unless we use a large amount of hay."

"For us, feeding hay to 5,000 or 6,000 head of steers is just not feasible. Since Dr. Lippke wanted his 20 acres planted in rye grass, I put the entire circle, 300 acres, in it. It was wonderful, no bloat, good gains, and I was a new man, ready to keep going with winter grazing.

"This past year 1996 we planted 4,000 acres in rye grass. We had some bloat in just one field, and that was when we rotated back on lush grazing; But overall, we had very little bloat and 450 pounds average gain per acre as compared to 150 on oats."

"Now I am looking forward to the plans which Doctors Lippke, Holloway, and Forbes, are formulating for trials fertilizing rye and a stocking rate with hope of producing a 600-pound gain per acre.

"I will be glad to answer any questions later on but right now I am as nervous as a bird dog on point, so I need to get off this stage."

The footnote to Mac's talk came in June of 1999, the spring of his last roundup. The beautiful Braford steers at the Rancho Nuevo tipped the scales at an average of 890 pounds; they had weighed 290, at the time of purchase. On a pasture combination of oats and rye grass, they had gained 600 pounds; a dream come true, due

One of Mac's 900# steers - 1999, the year of his last roundup.

in part to the research and dedication of Doctors, Lippke, Gale, Forbes, Holloway and the staff of A&M Experiment Center.

San Antonio Rodeo

Experienced only negative reaction while staring down from the Frontier club window into the huge, gaping hole being excavated for the new dome arena.

Why do sports facilities always need larger everything? What will become of the dear old Freeman Coliseum? Will they just put a bomb in it one day and it will be gone in a puff of smoke? What about the thousands, perhaps millions, of people who have entered its doors during the past 50 years and the wonderful memories we have? Do we just toss it away like so many other fine edifices in America; do we just dispose of it like the weekly garbage?

Thinking back, I concluded I've attended perhaps 44 or 45 of the 51 years the San Antonio Stock Show and Rodeo has been in existence. Many warm, wonderful experiences of my life took place there.

Perhaps my first trip was with the Utopia FFA and FHA chapters. If so, Mr. Max Amman would have been driving the bus, and the FHA girls would have been escorted by Mrs. Frances Hicks. To be out of Utopia, with the rodeo, carnival, and stock show to explore and experience made for an exciting day in our lives. Some of the students making the trip from Utopia would have been: Mary Ann Tanipke, David Hillis, Sue Lewis, Ray Tampke. Bobby Thompson, Patsy Clayton, and Helen Reavis (those are maiden names, of course).

My junior and senior years were at Sabinal High School and Mr. Medford Keath drove the bus, while his wonderful wife, Doris, escorted the FHA girls. Some of us who attended would have been: Helen Reily, Jenelle Clements, and Mildred Arnim.

Think during my college days I must have missed several years of rodeo time but Mac and I never missed. When the children were young, the first two weeks in February were a high point in their year. The first person we'd encounter upon checking into the Gunter Hotel for the weekend would be Buck Pyle. He'd question Mac, "Woodley, when and where was the last sighting you had on Billy Hill?" Mr. Buck was a fixture at the Gunter during the last years of his interesting life.

Youngsters might be treated to a special "up-close" visit with Rex Allan, Lassie, or Dale Robertson. Julie, T.M., and Jamie always had a bevy of Kinsel, Roos, Wheeler, Light, Hindes, and Kuykendall children to pal about with, and they took full advantage of all the carnival had to offer.

In the Gunter lobby, we'd visit with the tall friendly announcer, Pete Logan from Oregon. He was also in the cattle business and supplemented his ranching by following the rodeo circuit in the winter.

Louise Roos Wheir, Ruby Roos, Charles Roos IV and Charles Roos III (seated) celebrate.

From our seats at the Rodeo we would spot familiar faces: Dorothy and Richard Nunley; Dolph and Janey Briscoe, plus various members of their family; darling Delia Kincaid Light and Cuatro; the blond Woodward sisters; Fayrene and Charley Colvin; different and assorted members of the Bub Mauldin family; and the Jimmy Speers, to name but a few.

Over time the performers which stand out in the in my mind are: Rex Allan; Dale Robertson and his magnificent black, blaze-faced horse; eye and ear catching Reba McEntire, handsome and gentlemanly George Strait, Willie singing "Blue Eye Crying in the Rain," and Tony Bennett who I watched as a guest of Merrill Nunley.

Can't forget the year I took our 3-year-old grandson, Mason, for his first carousel ride. I was holding him on the pony when he decided he wanted no more part of that wooden horse or the entire merry-go-round. That boy was outta' there. Together we slipped, slid, skidded and stumbled until the operator took pity on my dilemma and stopped the whole affair so we could make our exit.

Another year our English farmer friend, Oliver, attended the performances with us. After he finished his order of calf fries at the Frontier Club, Mac asked if they were what he had expected. His reply, "Actually, I found them to be a bit bland."

It is tough to bring up in the think-bank all of the top-notch performers we witnessed over the years: Fred Whitwell winning the calf roping in his white starched shirt; Roy Angermiller heading steers; Jim Shoulders riding bulls and broncs; Larry Mahan doing the same; our friend, Phil Lyons, excelling in many events; Texan Joe Beaver wrapping up a calf in 4.5 seconds; and Fannie Grace and Roy Hindes's grandson, Cuatro, participating in the steer roping.

One of my favorite characters has been everybody's friend, Leon Coffee. This year Leon stated that the only difference between a huge, angry, Brahma-cross bull and his exwife was about 30 pounds.

But to my mind, the all-time outstanding act over the years has been the striking team of matched Clydesdale horses and the Budweiser wagon. They are always an elegant reminder of days gone by.

This year had a short visit with friends Evelyn and Jack Kingsberry of Crystal. Jack promised me his new book would be out soon.

The 2001 opening ceremonies were dedicated to Mary Nan West. Her flaxen Palomino was led around the arena; its saddle blanket lined in yellow roses; a fitting tribute to Mary Nan and all her efforts to make the SA Stock Show and Rodeo an outstanding event.

And so, will the Freeman Coliseum stand or fall? Is this Texas or Russia? Isn't there a Texan in the White House? Will anybody who is actually in the cattle business have the price of the fancy new seats? Let's complain, or the next thing we know steer ropers may be incarcerated by the animal rights people and the only entertainment at the Fairgrounds will be basketball games.

A Magical and Blessed Time

Actually, I had not put any plan into motion for spring break, but then all the stars lined up in their proper positions, and conditions came together to form a frame of time and events which were magical and blessed.

It all began when I boarded Southwest Airlines to Dallas. Arrived at exactly the proper moment to accompany Taylor Brewton (age 3) home from a three-month ordeal in Medical Center Dallas. Taylor Anne's open arms greeted me with enthusiasm, and I caught my first glimpse of her baby sister, Tessa, born Dec. 30.

Chris and Larissa (Taylor's mom and dad) had the two vehicles loaded when the proper medication arrived, we snapped the girls into their car seats and headed north on the tollway. It was Taylor's first glimpse of the outside world since Dec. 12, 2000, and she took note of the green grass and flowering pear trees.

When we turned onto their street, we saw pink ribbons waving from every tree, and in front of the Brewton home balloons danced everywhere. When Larissa lifted Taylor out of her car seat, a roar of applause arose from the huge crowd gathered to welcome the brave little girl home.

Once inside we all set about the pleasure of opening the Christmas gifts, which had been ignored since the holidays, awaiting Taylor's return. Taylor's other sister, Trystin, (age 2) joined us; it brought tears

Luke Woodley, Dorothy Kinsel, and Mason Woodley at the Kinsel Ranch

of joy to our eyes to see the small children dancing around the living room, exclaiming, "Sissy, Sissy, Sissy!" In the past few months, Trystie had only glimpsed her older sister, Taylor, through a hospital window.

After an intense time of cooking, laundry, baby-sitting, and cuddling tiny girls, I grabbed my bags, met grandsons Mason (age 12) and Luke (age 9), and together we jumped on a Southwest plane and headed south.

Next morning shortly after 9 a.m. the three of us (following Mac's admonition to always get an early start on the day's activities) embarked on our adventure at Sea World.

First we inspected the docile, wonderful Clydesdales, and sure enough, being spring, there was a baby colt in residence. We had to restrain ourselves from jumping the fence to hug the baby; the colt's white face and feathers were so appealing.

On to see the alligators sunning themselves and, for the boys, to test the water slide at the Lost Lagoon. Then suddenly it was time to join our "Behind the Scenes Tour."

Our knowledgeable guide introduced us "up close and personal" to eight Shamus (killer whales), all sorts of seals, sea lions, sharks, dolphins, exotic birds, and a Beluga whale mama and calf. Now we had a small glimpse of just how Sea World works.

Time to eat. When you take your grandchildren to this adventure park remember travel light and pack lots of dollars. You're inside and an ordinary hamburger is the price of a choice T-bone.

Our energies renewed, we sat in the splash zone awaiting Shamu's show. And what a show they gave us! Those exceptionally beautiful whales have a personality so appealing; you'd love to give 'em a hug and a kiss.

Poor Luke's ambitions to ride the Steel Eel were never realized as neither Mason or myself could summon up the courage to accompany him.

But we did board the Rio Loco raft, from which Luke and I emerged drenched through and through. Were still damp when we arrived at La Loma hours later, but, the boys loved the ride and we giggled over being caught directly beneath the waterfall all the way home.

The next day we watched the Riley Vanham's baseball team defeat their opponents, then the four of us did some serious fishing. The realization that our many, many efforts with our children pay off came when Riley manned the electric knife and did an excellent job of cleaning the fish. Riley is a true hero to Mason and Luke, as they observe him living life to the hilt, all the while struggling with diabetes and never complaining.

Wednesday a.m. found us driving south in a heavy downpour, headed for Ben's Western Wear. Many, many times I've traveled to Cotulla, but can never remember any occasion when the countryside was soaked with rain.

Inside Ben's we set about spotting Poppa Mac's hat among the South Texas Hall of Cattlemen's headgear. Mason requested we snap a photo of that soiled Resistol. Then we got busy getting the boys outfitted in boots, shirts, and Wranglers.

Aunt Dorothy treated us to an afternoon of fishing on the Kinsel farm. It was a profitable time. All my efforts to show Mac's grandsons a grand spring break were rewarded when I reached down and grasped a big bass by the mouth and Luke excitedly exclaimed, "Aunt Anne, you're a Real Man's Girl!" Thank you Lord.

Cattle Raisers Meeting

The last week of March always meant the Texas and Southwestern Cattle Raisers convention for us, and we would journey to Fort Worth, Houston, Dallas, San Antonio, sometimes Corpus to attend. But the past few years involved illnesses that prevented our presence, so I was glad to send in my deposit and make plans to be in Austin beginning March 23.

Headed out early in order to be at Bud (Dr. S.H.) and Evelyn (Woodley) Dryden's in time to attend 11 a.m. services at University Christian Church. Enjoyed the sermon, but being with Bud and Evelyn was a special sermon in itself.

Being entirely dedicated to the UT Longhorns, Dr. Bud always drives a vehicle with a special orange and white paint job. Enthusiasm and zest for life guide him in living life to the hilt, despite a few complications along the way. Last May found him in British Columbia, bagging a bear. Bud has plans laid to return May, 2001– bears beware.

Evelyn is Mac and Fred's beautiful and beloved cousin, daughter of K.K. and Jane Woodley. She and Mac shared a special bond in their affection for Texas Christian University.

During the course of the afternoon, Dr. Bud called his neighbor, Mike Marks, who appeared with a treasure trove of "Old Sabinal" photographs his father, B.K. Marks, had snapped during the 1940s and 1950s.

Mike and I had made a vow to meet at the Sabinal Library, sort through the photos, and copy special ones for the Sabinal museum.

On to Dallas, checking into the hotel, my cousin and college roommate, Mary Tom Harper Hefte, already had our room comfy and organized. Together we hugged and babysat Carson and Harper Petty, while their parents, Kathryn and Scott, attended the convention functions.

Next day, M.T., Dorthy Kinsel, Linda and John Watts, Joan Petty, and I dined on prime rib while Kay Bailey Hutchison delivered the convention's opening address. Was my first in-person glimpse of Kay, and I liked what I heard and saw.

She is most attractive, intelligent, and articulate. Kay noted when she is guiding visitors on a first-time tour of the state she advises them: "If you say Gig 'Em Horns," you're not from Texas. Cattle guards are not men dressed in uniforms, and Yes, we talk proper English, we sound this way because we do not want to sound like you."

At the Trade Show we visited with Albert and Dorthy Gates, daughter Louise, and her husband, Ernie Davis. D.K. and I reminisced with Ernie about the hunt he organized for Dan, Dorthy, Mac and myself

Dan Kinsel, Jr. with Matt Kinsel fishing at Piedra Ranch

to the Deseret Ranch in Wyoming. The two of us hold fond memories of that adventure.

Hugged Billie Rae Light as she and George conversed with Joe Finley, Jr.

So delighted to see how tall Jody Clark had grown. Jody and his Dad, Robin, always assisted on roundups at our ranch.

Jody's sidekicks were Matt and Hailey Kinsel, Dan III and Leslie's two.

Stuart Sasser told us his mom, Augusta, was in Corpus with their three children in order for Stewart and his wife to attend the convention. Stuart spent many weekends at La Loma with Jamie during their TMI days.

Jeanne Evans was the Cattle Women's representative from our area; she puts in many hours promoting the industry.

For the social event at the UT Alumni center, Mary Catherine Bailey joined our group. Jamie Woodley had arrived from Dallas, and I enjoyed a long visit with friends Margie and Tommy Hagelin of the Chaparrosa.

Next a.m. our tour departed in the pouring down (literally) rain, for the National Wildflower Center. Tried to hide my disappointment, as during the summer of 2000, I made a personal vow to never complain about wet weather. What a marvelous building and facility, must return for a long and detailed visit.

One reason I have always enjoyed attending TSCRA get-togethers is it is an organization of people who are true individuals trying to wrestle a livelihood from the land. Most of them do not fit into a mold. One young man was struggling with a very large picture frame when we boarded the bus.

"Did you purchase a painting?" DK inquired.

"No, ma'am, my grandfather did. I'm just the brawn in our outfit, Grandpa's the brains."

We advised the young fellow to stick with Grandpa who was fully in charge of the situation and directing the proceedings with his sorting stick.

Spring blossoms in the Hill Country

Spring season of 2001 deserves a special label or place in history, perhaps Primavera 2001 would be appropriate.

Its beauty and bounty are the topic of discussion wherever one happens to be these months of April and May. Had an opportunity to explore the Hill Country roadsides and its wild flower show during a weekend ranch visit near Fredericksburg.

Within the town itself we viewed Varney's Herb Farm which was more resplendent than I had ever witnessed. Old fashioned roses, both climbers and florabundas were drooping under the weight of their blossoms. The "Herb Star" was comprised of oriental poppies, shasta daisies, snapdragons, and several colors of verbenas, creating a spectacular show.

Wildflowers at Rancho de Loma, 2001

Stopping for an afternoon's refreshment, we were served the farm's special raspberry tea garnished with a miniature rose and a snip of spearmint. Biggie Wentworth and my aunts always had spearmint growing close by a water faucet, and they served it with iced tea at every meal.

Varney's is on the edge of town, and is easier to navigate than the Wildseed farm, which is usually overloaded with tourists on the weekends.

Leaving the ranch, my route took me down Edgar Fiedler Road in Gillespie County, and over the lovely Pedernales twice. Progress has yet to show its face in this area; a lonely ranch cemetery was decorated only by native blossoms.

The wild cherry trees were blooming profusely, firewheels (or Indian blankets) along with thelsperma were so abundant, acres of pasture lands were solid golden yellow. The pink primroses grew several feet high in the bar ditches, and were still fresh with morning dew.

Everywhere mustang grapevines were growing rampant, and the Spanish oak and post oak were weighed down with their verdant green foliage. But the dry times and summer of 2000 had taken a large toll on the live oak motts.

Angus herds were so content they had bedded down at mid-day.

Entering Kerr County marks of progress began to appear. Why would anyone construct a French mansion in the Texas Hill Country?, I pondered.

Mealy blue sage was every where as was purple verbena growing in fields and "set-aside" land.

Easing out of Kerrville, I took Hwy. 39 past Ingram and Hunt. There was Heart of the Hills girls camp, looking much upgraded since the time we deposited Julie there 35 years ago.

Hunt Methodist Church looked so inviting – made a mental note to attend its services on my next venture.

Passed the Felix Fisher-Stevens road, and thought of Felix Real's sweet sister, Ella, and her husband Felix Fisher. Sophie and Eddie have told us of wonderful visits to the Fisher ranch.

Continuing down 39, I noted Crider's rodeo and dance pavilion, thought of the Saturday nights when a group of us would attend the dances under the huge oak tree. My visits could be counted on one hand as my parents Annalee and Henry Burns felt it was a treacherous highway, especially on Saturday nights.

Herds of Boer goats roamed many pastures, but nary an Angora was to be seen.

An appealing old-time rock house was made complete by tile goat sheds and cedar stay fences out back, which were kept in excellent repair. Wondered who provides the labor to keep them in shape. On my tape player Willie questioned, "Are there any more real cowboys in this land?"

Perhaps a few, I surmised and some of the familiar names appeared on gates: Auld, Patterson, Haby, Rex Kelly, and I remembered Snodgrass, Adam and Hamilton Wilson, Short and Hans. People who ranched out "on top" as our family would say,

Once we attended a Sheep and Goat Raisers party, and Ross and Clara Belle Snodgrass were in our group; in their seventies at the time, they rarely missed a dance "set."

Shall never forget Ross remarking to our men who were in a deep cattle discussion, "I don't know about you boys, but I came to dance."

Dropping down from the divide on 187 to the Sabinal Canyon, the gorge was decorated in leafy green and the sycamores were breathtaking. Must have been at least 28 various shades of green glinting and glistening under a friendly sky.

Coming back to the canyon always fills my heart, and the beautifully kept St. Mary's Catholic Church welcomed me as I gazed to the right. On cemetery road the sun was behind the shredded wheat shaped bales in a Boswell field, and the inland sea oats waved a welcome as I turned into the old white house with its red roofs at Burns-Bownds place.

Is there a more welcoming sight anywhere than home? Combined with the spring of 2001, it could not have been surpassed.

Making House a Home

All the changing and rearranging in life lately set me to thinking about the cost, effort, and time required in order to shape a house into a home. My, hasn't our mode of living changed since the '40s and '50s, as well as the spaces we call home?

Remembrances of our first home was the small, I'm talking four rooms, shotgun-type house which four of us occupied at the South San Humble oil refinery, where Daddy kept books and loaded out tanker trucks. Think we had two bedrooms with a small bath sandwiched in between, then the standard arrangement of a living room and kitchen on the other side of the house.

There were perhaps 10 of these small, similar gray houses, arranged together on Humble Oil property. Not many closets or storage spaces were required, due to the fact we did not own much to store. On the weeks when Henry pulled graveyard shifts, Mama, Taylor, and myself would spend large amounts of time out-ofdoors or visiting the neighbors, to let Daddy sleep in peace and quiet.

From SA we returned to the Sabinal Canyon to live in the large, old white house on Utopia's main street. It was wooden, had 12-foot ceilings, a fireplace, one bathroom carved out of a corner of the kitchen, and provided Annalee the perfect spot for socializing with all the canyonites. Also our town home had a wonderful old barn, windmill and water tank (red), the telephone office, and lots of acres to explore.

It was the perfect place to grow up. Winters we'd all huddle around the large gas heater in the dining room while trying to get dressed for school. Hardwood floors and 12-foot ceilings do not work well for warmth and coziness.

But Henry was always in the process of improving, as he loved to remodel our houses – never travel, but continually strive to make home more livable. So he set out to knock out walls in the George Dan Harper house (Annalee's name for our home), carpet floors, and add a water cooler, which provided us some small sort of relief from the '50s drouth.

As we grew and times improved, another bathroom was added, and yes, we moved the bath from the corner of our kitchen. The small, claw-footed bathtub is still in our family today.

Eventually all three of us had our own private bedrooms, a four bedroom house was a spacious home in the '50s. And from it each of us set out to make our way in life and to create our own homes.

When Mac and I married, we returned from Kansas City with three children and a miniature dachshund to Yucca Switch, Texas, situated on the Southern Pacific railroad. That small red ranch house was wooden, unairconditioned, had one bath, but the essential fireplace, and a large front porch.

Immediately I set about painting, even transformed the old refrigerator and cook stove from white to brown.

It is true paint covers a multitude of sins.

Sometimes at 3 a.m., you'd wake with a start and truly believe the Southern Pacific engine was headed right through the bedroom. Best feature of Yucca was it was the center of all the ranch activities, so workers, friends, and salesmen were usually present for a meal, visit, or to offer a helping hand. All except Nacho, the old cowboy, who would always hide in the barn when he saw me working in the flowerbeds.

Then we became serious about houses and began to construct our dream home on the hill where years ago Big Mac had remarked, "This would be the perfect place to build a house."

Isn't it remarkable what youth and determination can accomplish? Now I marvel at how we ever supposed such a large house could possibly be constructed, furnished, and maintained. But it was. And memories still surface of all the dedicated workers who helped accomplish the project: Señor Cuaves from Piedras, his three sons and son-in-law,

Douglas Fowler, who directed the cement work, Aubrey Inscore did all the electrical wiring, young Red Emerson, James Scales, Martiano, Jose, Nacho, and many others whose names escape the mind.

La Loma was a place of beauty, fun, family, wildlife, plants, dogs, cattle, and friends for 30 of our years. The brick floors were handsome but tough to maintain. Spiders loved the beams in the top of the 18-foot ceilings and my kitchen, constructed with handmade Mexican cabinets, was a cook's dream come true. The large windows let in the wonderful world of nature.

And these days I am proud to inhabit a Jack Graves designed home, sturdily and strongly constructed by the Weibolt family in the '50s. It pleases me that it is a place built during my years of school in Sabinal. Hope Libby would approve of the recent changes and the room colors.

Isn't central heating and cooling one of the best of all recent invention? No huddling around the fireplace during blizzards, or standing in front of the water cooler during sizzling days. And it's comfy to have carpet instead of brick floors. Any time I need entertainment, the activities on Hwy. 187 are out my kitchen window, similar to days at Utopia house.

Love the huge oak trees, the red kitchen, and naturally the fireplace; each and every abode of our lives has its own jewels and drawbacks, different neighbors and outdoor space. What are your special memories of the houses in your life? Stop by for a visit and tell me about them.

North Texas Travels

Days with my darlin' nieces are rare as Frisco, Plano, and Sabinal are located too, too far apart. But journeyed upstate to be present for Tessa Brewton's (daughter number three) christening.

Taylor Anne, Trystie, and Tessa's Mom has been house bound the past few months as Taylor is staying at home to avoid contact with strange and unwanted germs while recovering from a stem cell transplant in January. Her progress has been miraculous, and curly brown hair and long lashes have appeared, giving her an angelic look.

But mommas need a day out from the demands of a 3-year-old, a 2-year-old, and a 6-month-old baby. So Sis and I jumped in the car early one Friday morning and headed for Canton.

Have you ever traveled to deep East Texas for "First Monday" trade days? It is an experience quite like no other. It began years ago when country folks would come to town to trade chickens, produce, or whatever they have, and thus carry home a little cash.

Remember during the first years of Taylor's and Mary Jo's residence in Tyler, Annalee and Henry, Auntie Mauldin and Horace journeyed up for a visit and an outing to "trade days." That trip provided them with conversation subjects for years to come.

Pulling into one of the parking lots, we left our vehicle directly in front of JOEL'S POPCORN. Wearing our comfy shoes was a must. What we should have done at the first was fork up $5 to rent a push cart for all our purchases.

Setting out slowly and without any definite objects in mind, we began to examine the offerings of the many, many booths. We're talking literally thousands of booths, believe me, here there is one of something for everybody.

 Was intrigued by the place where all sorts of hardware was available mostly Texas-style pieces; stars, horses, chickens, armadillos all fashioned into drawer pulls or hooks, or racks. Since I'd just remodeled, it was fun to imagine an armadillo on front of the kitchen cabinets.

Honey from Waxahachie filled an entire space attractively bottled with eye-catching labels. And every type of soup and dip mix you could ever dream of was available from a place located in Henderson.

On down the aisles into yet another pavilion, we browsed through a huge selection of sun outfits for little girls, with three in Frisco, we easily dressed them up in proper summer fashion.

Can never pass an Mary Englebreit book or store, and here was a stall with her items halfprice; I'm a sucker for a sale. If it's on sale I feel sure I need it, so stocked up on paper doll sets. Anne Estelle for Taylor, and Gloria for Trystie. These dolls had a magnetic backing thus adhering to the fridge. The girls can play paper dolls while mom's preparing dinner.

Sis decided upon a cookbook holder, while I longed for a Provence cookbook, but remembered I'd just divested myself of at least 20 cooking manuals during the move.

Canton is not only a feast for the eyes, it offers almost any type of delicious food you can imagine. Corn-on-the-cob was a big seller this June. Replenishing our energies with fried shrimp baskets, I

especially enjoyed the homemade cole slaw of cabbage, purple onion, fresh tomatoes, and lots of wonderful mayo.

Everywhere you look are items you never knew you needed or wanted:
bird houses carved of gourds, artfully bottled baby carrots, dill, peppers, baby corn, asparagus, each preserved in vinegar; rugs of cow-
hides, Mexican someros, thousands of old books, a John Deere martin
house. Would have been easy to squandered plenty on just personal
whims, fortunately, I was traveling SW with only a small bag.

But how could we pass up those funky sunglasses for five bucks
a pair? Lavender for Larissa, blue for Allie, and rose-colored for
Aunt Anne.

Arbor I and II pavilions are a decorators dream, and if you had a
house to furnish, you could easily do it here.

Found the fellow from Lindale whose "Just Piddlin" booth provided
church birdhouses for the entire family in years past. His fanciful
creations are more artful than ever.

Looked at probably millions of artificial flower arrangements, found
Talavera flower pots, and fingered turquoise jewelry.

Had an interesting conversation with a man selling scrimshaw
knives, every booth keeper is a salesman plus a conversationalist who
loves to discuss their product.

Children and senior citizens started to wilt in 2 p.m. heat. You could
see in the younger faces bewilderment as to why they'd been chosen
to endure this shopping marathon.

Just as we were considering searching for the car, a SALE sign over
a group of brightly colored tops, pants, and skirts grabbed our eyes.
What mom can resist outfitting beautiful size 6 daughters? Not me,
so we came away with bright pink for Sis, and powder blue for Allie,
perfect matches for the sunglasses.

Seeing the entire layout of Canton in one day, or one weekend is
simply not humanly possible, so there are always plans for "when we
return in October," or "we could do all our Christmas shopping here."

Best of all for Sis and myself, we whiled away some happy, carefree
summer hours together after a dark, stressful winter.

Cherish Your Family and Friends

Standing in front of the screen, I saw the second airliner crash into the lower center of the World Trade Tower. Instantly my reaction, "My God, there are hundreds of thousands of people whose lives are forever changed from this moment on." Changed by loss. Grief.

Those of us familiar with the ravages of loss understand completely what a friend is experiencing when a spouse, child, friend or family member's life is snuffed out.

For myself, God was generous and gave me time to prepare for the fact that the two men I loved more than my own life could not recover. For them, death was a sweet release.

But at 3 a.m. some times I wonder if my psyche would be resilient enough to withstand the sudden, shocking loss of a nearest and dearest one. How does one recover or reconcile to having a mate preparing dinner one evening, and tomorrow, forever gone? A child, playing around your feet, the next day, never to return?

Was fortunate to have made plans to attend a seminar on grief and loss, led by author and grief counselor, Paula D'Arcy. Special cousins and friends joined me at Alto Frio on Wednesday after the Tuesday a.m. terrorist attacks.

It was comforting to be in a group of people who found themselves struggling with irreversible change in their lives. Paula herself had lost her husband and 2-year-old daughter when a drunk driver crashed into their automobile, 27 years ago. From her own struggle to regain strength and stability, Paula has reached out to others in her writings, lectures and counseling.

One person who helped her tremendously was Dr. Norman Vincent Peale. She related how deeply he listened to her story. When she concluded he touched her with his powerful statement, "You lost

Henry, Anne, Annalee, Taylor, and Murray - Utopia, 1952

the purpose you wanted for your life, but not the purpose God intended for your life."

And so, Paula has found the purpose which God intended for her. Reflecting on these statements she gave us has helped me these days after our nation's tragedy.

"Keep standing up, keep walking, keep the grief moving through YOU."

"We are entitled to nothing, life is a gift,"

"Transform your own suffering into compassion."

"There is a huge difference in wanting to know about God, and wanting to really know God."

"Love is greater than pain."

Am writing this in Frisco, Texas, on a crisp, bright sunny a.m. outdoors, the sun is shining, the birds are singing.

Just an hour ago, I fastened Taylor Brewton's seat belt, handed her the stuffed horse, and kissed her adios. Hugged her beautiful, brave mother, and complemented Chris on his red, plaid shirt. We tried to be stalwart and cheerful, but we have lived through many traumas and are burdened with our knowledge of the struggle ahead.

At 11 a.m., this Sept. 24, Taylor Anne Brewton will enter Medical City Hospital of Dallas to fight again for her life. Her leukemia (acute myelgenous) has returned and she must undergo chemotherapy and another stem cell transplant.

Our family, yet once more, finds ourselves standing in deep need of your prayers. My own phrase, "In real life there are no insurance policies."

But while Taylor was dressing early this morning, she brought me a pamphlet advertising a hot air balloon festival near Plano. Each of us chose our favorite balloon. Mine was a red, white and blue American flag design. Hers was a duck, the floating bathtub type.

"Taylor," I questioned, "would you like to ride in one of these balloons?" "Oh yes," she replied, "if you and Mommy will go with me." My mind said, "Miracles Happen," remember Millie Brewton's story. "When you are feeling strong, you, Mama and I will ride in the balloon of your choice, I promise."

Today, worship your God, pray for our country, love your family, comfort your friends. Life is a gift.

Harper Wedding Anniversary

Her eyes are as blue and sharp as I remember them to have been in 1958 when visiting them while attending Sul Ross State University.

Frances Greenwood Harper led us by the hand and pointed to a green spot below a huge cottonwood.

"That's where I first saw Ted, right down there. He and Dad Harper rode up one Saturday afternoon. Ted had on a clean white shirt, Mother Harper always kept her boys dressed in starched white shirts."

"I had a date, and was anxious to get away from the ranch and on into town. But the Harpers were in the mood to visit, and I missed my date."

That occasion was more than 65 years ago, and apparently Frances forgot about the fellow who was waiting in town, because last week friends and family gathered at El Fortin la Cienega to celebrate the Harpers' 65th wedding anniversary.

You do not have the occasion to attend many gatherings markings such a long-term partnership.

And be assured, Ted and Frances have been partners all those years.

Ted Harper, Frances Harper, and grandson Sam

Frances Greenwood grew up calling the fort, La Cienega, home. Her grandfather, John Poole, purchased the ranch, 40 miles or more below Marfa, from Milton Favor.

The Favors were sheepmen who first settled the La Cienega and Cibolo ranches in the 1830s.

This is still wild country. Hard to imagine what it was like in that day and time.

And hard to believe La Cienega, along with the Cibolo, have been transformed into world class resorts.

For a price you can reside in the old Greenwood home, replete with family portraits of Frances, her brother Hart, and her parents.

Also, you can sleep in the small tower in which, as children, Frances and Hart played in and peeped out of the gunports.

So a large crowd gathered upon the green lawn under the same cottonwoods to mark the 65th anniversary of this couple who embarked on married life in 1936.

Persimmon, pear, and quince trees, which Mrs. Greenwood planted, still grow along the banks of the spring.

Ted and Frances signify the spirit of Texas.

At age 86, Ted still mounts up, although he acknowledges he needs a gentle horse which will "stand still." Both of Ted's knees are metal, and last year he had to be rescued by a Border Patrol helicopter. He had ridden down to the lower country alone, and his mount stepped into a deep hole.

Ted was badly injured, five broken ribs, and a broken collarbone. Fortunately, he had his cell phone and contacted his grandson Clete.

The Border Patrol arrived and airlifted him out. "Roughest ride I ever had," Ted remarked.

Frances chimed in, "I prayed the entire time he would make it through." Which he did. As soon as possible, Ted climbed atop his horse again.

Ted loves to recall bygone days, and told of how Dad and Mother Harper sold their store at Banquete, took the $500 plus a studio couch, and headed for West Texas. Uncle Rollie (as the family all knew him) purchased the Carazzal Ranch below Marfa with the money.

Thus the Harpers and Greenwoods became neighbors. And Ted and Uncle Rollie rode over on that fateful day to visit when Frances missed her date in town.

Life has held its ups and downs for the Harpers. One of the pluses was their involvement in raising Palomino horses. Every year they would ship a boxcar-load of horses to Lillie Fisher in Pennsylvania.

"Let me tell you her patronage helped keep us in the cattle and horse business," Frances remarked.

Tragedy struck the couple when they lost their daughter Amy in a car accident. Amy had three small sons, who Ted and Frances helped raise, and are all now fine young men. Clete lives in Marfa, Sam in Midland, and Sandy in Dallas.

Tana Surratt, the older daughter, lives near her parents and was the one who put together the lovely party. Hadn't seen Tana since our teen-age days at our Fisher family reunions

She and Johnny have three daughters, Amy, Maya and Tana, plus wonderful grandchildren.

Fun to see cousin Robin Roberts Walker, and husband Billy, who now reside near El Indio.

The handsome young man who looked so familiar to me proved to be Bobby Knight, Jamie Woodley's TCU pal.

Roxie Robinson Medley asked to be remembered to Ann Enloe when I next chatted with her. Fannie had an interesting visit with Roe and Jean Miller.

Roe related his World War 11 experiences as a bomber pilot over Japan.

Chatted with Barbara Wheelis, who I had seen earlier in the year at an Emmaus gathering. Mark and Barbara divide their days between Victoria and Marfa. Ted introduced us to Clay Tippett, the Border Patrol pilot who airlifted him out of the canyon.

As we were departing someone asked if Frances ever rode anymore. Her reply, "Ted came in several weeks ago and told me he sure needed some help gathering a set of steers. I said, 'I can't saddle my horse anymore.' His reply, 'I'll saddle 'em for you.'" And he did.

Together they gathered the steers.

Memories of the Fair

"We went to the animal fair, The birds and the beasts were there, The big baboon by the light of the moon, Was combing his auburn hair. The monkey got so drunk, He danced on the elephant's trunk ..."

Can't come up with the last verse to this childhood ditty. Will have to consult Annalee and Lola when I return to Uvalde County. It's one of the many songs they sang to us in our younger days.

And Trystie B. (age 2), Allie Burns Noon, and I sang it in the car as Doug drove us to the fair, The State Fair of Texas, is a grand affair on a sunny crisp October morn with a 2 year old in tow.

Recent events had greatly trimmed the crowds, so we had ample space for our stroller. First we hit the petting barn, where some feed salesman was getting rich, selling small (I'm talking tiny) cups of grain mix for a quarter. We had to invest in several as Trystie was most liberal with her portions.

City kids were delighted to stuff the goats, sheep, miniature donkeys, longhorns, llamas with more feed than Henry would have ever sanctioned. Our favorites were the young giraffe, miniature Zebu cattle from Africa (had never seen these before), and the alpacas trimmed similar to poodles.

Next we filed into the dog show to try and get a ringside seat. Many different breeds tackled the obstacle course, and demonstrated their prowess catching Frisbees. The huge trophy went to the blue heeler, who turned a flip before catching his Frisbee. Didn't catch his name but Trystie suggested Spot, which we deemed adequate.

Would have loved to have transported Spot back to Sabinal, as I now find myself dogless for the first time in 35 years. Nothing like an enthusiastic pup for entertainment and company.

Lunch time found us on the Midway, munching gorditos, corny dogs, ice cream bars and slurpees. Trys was in junk food heaven, liberated from everyday "eat your broccoli" rules.

As the younger three headed for the kiddie rides, I ducked into the creative arts building. Always love seeing the inventive crafts people over the state produce. Wasn't disappointed, the variety ranged from a rattlesnake concocted of barbed wire to a section of items constructed of Leggos.

Loved the collage entitled "Father and Son," which included mementos of two family members' Air Force careers, including the Purple Heart.

My choice quilt received only a red ribbon, but remember judging is only a matter of personal choice. This beauty was appliqued Texas wildflowers on an ecru background, expertly quilted with state of Texas motifs.

Noted the blue ribbon photography was of an 8 or 9-year-old boy standing on the banks of a stream, which could have easily been the Sabinal, Frio, or Nueces.

Nostalgia for Mac filled me at the sight of a heart-touching sculpture similar to George Lundeen's pieces. It was still in plasticine clay (not yet cast), life size, and depicted a young boy sharing a corny dog and caramel apple with his prize-winning goat. A perfect piece of Americana.

On to the Texas Agricultural building, where I studied the Millennium Quilt, twenty-four squares, depicting different aspects of Texas Agriculture were chosen to comprise this work of art during the Texas Department of Agriculture Quilt block competition in 1999.

Picked up a 2002 Farmer's Market calendar for son Jamie, who loves the place, which we visit together whenever I'm in Big D.

Purchased some wildflower seed packets and bluebonnet soap at the Made in Texas store, plus an "I Love America" sticker for the Durango.

Popped a couple of "Eat More Beef" magnets in my bag, but skipped the recipe folders. Figured I could cook more beef dishes from memory than it could provide.

Made a mental note to inform friend, Dorthy Kinsel, the gazebo in the center of the pavilion had Texas Women's University emblazoned over the top. A band from her alma mater was playing "The Yellow Rose of Texas;" DK will be pleased.

When you're traveling with a 2 year old, some exhibits must be sacrificed, thus we missed the miniature White House display. So we waved good-bye to Big Tex and headed for our vehicle. But secretly, I wished I would have been holding tickets for Elton John's "Aida" at Fair Hall. Perhaps next year, when circumstances are more calm for us.

P.S. Consulted Mama as to the words of the song. And sure enough, she provided the last verse.

"The elephant sneezed, And fell to his knees, But what became of the monk?"

Feeling an Other-World Sensation

Careening through the subterranean streets of Guanajuato gives one an other-world sensation, such as the many generations of miners here must have experienced. The underground streets (tunnels) are in actuality old river channels, engineered to move traffic efficiently along in this mountain city.

Years ago Mac and I, T.M., and Jamie drove to Guanajuato in the longest car we ever owned. Have to chuckle about how difficult it was to turn and twist around the small, winding streets constructed with burros and wagons in mind.

On that viaje Jamie (age 8), had a large longing to view the mummies. Following a Coca-Cola truck, our instant tour guide, through the maze of hilly streets, we arrived just in time to have the guards slam the gates at 5 p.m. Our pleas were only answered by, "Esta Cerra," And to this day Jamie has yet to view the mummies.

So time and circumstances collided and presented an opportunity for a return to Guanajuato and San Miguel de Allende, two colonial cities designated as national shrines of Mexico.

The cathedral in San Miguel de Allende

There seem to be only two schools of thought regarding Mexico and its culture, those who love it and those who do not. I fall into the first category as our southern neighbor has spoken to my imagination since the first day my feet crossed the Rio Grande.

Easy access to the state of Guanajuato is provided by direct flights from both Dallas and Houston to Leon, a sprawling and prosperous city set in fertile farming country.

Leaving Leon it is easy to spot the Cubilete Mountain which is the geographic center of Mexico. Crowned by a huge bronze "Christ the King," with extended arms, this edifice is visible from miles away.

Heading east the bus begins to gain altitude approaching "the hills like frogs," Guanax-Huato, giving an unusual name not only to the city but the state as well, home to the current Mexican president, Vicente Fox.

A glance tells you this is ranching country, very similar to the arid, indomitable lands of Alpine, Marathon, and Marfa. Almost all of the men who labored on the ranch in years past, claimed the state of Guanjuato as home. And they were adequately suited to the rigors, trials, and manual labor involved in agriculture.

Until the beginning of the 15th century, the area was the peaceful home of the Otomi natives, but all that changed when the Spanish discovered rich silver veins beneath the earthen hills. When all the wealth burst upward, Guanajuato gained prominence and prosperity as "one" of the world's most important sources of silver and gold.

Pulling into the attractive hotel, I knew it would be easy to find contentment here as a tremendous, "Old Mission," bougainvillea climbed the height of three stories, and then spilt its fuchsia brackets onto the walls and arches. Is there a more exuberant or joyous contrast than bougainvilleas against pale walls?

So the 6,300-foot altitude, and dry climate provided us the energy and stamina to explore and pray in the exquisite, elegant Basilica of Our Lady of Guanajuato. One evening a quinceañero was in progress, and the steps of the pale yellow cathedral were lined with flowers and illuminated with candles, creating a scene only Frieda Khalo could capture on canvas.

Colorful homes spilling down the hills fashion a setting which calls for an artist's brush. And the city is also a cultural center, home to museums of history, Diego Rivera, and Cervantes. Loved the delightful artist's interpretations of Don Quixote, and Sancho Panza, one of my favorite literary fellows.

Many students fill the streets during lunch hour and evenings, providing a Parisian touch of amor, embracing and kissing in the small plazas, caused one to reflect on carefree careless days.

And naturally the food called out and enveloped one in the fresh flavors of limes, chili, avocados, rich and creamy flan, and fresh corn tortillas. Saw the largest chicherone ever, a whole side of a pork, fried and flavored in its entirety. Where ever did they produce a pot large enough to fry the thing? Had to double as a wash pot.

A day in colonial San Miguel visiting friends who reside there year around convinced us, yes, this may well be the place to pass August, 2002. Center of a large artist's colony, the city, has much to offer.

Back in Guanajuato, loaded up with trinkets at the Hidalgo market. Was my third encounter with Gustave Effiel's edifices, the first his Parisian tower, the second the funicular in Lisbon.

Intriguing that Guanajuato was wealthy enough in the 1920s to employ an architect of international renown to design its central market. But this arid, truculent land coughed up 80 percent kilos of silver and 20 percent kilos of gold per ton of earth for several centuries. And those vast riches splashed out upon these hills and created a small unique city of color, culture, and compadres.

Welfare of Annalee

Friends suggested I might write a piece about Annalee as people are always asking and interested as to her welfare and well-being. Sometimes it is not easy to articulate on a subject very near and dear to your heart.

Turning it over in my mind, I know how very many of you are dealing with the responsibilities involved in caring for elderly parents or other family members. Sharing a few of our experiences might not be worthy of any more than the price of this paper, but hopefully it may be comforting.

How should one begin? Our lives were brightened and blessed by two parents who loved each other, we three, and life. Truly my one wish for every child born on this planet would be for them to experience the love, security, happiness, we knew in the old, white house on Main Street, Utopia.

And we grew into adults untouched by huge problems. Henry educated us, so each set out to seek our destinies.

Annalee and Daddy were able to retire and returned to Utopia full time in 1967. Mother was jubilant over the prospect of remodeling Bownds house, and living only a mile or so away from her childhood home.

She was one of the rare people able to find complete happiness in the place where she was born, grew up, married, raised her family, and passed her entire life.

Once, when I was promoting a trip to Europe she remarked, "But what you do not realize, Annie, is I'm able to visit Spanish castles in my head."

While attending a writing class, one assignment presented us was to compose an epitaph about our parents. For Annalee I jotted, "Mama had the good sense to realize Utopia, Texas, was Utopia."

All was well with our family until 1980 when Mary Jo Smith Bums

Annalee Burns at Utopia Methodist Church

was diagnosed with a malignancy. Annalee traveled to and from Tyler, to help and comfort Taylor, Larissa, and Allison.

Out of the blue in 1982, Daddy developed an unrelenting pain in his neck. By the time he was hospitalized, the coin had turned and Henry never walked alone again. Annalee did not leave his side during 60 long days and nights at Methodist Hospital.

For the next nine years, Mother dealt as best she could with his paralysis. God was gracious, and after a year's time we were able to secure help so they could return to living at Burns-Bownds place.

Have read convincing research that constant stress greatly contributes to memory loss, and I buy into that theory. Saw Annalee deal quietly and calmly with the tremendous pain Daddy experienced during those nine years, but the pressure took its toll on her.

Only once did mother give way and have to be hospitalized herself.

After we lost our Dad, she bravely went it on her own, always proclaiming, "Don't want to cry on my children's shoulders." People, as they always are in Utopia, were kind, helpful, loving to her. Mama has always been easy to love.

But the summer of '97 found her requiring two major surgeries within a month's time, recovery was slow and difficult. September of that year remains in my mind, as the week both Mac and Annalee were in Northeast Baptist. Should have had a pair of roller blades to expedite my travels between their rooms.

Anesthetic works against the mind's memory bank, and surgery is always weakening. One family member warns, "Stay away from the surgeon's knife if at all possible." I agree.

When Annalee returned home, Angelita Garza was her companion for two years. Together they made it nicely.

But August 1999 it became necessary to install 24-hour help at Utopia. Terri Ellis, Alice Bond, Beth Pringle, Kathy Ruiz were kind, capable and efficient.

But in July, 2001, my inner voice told me, "Anne, Annalee needs to be in Amistad."

Jeanne Burns arrived and along with Mary Reyes we guided Mother through the transition. She is now comfortable, secure, and playing "Blue Eyes Crying In The Rain," within Amistad's welcoming walls.

While earning my Ph.D. in care-giving I strive to keep a few guidelines in mind. Try to rationalize, "How would I wish to be treated if I were in this situation?"

"Work to spend as much time as possible with them, someday I'll be grateful I did."

"Remember they came through the Depression, World War II, Korea, and Viet Nam – they know more about sacrifice than we'll ever begin to comprehend."

"Nothing has to be accomplished in a certain manner."

"Allow them their dignity."

"A kind word is the greatest gift."

"Where they are now, we shall soon be."

The greatest challenge facing all caregivers today is financial. The prospect of caring for patients with long-term needs can drain fortunes, wipe out ranches, and put an untold strain on all family members. It is tough to save for the times when we will need an adequate financial reserve to cover the costs of disability. Every situation is different, but the reality is real.

Millie Brewton's Story

Corgis have been the dog of choice for myself and certain members of our family. They are bright, alert, small, and bred for working cattle. Some call them "heelers" for the manner they drive a stubborn cow, nipping at a heel and dropping flat to avoid an ensuing kick

The Pembroke Corgi migrated to the Welsh Highlands from Flanders, a few centuries ago. At certain times Queen Elizabeth has had as many as 11 for her personal pets. They travel with her on the royal jet, and she spoons their food into their personalized silver bowls (so I read).

Two years ago I was down to only one dog, and happened to be reading the classified section of the Livestock Weekly. TWO CORGI PAIRS FOR SALE caught MY eye, called the Midland telephone number and found a friend at the other end of the line, Palais Raines.

Yes, she had a tricolor (black, brown, and white) female and a red-blond female. If I'd purchase them both, the price would be reduced. First I bought the tri-color. She was a sweetie, and was promptly named Maxie.

When Larissa, Taylor Anne, and Trystie Brewton came to La Loma for a visit, they were enamored with Maxie, who gave them her best antics for entertainment. Larissa and Allie had had their own Corgi, Sugar, when they were growing up.

So we began to negotiate. First with the father of the Brewton bunch, Chris. "Could they have a dog for their new backyard?" asked Aunt Anne. "Yes," Chris replied.

I called Palias again, "Do you still have the red-blond female?" "Yes, and we'll deliver her to Uvalde," was the reply. Great. Now Taylor and Trystie could grow up with their own Corgi.

Millie was in top shape. Together she and Maxie were quite a sight. They could have easily turned heads while strolling down The Strand in London.

When the Brewtons visited the ranch, off Millie went to Frisco and her new home. She was most happy and took every opportunity to snuggle as close as possible to Taylor and Trystie. Corgis adore children.

All was as it should be, and Millie would accompany Sis and the girls on their afternoon strolls to the duck pond.

December 13, 2000, found Taylor Anne Brewton hospitalized in Dallas. The diagnosis was acute myelogenous leukemia. Immediately I flew to Dallas to offer whatever support and comfort possible. Millie was very cold and lonely in Frisco while her family moved to Dallas to be close to the hospital.

A Christmas tree stood in the Brewton's living room, but Christmas Day had passed without any gifts being opened. Taylor was still in ICU, critically ill.

On Feb. 13, 2001 the doctors determined her condition stable enough for Tay to undergo a stem cell transplant, it was her only hope for recovery. We all held our breaths and prayed for success of the procedure.

March 14, 2001, found Millie back at La Loma as the doctors had decreed both the cat and dog had to go when Taylor returned home from the hospital. Too much risk she could catch an infection from one of them.

So I welcomed Millie with open arms; Paloma (Mac's old bird dog) was less enthusiastic. I had lost Maxie to a strange snakebite.

Housed both Millie and Paloma in the red barn at Yucca while I was away for a few days the first of April. Upon returning, found

Taylor Anne Brewton and Millie Brewton at Rancho de Loma

Millie triste and trembling; seems as if Paloma had lost her cool and almost killed Millie. Will happened to be close by, heard the conflict and intervened.

Dr. Theresa Coble told me that old dogs sometimes become so jealous and dominant they will not tolerate a new canine addition to the family.

Several weeks later found me in SA on business, so locked Millie in the pen at Yucca alone for safety's sake; upon return no Millie was to be found anywhere.

I was frantic. We searched high and low, alerted all the neighbors and the vet clinics. Toni Hull kindly put out a bulletin for Millie's return over the radio. Placed an ad in the paper offering a reward.

Even saddled up (hadn't been on a horse in five years) and Cuco, Ben and I rode over the entire ranch. Will searched on his four-wheeler. No luck – no small blonde-red dog anywhere.

Everyday hope began to diminish a bit. My prayer, "Dear God, please bless Millie Brewton." How to tell Taylor Anne I'd lost her beloved Corgi?

Seventeen days later, on April 23, June Sights called me to say a dog such as Millie had just walked up to their house. Jumping in the Durango, I sped as fast as possible, praying, "Let it be Millie, God."

And it was. She was in perfect condition, not thirsty, hungry, or harmed in any manner. Miracles happen.

So we returned to La Loma, and continued the process of packing and beginning to move, while Millie and Paloma existed together in an uneasy truce.

One evening it was necessary to be overnight in Utopia, so I housed the dogs together in the ARC, before retiring, I could hear a huge row ensue. Racing outdoors, found Paloma mauling her small amiga.

What to do? Next a.m. 10-year-old Paloma departed for heaven, while Millie and myself prepared to move to Sabinal.

Labor Day week-end found the Brewton family, enlarged by darling Tessa, who arrived in December 2000, in Sabinal and Utopia. Their first visit in a year.

We swam, hunted, feasted, visited family members, and celebrated Taylor's renewed health. And when they packed up the Expedition and departed, Millie Brewton had a place of honor next to Tessa.

Whenever doubts or disappointments threaten to overwhelm me, a small inner voice whispers, "Miracles happen, remember Millie's story."

New Mexico's Magic

Skies over Ruidoso were clear and bright last week, the thermometer registered 45 degrees in the early a.m. but climbed to 85 by 4 in the afternoon.

Felt invigorating to be on New Mexico soil again after a five-year absence. There the sky is larger, the horses faster, and the air clearer than our own South Texas environs. For many years we'd travel to New Mexico to check the progress (or non-progress) of the set of steers which Mac would have pastured in he Northeast section of the state.

These journeys taught me the magic mix of Spanish, Indian, and Christian cultures. The best description and introduction I've encountered of the early days in and around Santa Fe is Willa Cather's "Death Comes for the Archbishop." Cather's account of the first Santa Fe bishop's life is perfect reading while residing in the state capital.

Took the Cloudcroft route on the drive up and enjoyed a delicious lunch at the stately and charming Lodge. Henry and Annalee used to join the Utopia group for annual visits to Cloudcroft. Flowers blooming around the pool were just as bright and brilliant as I remembered them to be.

The drive on to Ruidoso through the Mescalero Indian reservation was glorious, summer flowers in the meadows, horses bunched together, heads down in order to fight the flies. How pleasant to enjoy a cool, apple green world, with steams running clear, and puffy clouds drifting overhead.

Part of Ruidoso's allure for us is the number of friends and family in residence for the month of August. So we set about organizing our social calendar and checking the local events.

At the Bristols in the White Mountain area, George related how a mother bear and cub had visited their deck several days earlier. Mule deer abound in the higher elevations and some residents feed them, everyone has several hummingbird feeders out.

Some members of our group sat in on the Fiddlers contest and Antique shows at the Civic Center. Each fiddler was asked to play three different tunes, a waltz, song of choice, and a hoedown. Roy Hindes, being an accomplished fiddler himself, gave us tips on the rules and chose the groups he expected to receive high marks.

At the races we visited with Mary and Junior Roberts, Janice London, and long-time friend Tulisha Shanan Wardlaw, all of Del Rio.

Can't report any excellent results on our choices of horses, but it was grand to put heads together again with Peggy Moore and Kay Cauthorn on our wagers.

Saturday evening found us at the spectacular Spenser Theater. When we walked toward the marvelous building, it was framed by the perfect New Mexico sunset.

Being my first visit to the Spenser, I was awed by the fanciful glass creations of Dale Chihuly. His glowing "Sunset Tower" and "Persian Wall" are breathtaking.

Listening to Julia and Irina Elkina, Russian pianists who were also twin sisters, bring the two Stienways to life was inspiring, loved their Mozart presentation, while Fannie Grace was captured by Gershwin's, "I Got Rhythm."

Of course, Sunday afternoon called for a country drive, especially since the pastures were green, and the poplars tall and lush. Heading north, our first stop was Carrizo with its small adobe homes, and ole time main street, found several residences we'd like to remodel and resell.

On through Capitan to Lincoln which is almost a state historical shrine to Billy the Kid. Time seems to have erased the fact that in actuality he was a misfit and a killer.

But Lincoln is wonderfully restored, clean, and inviting. We toured the museum and grounds. Was deeply moved by the quote of the Apache Indian Chief, Victorio, when the Apaches faced relocation from the Lincoln area, "What is life if we are imprisoned like cattle? We are a wild and free people. Free to come and go as we wished, how can we be caged?"

Returning through the Hondo Valley, we stopped at the Hurd- La Rinconada Gallery to view the works of members of America's first family of painters. Our choice was a large watercolor by Peter Hurd of a farm in Dexter, N.M. Hurd's technique with watercolor is exceptional, and his love of the Hondo valley shines through his works.

After an evening with Houston cousin Janice and Stew Stewart, we promised to arrange a time when Janice and Fannie Grace could combine their talents on twin pianos.

Returning home to wonderful moisture was the almost perfect ending to the trip and this a.m. more good news came over the telephone. Our family is enlarged by another member, Max Murray Macieck, son of Laura and Kevin, grandson of Jeanne and Murray. Blessings abound.

Christmas Kindness

Each year when the boxes of Christmas ornaments are pulled out, I feel a rush of surprise and delight when unpacking them. Year to year you forget some, and each is a rediscovery, a rebirth of memories connected to the small, handmade delights. What other purpose could these frivolous pieces serve than to hang on a tree, adorning its branches bringing joy and gladness to friends and family?

We have been most fortunate over the years to receive gifts of oranges and grapefruit grown in the Rio Grande Valley. Now not only are the oranges sweet and juicy, but they come packed in the most wonderfully sturdy boxes proclaiming Pittman and Davis, Harlingen, Texas. These containers are always recycled as the perfect containers for the Christmas ornaments, keeping them safe from dust and mice until the next season rolls around.

Opening these mustard-colored crates in December I fell upon a mallard duck wearing a red kerchief on her head, and a bit of holly tucked under her wing. Her happy expression and colored wings have been painted by hand. A gold cord is attached to her back so she can hang jauntily on the tree. All hand and machine stitched, underneath there is a signature, Boalt.

How I love this small duck. She came to be ours one Christmas season when we visited Mrs. Woodley in New York City.

Walking up and down Madison Avenue during those frosty days, I came upon the most appealing of shops. The Gazebo was a wonderland of handmade quilts, pillows, woven rugs, comforters, and Christmas decorations with more patterns and designs than the mind could conceive.

First time into the shop was just to look, and touch, and smell as much of the merchandise as possible. How would it ever be possible to fit all of my choices in the budget?

Next trip inside I made three purchases after much study and careful deliberation. One, a rather large pincushion, was fronted with an ecru doily, hand crocheted, and tied with ribbons and silk violets. Oh, but how very hard to choose two, only two, handmade Christmas ornaments.

Should it be the Nutcracker ballerina (she was VERY expensive, being intricately stitched) or a fuzzy teddy bear, made of an old, really real mink coat? Then there were bunnies, and pups, Tom Thumb, kitties, and more characters and creatures than you could believe, and each one cried out, "Take me, please, take me."

Finally the choices were a small English cottage, complete with hand-embroidered roses over the door, and the little duck with her holly and red kerchief What a glad feeling to have at least two for our own, how sad to have to leave the others alone with no tree to adorn.

On the day of our departure from the Big Apple, I stole away an extra hour to return to the Gazebo, camera in tow. A few photos would provide ideas, and refresh the memory so some of these pieces could be recreated at home.

But my purchases had been small ones, and I was much too reluctant to boldly march in and begin snapping photos. After all, these creations were of someone else's origins, and they were making their livelihoods selling their charming ideas. And New Yorkers have a reputation for being most abrupt and rude when you displease them.

So – perhaps just a few photos through the windows would produce some ideas to take back to Sabinal. One snap of the tree decorated completely in white cages containing redbirds. "Oh, drat, will it be visible with the flash reflecting in the window?" Perhaps getting a bit closer would give a better view of the appliqued pillows.

"Pardon me, are you interested in getting some good photos of our merchandise?" My heart sank as I turned to see the dapper, gray-haired gentleman coming out to confront me. How sad and embarrassed I felt. What to say?

"Please do come inside and take all of the pictures you'd like," this elegant well-dressed New Yorker assured me.

Feeling confused, but happy not to be admonished, I stammered, "Oh, please, I hope you do not mind me taking a few photos, I love it all, and there's no way to remember each one."

"Not a-tall, now come with me, and I'll give you a tour of the shop; are you from the city or a visitor?"

How could I reveal to this distinguished urbane person, with a cranberry silk scarf in his suit pocket, that in reality I hailed from Sabinal, Texas - actually having grown up in Utopia? So I just stammered, "Oh, from Texas."

'Texas, my dear! Why, how very glad I am to meet you, my home was Wichita Falls, and I love seeing people from my home state. Exactly what town is your home?"

"Sabinal, west of San Antonio." was the loud and clear reply.

"Well now, would you care for a cup of tea? And tell me all the new and interesting things taking place in Texas. I miss it so."

Touring the shop, while we sipped cinnamon tea, he explained to me the quilts, pillows, tree Christmas ornaments were on commission by at seamstresses all over the City, who brought them to his shop to be marketed. A bevy of designers also drew up patterns and ideas for the women to stitch.

Time slipped quickly by and a plane to Texas had our seats awaiting. Offering thanks to my newfound friend, reluctantly I departed this dream world.

So now, the lady duck and English cottage are given places of prominence and importance on our tree. For they speak to me of a time when a country girl was treated like an old friend by a kindly, sophisticated New York gentleman. Where I had expected coldness and rebuff, there was instead warmth and acceptance.

"Little lady duck, seeing you again brings to mind a Christmas kindness which came my way many years ago."

The Holidays

The kaleidoscope of the Christmas season confronts us once again. Colors, carols, children, church presentations mingle and mix together and form contrasts such as strips of ribbon candy in our minds and thoughts. Each season provides its own individual glow, events, pleasures, memories, and life changes.

2001 has thus far been a wet holiday time, but those of us who have resided in this area most of our lives greatly prefer moisture over the blasting, freezing winds of a dry norther. Green oats and wheat color the fields, and provide HOPE for the farmers and ranchers. And HOPE is the foundation upon which Christmas is built.

Annalee and I absorbed Grady Roe's sermon on hope. Thought of what the Uvalde Methodist congregation suffered when their sanctuary was so deeply damaged and how they worked together to reconstruct its glory. Just sitting and drinking in the richness of the windows is a sermon in itself. Add crimson red poinsettias, the Christmon tree, and you see HOPE reflected from every angle of the building.

So many friends and family to meet and enjoy. While lunching with Barbara Machen, Susan Hildebran, Fannie Grace and Pam Hindes, I visited with the Charley Carsons.

Charley has much to celebrate this season as he is recovered from a terrific horse accident, as is Bill Lane also from the Barksdale area. Bill and Lea will be in Oregon with their children on December 25th – happy holidays to the Lanes and Ernestine and Charley.

Cattle women from the area gathered and lunched in the mint green Colonial Room of the stately Menger Hotel. What a gracious, Southern atmosphere the Menger affords, and the luncheon buffet daily is crowned by a succulent prime rib roast. Visited with Fredna Woods, Margo Hoff, Laurie and Dorothy Gates, and Louise Davis, Corrie Ann Copps, Lesile Kinsel, Jeanne Wheeler, Evelyn Parker.

Dorothy Kinsel had invited Beth McNutt of Mountain Home, now the state president of Texas Cattlewomen, and Beth brought me

Louis Wardlaw

up to date on their ranch activities. Jeanne Evans and I passed a time together, as we were both inconvenienced by the bridge which is out on the Frio River below Sabinal.

How festive and inviting Uvalde looks with its many ingenious decorations. The folks who constructed these fanciful designs are to be commended for their creativity and commitment to enriching Uvalde's image. Try to set aside an evening to enjoy the artfully-decorated town – if you live afar, it will give a lift to your spirits.

And yet during this season many friends and family departed for heaven's realm. Reading the Leader-News was shocked to learn of Louis Wardlaw's loss.

Louis was literally larger than life. He spent many years of his life trading cattle on the Mexican border, was well known in the cattle business. Louis and Mac spent many interesting times traveling together and talking on the telephone.

One January they set out for Cuarto Ciegnas together, and by nightfall the temperature began dropping and snow commenced to fall. Mac claimed the hotel room they had was colder than any place in Siberia. No heater was available, and not a blanket was to be had.

Finally, the two of them decided it would be better to tough out the remainder of the night in the car. Mac had to take the front seat, as there no way Louis's tall frame could fit there. For years whenever they would meet the two would recall the misery they endured stranded in a snow storm, in a place where snow rarely fell.

Mac's friendship and business associations with Louis enlarged our lives. T.M. and Jamie treasure the days when we'd arrive at the Hamilton Hotel, Louis's headquarters for many years, and being Aggie to the heart he'd begin razzing their Dad as to why anyone would choose to be a TCU Hornfrog.

And our Utopia neighbor plus dear amigo, Joe Ben Snider, left us this past week. Can't recall the exact time frame, but seems as 30 or more years have passed since the Sniders became part of Utopia community.

Our Dad considered Joe the best of friends, and Utopia profited from Joe's residence. He set about helping move the Senior Citizen's Center from a dream to reality.

When the center was completed, he and Elaine performed with the "Hill Country Hams," bringing pleasure and fun to canyon residents.

But most of all Joe was widely known for his Christian dedication, and study of the Bible. He kept a notebook in his pocket and would list prayer requests for individuals in it praying for those people daily. Utopia will greatly miss his presence.

What a turbulent year all of us in America have come through. Seems as everyone is struggling to regain their footing. So it was comforting as well as inspiring to sit in our home church, Utopia Methodist, and listen to the Christmas cantata. Joan Fisher Clark directed the choir, Joy Davenport sang a solo part and everyone was wealthier for being present. Saw Joan walking away with a bouquet of richly deserved red roses to commemorate her birthday and congratulate her on such a Crowning accomplishment.

Attending the Sabinal Methodist Pagaent, Carol Clary and I marveled at the ingenious construction of the palapa stable and the tall palms. Remember when your Mom had to scurry about for old bathrobes and headscarves, so we could participate in the Nativity scene?

Christmas 2001, Annalee and I send these wishes to you from a quote which came our way:

"To give without remembering

To receive without forgetting."

2002

Entering 2002

Ever wish you possessed the talents and accomplishments of someone else, if only for a short while?

Such were my sentiments when the vivacious blonde, Teresa Seidl, strolled onstage gowned in the perfect black sequined dress and began to sing "Vilja" from "The Merry Widow." Her highly trained soprano conveyed the joy and excitement necessary to bring out the zest of the Strauss piece.

"A Night in Old Vienna" at the Majestic in San Antonio was a thrilling setting for ushering in the new year. Who of us that attended movies there at a young and tender age will forget the blue sky with its twinkling stars? And the spectacular Andalusian balconies and pillars silhouetted against the indigo sky?

So it felt as a homecoming to sit back and let the strains of 12 violins and sweetness of the French horns provide a jubilant entry into 2002. The encore of "The Beautiful Blue Danube" brought to mind the day we floated down that mighty river past the apricot-colored abbey at Melk. And I wished for Annalee and Jane Mac to be present enjoying once more the melody of that waltz.

Again we enter into a slower pace after the hubbub of the holidays. But the newspapers and television tell us people did not shop as seriously in 2001, and spent more time at home with their families. Isn't this one of the main objectives of the season? Loved the line asking, "When did Martha Stewart become the queen of Christmas?"

My sisters-in-law, Jeanne and Joan, are always anxious for adventure when in residence at Burns-Bownds House, so we decided to seek Hill Country places. Taylor suggested we detour by to view the Karios barn situated off Highway 16, between Kerrville and Fredericksburg.

The frame, huge beams, of the barn was disassembled in the Amish country of Pennsylvania and transported to the Hill Country by artisan Robert Fuege.

A couple from Arlington had the vision to reconstruct the timbers on their Fredericksburg acreage, plus greatly enrich the interior with a huge fireplace of native stone. Now the barn is perfect for the modern-day purpose of a party house which is rented for wedding receptions, birthday parties, business group meetings or whatever the occasion.

The architect was awarded much recognition for his design, using modern-day materials to simulate an old structure. Another use of the barn is for art exhibits. I met the delightful owners at Laity Lodge. Beth is an artist, and Dr. Roy has established all of the landscaping himself. His arbors are the perfect settings for enjoying outdoor vistas.

On the outskirts of Fredericksburg we visited Varney's Herb Farm, as both J and J are serious gardeners as I used to be and intend to be again. But the herb star was down to its bare winter bones with only a few pansies peeping through the cedar shavings and providing a tiny touch of color. Rosemary plants were still dark green and pungent, but frost had nipped the lemon grass and thyme plants.

Over 20 years ago the Varneys purchased 14 acres on the edge of Fredericksburg and set about establishing this unique garden. Now a bed and breakfast, a day spa, restaurant and shop are intermingled with gardens, greenhouses and the Varney's private residence.

Our roast beef sandwiches on sourdough, complimented with creamy, fresh horseradish, were as tender and delicious as anyone could wish, and the garnishes of pansies and johnny-jump-ups delighted us. Their faces always so cheerful.

In the herb star garden many stones are carved with quotes, and I wanted to share the Secret Garden one with you.

"When full of flowers and herbs, symbolic of faith, hope and love, and with gentle scents attractive to wildlife, as if in the Garden of Eden, the cares and chaos of modern lifestyles are healed."

"A secret garden gives us a chance to create the moment, to labor or relax, to believe in the impossible."

Happy New Year's to you and yours, may we believe in the impossible in 2002, and may many joys and interesting experiences pass our way, and may all of us have the eyes and ears to recognize and participate in life's unexpected moments.

Doing the Cajun Country Circuit

Hadn't planned to celebrate my birthday at Mulate's, the original Cajun restaurant near Breaux Bridge, La., but when the opportunity presented itself, I certainly did not pass it by.

Who could resist feasting upon gumbo. crabs, crawfish etoufee, catfish and even alligator? Yes, the alligator was quite tasty; a bit chewy, but not too far off from chicken breast, or perhaps, rattlesnake. Might as well go ahead and be brave and adventurous when exploring new territory.

And the live Cajun music featured at Mulate's was toe-tapping lively, the accordion adding a special touch to the waltzes and two steps. One has to be in shape and quick to keep the proper beat on the dance floor. "Jolie Blonde" was the most recognizable tune, but "Grand Mamou" and "Marie" were just as danceable.

Arcadia, the southwest region of Louisiana, was settled by a colony of French Canadians about 1765; in 1785, another migration arrived from France. These Arcadians, or Cajuns, as they came to be called, created a unique culture, much of which survives today.

The town of Breaux derives its name from the drawbridge over the bayou Teche. My experience with drawbridges was limited to the one over the Corpus Christi ship channel, which raised up from one side, but the BB version is completely drawn up into the high frame, which tops the bridge, itself.

And the Teche has an interesting legend associated with the Chitimacha Indian tribe. A huge snake (Teche), caused the tribe many woes and much destruction. Finally the Indians were able to unite their forces and kill the massive reptile. As the snake's body decomposed, the area around it began to deepen and create the riverbed of the bayou Teche.

Driving the bayou route from Breaux Bridge to St. Martinsville on to Abbeyville, one is impressed with the prosperity and cleanliness of the countryside. The homes are well-kept and colorful, yellow being a favorite, and constructed in the southern manner with porches across the front. This is an agricultural region of rice, crawfish and sugar cane farmers, whose properties are neat and impressive.

In St. Martinsville we lighted candles in the sanctuary of the lovely St. Martin parish. Most of the descendents of the French settlers are Catholic, and the wonderful churches are a testament to their devotion.

Longfellow's immortal poem, "Evangeline," the story of two starcrossed lovers separated by the migration, never to be reunited, is marked by the Evangeline oak on the banks of the bayou Teche. It is the typical Old South oak, huge in circumference, and with moss dripping from its many branches.

In Abbeyville we purchased can syrup at STEENS mill. The friendly girl at the counter had grown up in Fredericksburg, Texas, and had married one of the mill owner's sons. She was pleased to visit with Hill Country folks. One of the pleasures of travel is meeting up with the many people who have ties to Texas.

Our Fredericksburg friend told us the cane mill is in full operation during September and October when the cane is being harvested and processed. It is an important crop in the delta region.

Every home, restaurant and public place was decorated with the festive green, gold and purple of Mardi Gras. Most of the small towns have their own celebrations during this week, including several parades.

The inhabitants all extended invitations to stay and participate in the festivities. The Arcadians are a friendly, sociable people who work hard, play hard and love their corner of America. During Mardi Gras they especially adhere to the Cajun phrase, "Laissez Les Bon Temps Rouler" (let the good times roll).

Heading home through East Texas, we stopped for lunch in Livingston, near the banks of the large lake. A member of our group had been advised to eat at Florida's, and grand advice it was.

Florida's menu, which proclaims, "the Best Home Cookin' since Abraham Lincoln was President" was no idle boast. My plate of pork ribs, potato salad, pinto beans, and cole slaw was so delicious, decided to catalog it as one of my memorable meals. Others feasted on fried catfish, brisket, and pondered over the long list of delicious deserts.

If you ever find yourself near the banks of Lake Livingston, do not miss having a meal at Florida's, it is worth the drive to East Texas.

Utopia 150-Year Celebration

The first of February is the season for the arrival of the martin scouts from Sao Paulo, Costa Rica, and other warm climes. And thanks to the Christmas gift from special friends, I'm prepared with an elegant new house. Had left my three other casas at La Loma because they were occupied with residents last June, which we did not wish to displace.

Purple martins are the birds everyone needs for their outdoor areas as they consume an incredible amount of insects daily, especially mosquitoes. Over the years they provided daily entertainment for us with their flying prowess and antics of the young struggling to begin solo flights. It is pure pleasure to sit on a May evening and observe the activities of resident martins.

Winter and summer are playing tricks with us, but soon garden season begins in earnest. Pruning your shrubs, trees, and rose bushes is the thing to accomplish this month, plus adding new plants to the landscape.

Have always longed for a grape arbor, so am hopeful to get one under construction this spring. Must decide on the shape, size, and type of grapes, wisest choice will be native mustangs, so they'll endure the drought.

1 find arbors attractive additions to buildings in hot climates, always remember a small village in southern Spain where the front of every home was shaded by an arbor and being September the grapes were ripening overhead. The residents used the arbors as outdoor living and dining areas as they provided a respite from the heat. Many older Hill Country homes had arbors instead of porches to provide shade and grapes for jelly making.

Utopia, 1909

While reading the "Sabinal Canyon, 150 Years," memories came to me of the many hours Mama spent compiling information for the Centennial booklet. What a major event the 1952 Centennial celebration was in our lives.

These are a few of my memories, am anxious to compare with you what role you played in the event.

The Park Association hired Fritz Topperweing of Boerne to write, direct, and stage the pageant, which would take place in the rodeo arena. In order for the arena to lighted our Dad made his contribution by working for months climbing those tall, tall poles to install the wiring and electrical equipment. Kathryn Redden told me Paul assisted him.

Handsome Governor Allan Shivers led the parade riding a golden palomino complete with a silver saddle. He was accompanied by O.J. McCullough, Neal and Pearl Horsman, also mounted on palominos. Perhaps the Governor was carrying the Texas flag and Mr. McCullough the American one.

To this day I can see Colie Thomas astride her striking sorrel horse, and wearing a huge Mexican sombrero. Evelyn Fisher LeBouf rode the venerable Fisher horse, Champ, and I was on my mare, Chulita. Neither Ev nor I feel we were properly outfitted for the occasion, although I did have Doris Smith Kruger's boots which she had loaned to me because we couldn't just run out and purchase a new pair of boots for a parade.

The Methodist Church float was constructed to resemble a brush arbor, and upon it rode Grace Fisher, my grandmother Wentworth, Aunt Ella and Uncle Rollie Harper, Mama, Mr., and Mrs. Frank Jones, and Aunt Lucille Matthews was playing a small organ. Philip Dibrell was the Methodist minister at the time.

Ev has perfect recall as playing the part of a prickly pear in the pageant, but for the likes of me, can't remember my role. Know we traveled to Gibson's costume warehouse in SA to rent a long dress and bonnet for Mother also one for Biggie Wentworth.

Annalee worked for a year or more before the Centennial date traveling up and down the canyon, interviewing its citizens, and writing their stories. One of her favorite storytellers was Casper Schweinfurt, and we paid several visits to his home while she chatted with that canyon pioneer.

Another colorful source of stories for her was the Thompson brothers, Lonnie, Hub, Johnnie, and Curly. To me, one of Mamas most memorable articles was the tribute she wrote to Johnnie Thompson which begins, "There is an empty saddle in the canyon tonight. One of the greatest old-time cowboys was laid to rest in Vanderpool cemetery this afternoon."It is included in the "150-Year" book.

Make a note to get yourself a copy of this interesting and absorbing book; it will bring back wonderful memories to those of us who call the Sabinal Canyon home. And begin to make preparations for the celebration, which is scheduled for the third weekend in June. It will be a glorious gathering of friends and families.

Traveling Around South Texas

Sitting in the Blessed Sacrament Church, Laredo, for the Feast of the Epiphany, it was easy to reflect upon the turbulence of 2001, and gaze eagerly forward with hope toward the beginning of 2002. The beauty and radiance of the ceremony related the travels of the three Kings of old seeking the Christ child, and I, a traveler, too, was grateful to be present.

When we are young it is tough to make intelligent decisions concerning college, and courses of study, at least it was for me. After a year at Sul Ross, Alpine seemed too remote and far, far away from Utopia and the Sabinal canyon for my comfort. So I changed schools in order to room with cousin and lifetime friend, Mary Tom Harper. We enrolled at Texas A&I University (now part of the Texas A&M system), and now years later the two of us keep in touch, visit, and make excellent use of Southwestern Bell's telephone facilities.

But a period of several years had passed since my last visit to MT's home, so headed the red Explorer south. Together the two of us can while away many pleasant hours shopping for notions for the quilt I've been putting together for her granddaughter, browsing in bookstores, comparing titles which we've recently read, and this time attending, a movie.

We hadn't properly prepared ourselves for the power and magnitude of "A Beautiful Mind." The film is a biography based on the life of Dr. John Nash, a mathematical genius who was ultimately awarded the Nobel Prize for his work in international economics.

But Dr. Nash had to struggle for years to conquer the debilitating effects of schizophrenia. The film director handled the subject in a most creative and imaginative manner. If you've ever had experience in dealing with the ravages caused by this disorder, it is easy to relate to the problems John Nash experienced.

Such a powerful theme, but it gave us much to ponder and discuss. I recommend this thought-provoking movie to all of you.

After a respite near Corpus, and gazing out upon the Nueces watershed, I packed my bags, and prepared to travel west for an interlude with another college amigo.

While Linda Ronstadt belted out "Mi Ranchito" on the cassette, I pondered how many years had slipped away since last seeing the fertile fields around Banquete, Agua Dulce, and Alice. Farmers had bedded up the black clay soil, and were awaiting adequate moisture for planting corn, milo, and later, cotton. Persistent drought has plagued these competent people for the past five years, and many are struggling to survive.

San Diego, George Parr's old stronghold, looked sad and abandoned. Freer was full of oil field equipment, and signs advertising the "Muy Grande" deer contest.

Was amazed at all the pumps indicating ample oil and gas activity between Freer and Laredo. Tigerstriped cows grazed dry buffel grass pastures, but it was easy to discern that high fences for raising trophy whitetails were much more prevalent than ordinary cattle ranches.

On the outskirts of Laredo, was startled by the tremendous outlay of attractive buildings situated around a man-made lake. The area proved to be the Laredo site of Texas A&M University. The Killiam family donated 300 acres for the campus which is tastefully constructed in Spanish style. What an educational asset to this isolated area of Texas.

A few statistics concerning the rapid growth and changes in Webb county. Four international bridges channel 15,000 to 18,000 tractor truck rigs daily across the Rio Grande. Laredo is the fastest growing city in Texas, and the second fastest growing one in America. All this commerce and international business is the result of the NAFTA trade agreement.

Huge new highway interchanges are being constructed to handle the flow of trucks carrying materials to and from the maquiladoras in Mexico. Much of the area north of the city is covered in a sea of warehouses where the merchandise is loaded and unloaded daily.

New developments of expensive and luxurious homes on what was formerly dry ranchland testify to the booming prosperity. My first remembrances of this border community began when we would travel to Mirando City checking cattle and pasture conditions. Laredo was always pleasant headquarters for it offered excellent food, lodging, a crossing point for Mexican steers, and provided the entry for traveling to the interior of Mexico.

My friends and I admitted we find ourselves somewhat overwhelmed and awed by all the traffic, building, and population which is transforming their lifetime home. Somehow it is both exciting and invigorating, but also scary.

A memorable meal was steak Milanesa, served with fried potatoes, refried beans, and Spanish rice. In all my years of eagerly consuming Mexican specialties, never had I tasted this exact cut of beef. Rosina explained the procedure for preparing it properly.

Order a thin, not over a half-inch thick slice of loin, available in Laredo markets but not known to our butchers. Dredge the steak in an egg and milk batter, then coat with finely crushed cracker crumbs, cook it very quickly on a hot, slightly oiled griddle. You do not want it to be overdone.

Shopping on San Bernardo for a recuerdo to remind me of this time with amigos, we found the perfect flower pots, one rana (frog), and two conejos (rabbits), perfect for potting petunias.

For the drive to Cotulla on 1-35 North, my compadres provided me with the perfect dicho to consider.

"Lo comido y pasado nadie te lo quita."

"What you have eaten and where you have traveled no one can take away from you."

Remembering 'The Greatest Generation'

Hope Tom Brokaw will not be offended by my borrowing his book title, but as I sat down to type this, I realized that my subjects are all of the generation of which he wrote so eloquently.

In early December, Deloise Reagan chauffeured Pat Rochat, Sophie Falkenburg and myself to the ranch home of Linda Thorne and her family near Kerrville.

Linda is the daughter of Lillian and Felix Real of Utopia, and the occasion was the celebration of Lillian's 80th birthday. The crowd included a mixture of friends and kin from Fredericksburg, Kerrville, Utopia, Sabinal, Knippa, and Uvalde. Each one of us was acquainted with Lillian's warm, welcoming personality, and the Real's special type of hospitality.

2002 was also the time of Lillian and Felix celebrating sixty years of marriage. Some of the cousins reminisced, "The two of them always worked together. If Felix was driving a

Lillian Real, bride of Felix, 1942

tractor, Lillian would be riding with him." From my visits to the Real Donoho ranch, I am well aware of the many projects this team has accomplished.

Linda, Robin Roberts, Sandra and Casper Real, Lillian and Felix's children organized the birthday party. From the windows of the rambling ranch home we could see the flock of fine wool sheep Linda and family still maintain on the property. They are line-bred descendents of the original strain of fine wools, which Felix Real (Linda's great great grandfather) introduced to the Hill Country many years ago.

As we chatted over delicious desserts and coffee, the present day Felix drew our attention to a blue darter (Cooper's hawk) harassing the birds at Linda's feeders. All sorts of feathered friends were drinking from the native rock fountain designed and constructed by Felix.

The Reals have enhanced and enriched our Utopia community since moving to the Real-Donoho ranch in the '70s. Am happy to have an exceptional piece of artwork masterminded by the two, and always leap at an invitation to the ranch where Felix and Lillian have created a haven from native materials.

Was sorry and saddened to learn of the passing of Marvin Angermiller, although I knew he was not able to recover from the disease that claimed his life.

Marvin was a true product of our part of the world, and his smile was as wide as Uvalde County.

He was one of Mac's longtime amigos and from time to time they would organize a hunting party to pursue bobcats, panthers, or whatever type of predator Mac might have spied along the banks of the Sabinal, Blanco, or Frio.

Once while we were still in residence at Yucca Switch, Mac warned me not to wonder at what time he'd return as he, Marv, perhaps J.L. Haby, and other friends would be out hunting a big cat Mac had sighted at the Hiler ranch.

About 3 a.m. Mac returned to the red ranch house, weary, dejected, and tired of the hunt.

"So you all gave it up?" I asked.

"Hell, no. Marv's still down there; he may work at it for another two or three nights, but he's a lot tougher and more dedicated than I am."

Ten or more years ago we had our grandson, Mason Woodley (age 4) dressed in boots and hat at the Cypress City celebration. Cowboys fascinated Mason at that stage of life, and when we sat down to eat our barbecue lunch with Helen and Marvin I told him, "Mr. Angermiller is a REAL cowboy."

And he was. One of the generation of which we shall not see the likes again. Helen, I send heartfelt sympathy to you and your family. it's tough-to lose a guy who is an original. They aren't making anymore like Marv.

Wrangled an invitation to Bub Wheeler's 80th birthday party by escorting Fannie Hindes to Pam and Lee Wheeler's attractive ranch home.

Have known Bub from the time my name became Woodley. Mac became fast friends of all the Wheelers while attending TMI with Gus. Still have a photo of Gus and Charley (Bub's brother), Blackstone and Caldwell Dilworth, Mac, and Dick Horton all together at Tilden.

When we passed the sign, "Entering the Free State of McMullen County," I knew we were in Wheeler country.

Bub greeted Fannie and myself with gifts of 2003 calendars from the Live Oak Livestock auction, which were a salute to the veterans of the area. Sure enough, on the Septiembe page was Bub outfitted in his WWII uniform.

Always dressed in his high top Luccheses, Bub is the most genial of men. After giving us a tour of the fabulous deer heads in the hunter's lodge, he joked, "Yup, it's easy to see who is the smartest in our family. Lee wanted to put up high fences, and I wanted to stay in the cattle business."

Mac had an endearing story that reflects Bub's kind nature and easygoing attitude. When Lee Bracken Wheeler was about 5 or 6, he kept insisting to his Dad how very badly Lee's horse wanted to see the train. Finally, after Lee kept pursuing this matter for a period of time, Bub hitched up the trailer, they loaded the horse (can't remember the name), and hauled that ole' pony from McMullen county up to progressive Pleasanton and let him have the pleasure of watching the train pass by.

Bub is in that category with Marv, a South Texas original. His own man.

★

Spouse-Partner Relationships Exalted

Had it in mind to write about Dale Evans and Anne Morrow Lindberg passing away during the same week. They were both two of my real-life heroines, and I have read most of the books written by or about each of them.

Low and behold, I sat down one evening to watch the PBS Evening News, and Roger Rosenblatt had beaten me to the draw. His essay on Dale and Anne's lives was insightful and thought provoking. He pointed out several parallels in their lives. Each had experienced tragedy through their children, both were highly successful authors. Dale wrote over 20 dozen songs, the most memorable, of course, "Happy Trails To You."

Anne Lindbergh was the author of many books and diaries, her most famous being, "A Gift From The Sea."

Roger pointed out that initially both women owed their fame to their husbands, but as

June Fisher and Henry Fisher, 1972

time passed each became famous in her own right. He felt Anne and Dale each had nerve, a spirit to push forward with their own ideas and ambitions, a special gift of "moxie."

Rosenblatt concluded these women who married "media kings" had the will to forge a partnership with their husbands, thus creating a team which enlarged their relationships with their famous husbands. As a result the women became as well-known as their men.

Reflecting on Roger's remarks concerning the greatness and vitality which can result from building partnerships within the framework of marriage, the names of "real-life" teams sprang to mind. The following are but a few of the spouse-partner relationships I've witnessed over the years.

Chris and Kerry Melson – after Chris sorted and loaded steers, Kerry weighed the trucks, figured the weights, and wrote the checks.

Betty and Gary Hart – he builds outstanding mesquite furniture. She tends the store and puts a glistening finish on his creations.

Halydene and Jerry Aaron – Jerry keeps the equipment in perfect running order as Halydene drives either the truck or the combine as they harvest crops over Texas.

Lowell and Jamie Tubbs – he was the superintendent and coach at Utopia schools. Mrs. Tubbs taught English, and together they saw that we all received an education.

Jack and Evelyn Kingsbery – Jack ranched and built safes on the side. Evelyn was the librarian at Southwest Texas Junior College, together on horseback they still gather their Beefmaster herd.

Fannie Grace and Roy Hindes – Roy built high fences, and pioneered growing outstanding whitetail bucks. Fannie cooked for the hunters and entertained them with her piano.

Dorothy and Dan Kinsel Jr. – Dan would put together the grass leases and steers while Dorothy (always smiling) drove him all over Mexico and the Western United States.

Henry and June Fisher – Henry tended to his ranching and Methodist church affairs, while June cared for her home, children, grandchildren and great grandchildren.

George and Barbara Bush – while George was at the helm of our country, Barbara managed the White House, cared for her family, wrote books, and defended George.

Henry and Annalee Burns – Daddy repaired telephone lines and sold insurance, while Annalee cooked, kept house, played the piano and wrote for the newspaper. Together they taught us there is magic in marriage when there is teamwork.

Ann Morrow Lindbergh wrote:

"How are the waters of the world sweet
If we should die,
We have drunk them.
If we should sin or separate
If we should fail or secede
We have tasted happiness
We must be written in the book of the blessed.
We have had what life was to give,
We have eaten the tree of knowledge.
We have known
We have been the mystery of the universe."

"Happy Trails" to Dale and Anne, and gracias for the life lessons they taught us.

The Convention in Cowtown

"Put on your new shoes, Put on your gown, Shake off those sad blues, The big ball's in town."

The Braeford pear trees were struggling bravely to bloom in the inclement weather, which attacked Fort Worth last week. But by Friday all the blossoms had been blown, beaten, and washed from the tree limbs.

The Texas and Southwestern Cattle Raisers chose to convene in Fort Worth for their 125th meeting. The group's very first gathering had been in nearby Graham, Texas, and the year was 1877.

On Monday morning we listened to Gov. Rick Perry speak. He is down to earth, Texan to his core, and one of us, but he faces a fierce fight for his future in the upcoming election.

The best aspect of cattlemen's gathering for me is seeing faces from our past. Dr. Lev Gayle manned the Texas A&M Veterinary Medicine School booth, and is now the head of the vet school diagnostic lab. His experience and expertise guided Mac through many a cattle health crisis.

Deets Finely and Augusta Sasser's youngest son Stewart greeted us early Monday morning. Stewart promises his Mother, Mrs. Kinsel,

Mrs. Hindes, and myself a tour of his South Texas acreage if we'll just set the date.

Robin Clark was sporting a spectacular tie presented to him by Sheriff Terry Crawford. It was yellow, with the Lone Star in the center and symbols of Texas all around. He was headed toward the Mercedes boot booth with the pair Mac had presented him. Time passes and those boots needed repairs. Robbie always was horseback when we shipped steers, and along with labor he provided the humor during those busy times.

Had lunch with friends Margie and Tommy Hagelin of the Chaparrosa. They reported a completion of most of the building projects on the ranch, and now, like most of us, are praying for rain.

Spotted Dr. Bill Holloway of the Uvalde Texas A&M Experiment Station, at a distance, but never had the opportunity to say "Hello."

Belito Donnell brought us up to date on his son's marriage this past summer, Kathy's teaching, and drought in the Big Bend area. Together we laughed over the remembrances of the pheasant hunt the Donnells, Woodleys, Kinsels, Hargroves, and Taylors experienced in the Texas panhandle. Dorothy and I still have the trophies of that expedition.

When young people seek you out my spirits are always refreshed. So seeing Joan Petty, Nancy Bracken Walden, Tom Arnim, Tex and Annie Vestring was special as each of them visited at la Loma when T.M. and Jamie were growing up.

Mac Woodley, Jr. cutting steers at Rancho Nuevo, 1998

A tour to the new Philip Johnson designed building housing the Amon Carter collection of western art was inspiring. Naturally, Russell's monumental sculpture, "Coming Through the Rye," is in the foyer, as is Remington's unforgettable painting, "A Dash for the Timber." Personally I was drawn to the two rooms housing Russell's miniature sculptures. Try to schedule a visit to this mother lode of western art if you are in Fort Worth.

Returning to the Stockyards Hotel and Exchange building brought back memories of the year Mac made the decision to offer our set of steers for sale through

Superior satellite. We were nervous, never having used this method of marketing before. What if no buyers came forth? Would the market hold up? Could we make the deal profitable?

That year Mac and Will had worked especially hard to divide the cattle by color, so the sets of yellow charbray, black angus and brangus, and red brafords showed up spectacularly over the many television sets in Superior's offices. Bidding was spirited and when it was all over we had a satisfactory price for the cattle, and a new tool for marketing them.

That evening we celebrated across the street at the White Elephant Saloon, with Buddy and Harriet Jeffers, Dan Kinsel III and Leslie, listening to Don Edwards sing "Faded Love," "A Maiden's Prayer," and of course "Big Ball's in Cowtown."

"Big Ball's in Cowtown.
We'll all go down, Big ball's in Cowtown, We'll dance around."

Growth, Change in Area

Naturally you're aware of the sweep of changes in the Hill Country and our own communities. Those of us who grew up in Uvalde, Real, and Bandera counties marvel at it daily.

And as Annalee notes, "Progress is not all bad, not all good." But she would also hasten to add, "Better to be growing and changing than diminishing, and drying up."

Lately both Sabinal and Utopia are experiencing the seeds of change, and new life is flowing into our small communities which at some periods have sat too long stagnant.

A jewel for Sabinal is the newly renovated Nunley Brothers building, the original Sabinal State Bank building. Upstairs it houses the Nunley ranch offices, furnished with original mesquite furniture. Downstairs Kim Brown (daughter of Betty Kincaid Mathis) has established an inviting soda fountain and pharmacy. Our community was deeply in need of a place to gather, lunch, purchase greeting cards and gifts, and order prescriptions.

We have Rich and Bob Nunley to thank for such a tasteful, attractive building on Main Street. Best wishes Rich, Bob, and Kim; your efforts have enriched our community.

And Frankie Odgen's Main Street Diner is the perfect plate to savor a home cooked meal while visiting with family and/or friends. Frankie and I became soul mates during a difficult time in our lives,we spent many hours on the telephone encouraging each other.

Frankie's son Chuck Van Pelt is still in the process of recovering from an almost fatal burn, so special wishes for success with the Diner are in order for Frankie and her entire family.

Standing in my new kitchen it is easy to gaze out upon the activity at R B-B-Q, located 1200 North Center Street, owned and operated by the Rodriquez family. So another nice new choice is available for those of us who enjoy eating out, our best to Robert, Irma, and boys.

Soon Utopia will sport a larger, new efficient building to house the branch of the First State Bank of Uvalde. So convenient to have a bank in town, this service was not available during my growing up years. Remember Henry would rise from the dinner (lunch) table and announce, "Have to make a quick trip to Sabinal before the bank closes. Does anyone want to ride with me?"

And the First State kindly and graciously donated the old bank building to the Utopia library. So the old bank building has been moved to a new location and is in the process of being converted to a modern book establishment. What a wonderful addition for Utopia. Heartfelt thanks to the bank board for making this possible.

In his book, "Walter Benjamin At The Dairy Queen," Larry McMurtry remarks he grew up "bookless" in Archer county. Could easily relate, to his experience, as the only books easily available to us in the '50s were the small selection in the school library and Annalee's subscription to the Book-of-the-Month Club.

Now through the library, Canyon citizens have access to use of computers, the Internet, and huge selection of current periodicals and books. We are "bookless" no longer.

Not to let Sabinal surpass them, Utopia has its own new Bar-B-Que establishment, owned and operated by Jim and Carol Magnum. Carol grew up involved in the business, as her parents operate a similar establishment near the Austin area. Annalee, Betty Leighton, Alice Bond, and other family members plus myself have enjoyed pleasant Sunday lunches in the Mangum's attractive establishment.

Can't miss mentioning the beautiful and exciting Main Street Utopia shop established by Wanda Waters and family, and presided over by Diane Causey. Every visit here is exciting and second only to a trip to Provence, the origin of much of the merchandise. If you have not visited, save your $$$ as there are many special items here.

And our family is anxiously awaiting the construction of the Burns-Bownds sports complex for the Vanderpool-Utopia community.

Our Dad loved the game of baseball. Am sure his only equipment during his childhood years was a worn glove, perhaps a ragged ball, and hopefully, a bat. So it pleases us that soon Sabinal canyon youngsters will play ball in style upon Daddy's fields.

Sports are an avenue of enjoyment, cooperation, scholarships, and teamwork for boys and girls. Hopefully, the Burns-Bownds field will offer an opportunity for fellowship and fun for the people who still love to "Play ball!"

The above are only but a small few of the many new businesses and organizations opening in our area. Forgive me for not listing each and every one. Best wishes and Godspeed to each and every individual and civic group who have stepped forward and invested in the future of our area. Hopefully, all of you will prosper and flourish in the next several years.

Cold Weather Brings the Blues

Dry, frigid northers blowing off the Yukon have always given me the blues. And as I write, a huge one is howling around the doors and windows, promising to wreak more havoc to our already parched, frozen land. My grandmother Burns ranched solo for 15 years, and would have referred to this weather, as "nights which would freeze the horns off billy goats."

Perhaps growing up in the dry years of the '50s give rise to these feelings. To my mind the cruelty of drought deals a tougher hand than wet weather. Those of you in my generation are sure to recall the dust storms, which literally blackened the skies during those years. And our Dads (mine had to get down in the well himself) digging the water wells deeper, selling off their livestock and struggling to survive economically.

My thoughts are with the agricultural producers who are forced to deal with this inclement weather during March, when we should be experiencing spring temperatures. In a high dollar investment business, with markets producing low pay-offs, the unknown risk factor of weather can put people out of business overnight.

One year Mac and our Dad were experimenting with a new forage crop, tricale. It flourished under their efforts to properly fertilize and water that winter. They thought they had hit upon the perfect answer to winter grazing problems.

One afternoon an arctic front blew in from Alberta and the next morning the thermometer registered 15 degrees in our kitchen window and 10 degrees at Bownds house, Utopia. The tricale was flattened, frozen completely through to the roots, naturally it was stocked to the hilt with steers. Overnight our business label changed to the "Out of Grass Cattle Company," and we had a set of cattle with nothing to eat.

And all of you farmers and ranchers reading this could recite dozens of your own stories of similar experiences.

Greatly enjoyed seeing Dr. Hagan Lippke and Dr. David Forbes' "frontal grazing" system in operation. Millie had called to invite me for a look and lunch. So interesting to watch the 47 steers line up behind the sprinkler, which introduces them to untouched rye grass forage four different times daily.

This type of learned animal behavior and controlled pasture area provides a situation in which all of the fresh feed is utilized to its potential, and produces more pounds of beef per animal. Hagan and David are working to fine tune the cost factors and adaptability of this concept. As in all experiments, it has great benefits but the economics of making it work on the ranch also come into play.

Drs. Lippke and Forbes have labored together the past 10 years to research the many variables in grazing forages for our area. Their efforts were greatly profitable for Mac's steer operation. All agricultural producers in our area have benefited from the many programs conducted by the Uvalde A&M Experiment Station.

During lunch, Millie, Hagan and myself discussed the future of American agriculture. We are most aware of the economic pitfalls in the industry and realize the terrific struggle farmers and ranchers are facing to survive. So many question as to how new markets can be created, and the huge expenses of operating costs driven down.

None of us had any concrete answers, but we expressed a pride in being associated with an industry that has been the backbone of our nation since its inception.

Hopefully the cold weather will abate, rains will fall softly upon our country and cattle and grain prices will rise. It is such a tough business, but it does have its bright sides, most of your are your own boss and you're not stuck on the freeways every morning and afternoon. Best wishes to every farmer and rancher.

Where Is Spring?

Keep remarking to everyone, "As soon as the sun shines it will be spring," but it doesn't and it isn't. Sad all this drip and drizzle hasn't produced any measurable moisture for most of us.

But did get started on springtime adventures by placing some tomato plants in large pots, had to race out and haul 'em into the kitchen when the icy spell hit.

Forgot to cover my kalanchoes during those chilly 24 hours, so now have four pots of mush. But am not going to cry over kalanchoes, they are easily replaced.

Outside my living room window, the first of spring flowers, scrambled eggs (southern corydalis), are flowering and covering the turn-rows, and a few primroses and verbena are appearing as well.

Driving along in Webb County, acres of popping weed (bladder wort) were creating yellow vistas, and golden huisache, plus creamy catclaw were beginning to bloom. Now those native plants are beginning to flower here as well.

Joan Woodley and Anne at Fiesta fireworks party

Had a most informative and entertaining morning at the San Antonio Garden Center thanks to my sister, Joan Woodley (yes, she is my sister-in-law), but I think of her without the hyphens.

We heard three well known garden writers speak of their personal gardening passions, using slides for illustrations.

Ken Druse, author of "The Natural Habitat Garden," advised us, "Don't be afraid to stick your head out in your gardening endeavors because you might get it chopped off. If you don't stick it out, you'll never get ahead."

Ken wants us to get out and use those plants indigenous to our area, which will not have to be constantly kissed and cuddled in order to flourish.

Listening to Jill Nokes was a delight; she grew up in West Texas and knows her bitterweed from a desert willow. Now her home is Austin where she operates a landscaping business.

Jill struck a note true to my heart when she cried about the urbanization of our native state, and the mass plantings of trees and shrubs not adapted to our area.

Her well-researched book, "How To Grow Native Plants of Texas and the Southwest" is a treasure for all of us seeking to identify plants in our part of the world.

She loves landscaping with Lindheimer's mulcy grass, sotos, aloes, lantanas, laurels, oaks, junipers, and other hardy Texas natives. But she also warns we have many "thugs" in our natural environment, which need to be eliminated.

Am unhappy with the sterile, flat, mown look of my place. So am going to begin by adding some cenizo, guajillo, sotos, and Lindheimers in the corners, hopefully softening the edges.

What a glorious spring lies ahead. The bluebonnet plants are as large as plates, thanks to abundant winter moisture. Every wild seed in the state should be sprouted and soon be showing its face.

2003 is the spring season to leave the dishes in the sink, the vacuum in the closet, and get outdoors. As my wise cousin Betty remarked, "It isn't about the house anyway." Mother Nature is going to strut her stuff, and I for one am not going to miss the show.

Ranch People Face Daily Dangers

Cattle trucks rumble by early momings and hours later return loaded moving toward Highway 90. Late April, early May the winter grazing, oats, rye grass is giving out and cattlemen are shipping steers and heifers north to Kansas grass or panhandle feedlots.

The amount of men, horses, helicopters, trucks, truckers needed to accomplish these tasks are tremendous, dangerous, and difficult. First of all you can bet on being short handed, usually there are not enough trucks available, and sometimes the cattle do not work the way you had planned.

Such a situation developed in our community when Robert Driskill roped a steer from his mount; the steer (perhaps 600-700 pounds,) cut back, jerked the horse over on Robert and knocked him unconscious.

Fortunately the man working with Robert was able to find George Driskill, and in a short time Rob was airlifted to University of Texas Hospital, San Antonio, trauma center.

Daily family and friends wait and pray for Robert to seek his way back to consciousness, and to regain movement of his limbs.

Many families in our part of the world are familiar with horse and cattle wrecks, and have experienced the anxiety of waiting such as the Driskill family is now enduring. Three years ago Barksdale neighbors Charley Carson and Bill Lane wound up in unrelated horse accidents and in the University trauma unit. The certainty of their recovery was unknown for many weeks. Thanks to modern medicine, many prayers, and God's grace, those two are back in Barksdale, living normal lives. Bill's family keep him on the ground, away from the saddle and horses; don't know if Charley still mounts up. But cousins Ted Harper and Billy Fisher do. About two years ago Ted saddled up one morning and headed for the "lower country"

John Driskill II, Robert Driskill, George Driskill around John Driskill, Sr.

section of the ranch. His mount stepped in a hole and Ted ended up with broken bones. Fortunately he had his cell phone, contacted grandson Clete, and the Border Patrol helicoptered Ted out of the canyon.

This May Ted will be 88, he and Annalee are first cousins, and share the same birth date. He still mounts up with two artificial knees, but all our family knows you can't keep a Harper off a horse.

Billy suffered horse injuries this winter, but when I questioned him several weeks ago if he was riding again he replied, "Well, Annie, you know we all got to do what we can to keep going."

Years ago when Evelyn and Bub Mauldin's young Linda was terribly broken up while riding, they called Henry to come quick. Daddy was always Cool Hand Luke in a crisis. He picked up Linda, loaded the distraught parents, and drove as fast as the car would run to Uvalde emergency.

Gene Ilse told me the details of a horse mishap in his youth, and how weeks later Dr. Walter Meyer performed surgery on his leg which had developed gangrene.

Many of us around Sabinal remember the terrible injury Jack Kincaid suffered years ago. His mother, Jewel Kincaid, never let go of the belief he would recover, and he did.

My sweet friend Barbara and husband Gary Machen lost their son Cap during a cattle working, a freak accident claiming that young man's life.

Whenever the loss of Kathy Soyars comes to mind, tears spring to my eyes. She gave her life helping her husband with his business, trying to make his load a little lighter and easier. I'll always love her for those reasons.

All of those of us involved in the ranching and cattle business know how dangerous it can be to work daily with animals. But we tend to take it in stride and go on about our business.

Remember every day when we were in the process of delivering steers I'd pray, "Dear Lord, keep Mac, the men, cattle and horses safe. Let the cattle arrive safely at their destinations." Sometimes they did, sometimes they didn't.

After Robert's injury have given much thought to the perils which stockmen and ranch expose themselves to daily, although their product does not earn a premium in the marketplace.

And yet, the cowboy, cattleman's way of life still holds an aura of romance and allure. Our amigo, Alberto Musquiz hit the nail on the head with this statement in "Voices of the American West," "I never met a rich man who didn't want to be a cowboy or a rancher."

Perhaps this quote from "Voices," explains a bit of the satisfaction of western life, "People are always telling me, 'Dang, you won't even be able to walk when you get older,' and I tell them, 'Yeah, but I'll have a whole lot more to talk about than you will,' Scott Gilbert, rodeo, cowboy."

Keep the Driskill family in your prayers. They face the difficult struggle of helping Robert regain his life. But they have faced adversity in the ranching business every moment of their lives and thrived upon it. They will handle this situation competently.

My Hospital Visit

Recently I made the first hospital visit for myself since the year I was ten years old, and the time had come to have my tonsils removed. For days ahead of time I cut and prepared my paper dolls in anticipation of this large event looming in the future of my life. The paper dolls were correctly arranged in a shoebox in readiness for their trip to the big city, where I would have ample hours to dress them, and not be concerned with school assignments.

After the surgery I was too ill to hold my head up off the pillow, much less even cast an eye in the direction of the dolls. As in many matters of mankind, things did not go as I anticipated.

Two months ago I made a trip to the dermatologist to determine the nature of a large lesion, the answer: no problema, but please pay 268 dollars for that conclusion, and pay it NOW, before leaving the office.

Two weeks after the dermatologist visit, I was struck with stabbing pains shooting around my midsection, so severe that I called for a friend to drive me to Northeast Baptist Hospital ER. We left at 5 a.m., arrived at 6:30, the doctor came in at 7. Dr. Bell assured me they'll get to the root of the problem, admitted me for tests, and I wound up in the ER waiting room the last week of April on the other side of a very thin curtain from a fellow who looked as if he's been celebrating Fiesta every day since 2001. He was very vocal concerning his aches and pains.

Doc ordered a sonogram and X-Ray for me, and soon the nurse arrived with eight glasses of water to drink, eight is the number a normal person is supposed to drink in the course of a day. Ok, I got the drinking accomplished; off they rolled me for the sonogram. "You No Drink Enough Water,"the technician loudly admonished me. "Okay, I replied, give me two more glasses; I'll drink 'em.""Oh, No, You No Do That Here!" he got louder each time.

Rolling along the corridors and staring at the ceiling, I realized this was my first ride on a gurney; I've followed many, but never was the one taking a ride.

Next I'm back in the small space with the Fiesta amigo who was cursing, carrying on as if every breath is bound to be his last. I considered using my best schoolteacher admonishment tone on him, but decide it wasn't worth the expended energy, and would not work anyway.

Okay, two more glasses of water and many, many minutes later I'm back in the sonogram section, "You wanna see your kidney?" the tech asked. "Not particularly," I replied. "Oh, it look mighty good," he assured me. "Well, I'll take a peek if you insist." And he gladly showed me the image, and was so pleased with himself, I reassured him, "if you'll make me a copy, I'll have it framed." He flashed me a large happy smile.

Four hours and two prescriptions costing $176.82 later, we returned to Sabinal, and I had the dim, discouraging feeling of not being taken seriously.

Next week I journeyed to San Antonio for 2 other type of medical tests I waited five months to have because the doctor was too busy delivering babies (and making money) to worry about me.

I was in the capable hands of Mary, and it was so nice not to have to drive myself. Tests went off fine. "You're fit as a fiddle, Mrs. Woodley, go home and enjoy the wildflowers." Thanks be to God, no more medical worries, Mary and I decided to celebrate at La Fogota, one of my favorite Mexican havens. Thought my order of the combination of rajas and enchiladas would either kill or cure me, and I did not want to miss these heavenly dishes.

Back at Casa Anita in Sabinal, all was well, each day filled with hustle and bustle. I set out new plants, completed the red and white baby quilt, and transported Annalee for a pedicure, and naturally she chose red polish.

Home again, jiggy-jog. Bedtime, and later in the small hours those little arrows began shooting around my midsection, then danced in my cabesa, and occasionally crawled down my right leg. BUT, I must be NUTS, because after all three different doctors have proclaimed I was in fine condition.

After a very few hours of sleep, I jumped up, quickly packed my bags, and headed the red Explorer for San Antonio and the Fiesta festivities.

Enjoyed a festive evening complete with mariachis, excellent food, and visiting with friends I only see occasionally these days. My amigas, Blanca Laborde and Cornelia Musquiz brought me up to date on the recent events in

Alberto Musquiz, Jr.,
Musquiz Ranch, Mexico

their part of the world. Cornelia is much younger than me, but we had much in common as she lost Belito seven years ago. Beto flew Mac and Louis Wardlaw many miles over Mexican cattle ranches. I always think of Beto's quote in "Voices and Visions of the American West," "I never a rich man who didn't want to be a rancher," was a true statement.

Blanca and I discussed the many problems involved in caring for parents, I assured her, "Where you are I have been."

Returned to my SA abode, high in the sky, all was well, and I stared out at out the Fiesta filled skyline, and drank in the exuberating sparkle of a thousand lights. Life was good.

As the hall clock struck 12, my foe, the sharp pain ran around my middle, continuing gleefully down my right leg, ending in little electric sparks such as sparklers produce. This continued throughout the remainder of the night, and my only respite was to roll around on the woolen carpet, feeling lower than a snail.

At 9:03 a.m. I was on the telephone to the one of the doctors who had proclaimed me a picture of health. "Come in for another test, I'll give you a prescription for pain, BUT I'll be leaving today at 3 p.m., and not return until 1:00 Monday," translated, "Lady I'm out of here for the weekend, take the pain pills and it'll all work out."

My friend appeared in her red brush-country suburban and we headed back to Northeast Baptist. Somehow the deer guard on the SUV looked out place among so many city Lexus, Mercedes, and Cadillacs, but that was no never mind to us ranch gals.

Another CAT scan, I could have spent two weekends luxuriating at the Acapulco Princess for what this will cost. The nurse advised me, now wait until Monday afternoon and the doctor will call you with the results.

Return again to my SA headquarters, thinking I'll attend the big party tonight, but about 3 p.m., I received a gentle warning and bowed out of the engagement – gracefully, I hope.

At 12 p.m. the demon staged a strike against my middle, crawled fiercely down my right leg, and crept up the rib cage. Was I losing my marbles? Remember the doctors say you are in great health.

3:00 a.m. – I thought of flinging myself off this seventh story, making the headlines, and not having to pay the medical bills.

4:00 a.m. – My body was introduced to the agony of pure exquisite pain; I made a pact with myself, to give our family friend, Dr. Chris the luxury of sleeping to 5 a.m. before calling him.

5:01 a.m. – after dialing Dr. Chris's number, he immediately answered, instructed me to enter St, Luke's ER, and he'd have all the wheels turning to admit me.

Creeping along Loop 410, I gave thanks there was the blessing of no traffic, and sweated out each shooting star of pain. FREE PARKING FOR WEEKENDS, the parking lot meter exclaimed, the first real break in this entire episode.

"Mrs. Woodley, we're expecting you,"the ER nurses told me, now here' a wheelchair for you. "For Me?" I've never ridden in a wheelchair in my entire life.

"A private room, what is that?" answered my first question as I was rolled into 130B. At St. Luke's the day was just beginning. "You want pancakes with bacon?" a lady asked. "Please, no food, but lots of coffee."

Dr. Chris appeared, his kind manner in tact, "More tests, Anne."Off they wheeled me in the chair to the basement of St. Luke's, my first MRI proceeded nicely.

Returned to 301, much family was visiting the roommate; we're all packed in very close quarters, and everyone was speaking loudly.

The day drug by, consoled myself that at least I was by the window and was able to see clouds, a tree, and an occasional bird. How I hate being closed away from the outside world.

The demons danced around in my head and threatened me with pitchforks at intervals.

"The doctor has ordered yet another test," the nurse informs me, "Searching for kidney stones." The procedure will go like this: dye will be injected into my blood stream, NO FOOD for the remainder of the day.

9:00 p.m. – back to the basement for the scan, I got settled on a layer of cold steel, it was so icy you could've hung a beef in the room.

Hey!!! The technician questioned, "They no give you no prep?" "Nope,"I replied 'Not one person mentioned it." "Well, you gotta go back, wait till tomorrow,"he declares.

10:30 p.m. – back to 130B, the roommate was most interested in every small detail of my trip and anxious of making me aware of her many medical problems; I made a great effort to be congenial.

12:00 p.m. – just at the same hour as Cinderella turned back into an ordinary chore girl, the demons leap out and took control of my body.

2:00 a.m. – the nurses provided Loratab which sort of pushed the pain two feet away, but it managed to reach out and snap at my ribs, sizzle down my right leg, and explode in my foot.

4:00 a.m. – the one and only competent nurse in my entire ordeal declared, "I'm calling the doctor."I contemplated my bad luck of being on the ground floor, if only it had been the fifth floor I could have jumped out the window.

The blond, no nonsense nurse reappeared, and administered my first introduction to big-time pain killer, Demitrol. The present world and reality began to slip beyond my grasp, and I entered a mythic place where friends and family floated by against an airy background of fields, green rye grass, and waving yellow coreopsis. Annalee was playing "In Your Easter Bonnet," as Lola, Georgie, Auntie Mauldin, and Lucille harmonized. Mac inquired, "When will lunch be ready for the cowboys? Good luck was on their side, and they finished early this morning." Taylor Anne Brewton flew by on her angel wings. Mary Tom, Murray, Jeanne, myself all strolled down the Champ d Elysses, the Eiffel Tower now gold instead of black. Henry laughed his hardy laugh at a friend's joke. Rebecca assured me she is saying some novenas for the return of my health. A deep dark sleep overwhelmed my consciousness.

The next day rolled around, the doctor was baffled and hinted at surgery, friends and family appeared and were concerned, and my dear Mary arrived to care for me. The day passed slowly as I drifted in and out of a faraway world. LVNs pushed me back to the basement for yet another test; fortunately I am drowsy enough now to take much note of the proceedings.

It became night again and after drinking what seemed to be gallons of water, I must manage to get to the restroom with my IV pole and my dizzy head. Just as I was about halfway to my destination, a large cockroach hopped out of the woodwork and offered to tap dance a tune for me.

9:30 a.m.: now somehow it was the next day, no answers as to a diagnosis, and Mary again arrived and helped me into the shower. The water felt warm and comforting, and suddenly Mary remarked, "Mrs. Woodley, you have a rash." I peered at the red bumps, and it struck me, "Mary, it's the shingles!" About that time the nurse appeared, and we informed her of our discovery, "Oh, the shingles!" she shouted, and reached down to touch my lesions without her plastic gloves on.

Now everyone got busy and administered the antibiotic which was needed to kill the shingles virus. They were happy because no surgery was required as the doctor was considering. They're happy; I was ecstatic. Little did I know my involvement with the shingles that would land me in the hospital two more times, and cause serious side effects which I must battle until the end of my days.

Burns-Bownds Sports Complex

Isn't this a wonderful place?

Our Dad and Robert would be so very pleased. Heartfelt thanks and our gratitude to all who donated their time, labors, means, expertise, land, and materials. As you can see they have come together to create an outstanding facility.

Our Dad, Henry and Robert Bownds were lifelong friends. Robert spent many weekends and summer vacations at the Burns ranch, trailing Daddy around and eating Burns's delicious fried chicken, together they were sort of a Mutt and Jeff pair.

Daddy was the Jeff counterpart – tall, lanky, and very quiet. Robert was more like Mutt, smaller in statue, rounder, and a born storyteller.

All our lives whenever we were together, during the Christmas Holidays or the Forth of July, someone would request Robert to tell the Jim Christmas story and he was always glad to oblige.

Ole' Jim Christmas (yes that was his actual last name) was a crusty bachelor, whose ranch joined the Burns ranch on the back or Frio side. It was

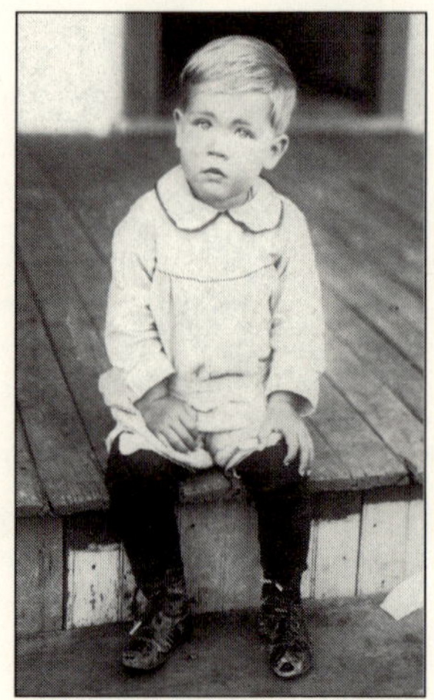

Henry Burns at Payne Ranch, Real County, 1912

his custom to come to Utopia for supplies on Saturdays, and to visit, find out the news, and pass a few hours with friends. During the winter Jim would wear a large army surplus type of raincoat, which boasted huge side pockets.

Now Daddy and Robert were great lovers of jokes and pranks at that young age. So one Holiday Season they happened to be in town on a Saturday afternoon when Jim was making his rounds, and somehow were financial enough to be able to purchase some firecrackers of considerable strength. Spying Jim visiting on the street was a temptation the two together could not resist.

Robert, the conversationalist engaged Jim in a visit while Daddy slipped up from behind the old rancher and quickly and deftly dropped a lighted firecracker into one of the raincoat's large pockets. According to Robert the explosion was magnificent, and became more spectacular with each telling. It achieved just the effect the pranksters had intended.

Robert's account included the aftermath of the incident, every time Daddy and Rob would encounter Mr. Jim in town Robert would sidle up to the ole' fellow and question him, "Mr. Christmas, did you ever find out who put the firecracker in your pocket?"

"No," Jim would reply, "but if I ever find the fellow, I'm going to give him a whipping he'll never forget."

To this day I can still see Daddy laughing, sometimes to the point of tears in his eyes, when Robert would relate the story.

And poor ole' Jim Christmas went to his grave never knowing that it was Henry Burns and Robert Bownds who had blown the pocket off his raincoat.

Our family is grateful to have our Dad and his childhood friend remembered in a manner where young people and their families can gather, participate in games, learn sportsmanship, and enjoy the beauty of the outdoors.

The construction of this wonderful facility has been a community effort which will provide benefits for generations to come. It is a testament to the fact that Utopia is a true community where its people can work together for the good of its citizens. Thanks to each and every one of you who have given your best to make this park a reality.

Flood Damage Is Hard to Fathom

Trying to convey on paper a tiny glimpse at the devastation in the Sabinal canyon is not truly possible. Unless you are able to witness the scene with your own eyes, one cannot comprehend the powerful force of water raging out of its usual course, and invading homes, businesses, across roadways, through fence lines – all of the ordinary boundaries of every day life.

Residents each have their own stories to relate, which could be compiled into a volume of harrowing emotions, experiences, and losses. Only one resident of the canyon lost his life in the torrential rains, and a sad tale it was too as he was returning on his tractor to reach his faithful dog.

But viewing the areas where the waters raced out of control, it is hard to realize that more human life was not lost, for this all of us feel a great sense of relief and thankfulness.

While driving to survey the Burns-Bownds house, my heart was fearful this mighty flood had found its path into the home and barns constructed in the 1920s. But by some miracle and forethought of the builders, the river left the structure high and dry, rolled out to the east, taking out the fences, but leaving all the buildings intact.

Billy Moore, Fannie Grace, and I visited on the east porch over coffee, as Billy related how a number of the wonderful Simmental bulls pastured in the "Jones cemetery field" were swept away and lost. All of the fences at the Boswell were down, and the tiger-striped cows were wandering at will over the surrounding countryside.

"The river was spread from the top of my front porch to the town of Utopia," Billy remarked. So difficult to imagine this three mile area entirely under water.

Could not help but wish for Henry Fisher, Auntie Mauldin, and Annalee to be present, so they could relate to us the paths and stories of previous floods, such as the one of 1936.

Henry, Mama, Gladys Fisher, and Orceneth Fly would have been sad to witness the condition of the Fisher Camp dining hall where the river tore through the north kitchen wall, took down the tin roof, and floated the old red refrigerator out by the highway.

We Fishers can band together and put our camp back into some sort of usable condition, but the people who lost homes, contents, automobiles, and life-long possessions are faced with a much more demanding struggle.

The Utopia EMS supplied this list of families and people affected with water damage. They note it is not complete. The names marked by asterisks were severely affected.

David Sheedy, Duane Crawford, Utopia on the River*, Mark D'Spain, Sid Mauldin*, Nancy Thompson, Westerfield, Teny Jo Tynes, Joe Farris, David Barnett, Scott Dethloff*, Ray Redden*, Lonnie Bomer*, Emma Bomer*, John Busse*, John Jurnery*, Jack Preston*, Betty Yeager*, Clarence Lebouf*, Ryan McNair*, Helen Newkirk*, Kenneth Smith*, Joe Burke, Jay B. Taylor*, Wayne Wilsher, Bill Fernald, Norbert, Lyssy, Bobby Thompson, Raul Rios*, Michelle Duclos, Vi Strand*, and Johnny Boultinghouse. Please know this list is not complete.

Visiting with the volunteers at the EMS headquarters in Utopia, they stated individuals wishing to offer financial help to victims should choose a family and make contributions personally. This would eliminate setting up a fund which would have to be distributed through their agency, and will more quickly facilitate getting contributions to the donors of choice.

Also the EMS asked that no more clothes be donated as they had a larger amount on hand than they could manage at the moment.

When we delivered sacks of sandwiches to provide lunch for mud-cleaning crews, we also volunteered some hours to sorting and moving the mounds of accumulated clothes in the EMS building. While we were working, a group of young campers from Alto Frio arrived, and put their strong backs and alert minds to the task of transporting the clothes to the Senior Center, where they could be sorted and distributed.

Our neighbor Helen Newkirk and daughter gave me a brief summary of the damage Helen's house sustained. Her trailer, which doubles as a bed and breakfast, or perhaps a cabin, was secure, but the house is severely damaged as a tree struck it.

Helen was smiling her brave smile while stating her future plans are still in the process of unfolding.

Ruth Preston interrupted her grocery shopping to fill us in on some of the details of their loss. She was expressing her gratitude to an out-of-town couple who have graciously offered their home to them for the time it will require them to put theirs back into living condition. Everywhere people express gratitude for lives being spared.

Viewing the river itself, you can note the immense height the water reached on the stately cypresses, and the tons of gravel moved into different watercourses, and the debris scattered all along the banks. It will take much time and effort to clean the country of litter. And another huge menace is the angry fireants lodged in the wash along fence rows. Some people sustained bites from the vicious little creatures when the waters entered their residences.

And to think we are speaking of destruction along only one of the Texas watercourses; along the other rivers many more problems exist. Our state is the business of rebuilding from the massive amounts of rain the July low-pressure system dumped upon the center of our state.

Many friends from outside the area call to ask what they can contribute. Utopia EMS volunteers suggest it is best to choose a name and assist a certain family or individual.

Utopia Trip Evokes Reminiscences

Sometime ago we took in the production of "My Fair Lady" at the Opera House. What a spirited group, who gave their best efforts to Shaw's tale of Henry Higgins and Eliza Doolittle's encounter and adventures.

Betty and I loved Terry Harrison's dominating Henry and Crystal Hollaway's delightful Eliza. And who could forget Gary Cuny's Alferd P. Doolittle? Am still humming, "With A Little Bit 'Of Luck," these several weeks later.

So after Betty's overnight at mi casa, I made a date to return the time at her wonderful abode on the banks of the Sabinal in downtown Vanderpool.

Arriving in Utopia, I first noted the Jurney home is now history, much of it was stacked on the highway right-of-way, and the lot clean. And next door to us much burning, raking, cleaning had taken place on the Boswell ranch, leaving a large, clear area for the river. to sprawl over, hopefully not soon. Looked so inspiring to have much of that litter and debris cleaned away; am sure Billy Moore and crew were responsible.

Next stop, the LeBouf home on the banks of Long Hollow and the Sabinal, had to check on the headway that brave and determined couple were making in the process of rebuilding their flooded home.

So inspired and delighted to find the walls completely re-sheetrocked and awaiting texturing and new paint. Dear Robert

Murray Wentworth Family Float, June 2002

Garnett, husband of Susan Garnett, son-in-law of June Fisher Bible had arrived with 14-year-old Drew from Dexter, N.M., to offer their expertise, labor, and encouragement.

Slowly, the LeBoufs are making order and renewal from the chaos of their dream home. My admiration for their efforts in face of tremendous odds facing them is huge.

The shouts and sounds coming from the swiftly flowing Sabinal were the delighted cries of the Bible children, splashing and swimming. A rare treat for them, hailing from land-locked New Mexico.

At Vanderpool, Betty had prepared a delicious supper for Elaine Snider and myself. Chicken salad fit the menu perfectly as a collection of many various chickens of doubtful origins paraded around the dining room.

Saving our dessert until later, we hopped into our vehicle and headed for a late evening tour of old Humble Station C on the divide. Very dim in my memory is a time when our parents and the three of us attended a festive barbecue and dance there.

Bet explained this was the location the main Humble Oil pipeline extending from West Texas to the coastal plant. The "station" was constructed to check the pressures and gauges of the pipes was laid out in orderly fashion, seven homes, four on one side, three on the other facing a single center street. Also there was a clubhouse where meetings and get-togethers were held for neighbors and members of the Utopia-Vanderpool community.

Sterling Fisher, Betty, Billy and Marjorie's Dad worked at the "Station." "We would drive Daddy up on Monday mornings (early), or late Sunday afternoons, and return for him late Fridays. His job helped bring us through the depression."

The divide country looked lush and green with yellow thelsperma daisies blooming in the pastures, but no sheep or goats grazed there, and only a few cattle. Spotted a flock of half-grown turkeys with their heads turned curiously toward us.

Next a.m. I studied Bet's photo album of the spectacular 150th celebration parade at Utopia. Had intended to compose a column on the celebration, but my intentions sorta got washed away with the flood.

First were parade marshals, Beth Crane Davenport, Martha Hans, and Charley Chaney; identified Mary Ann Metz and Inez McClain on the Arts and Crafts float.

The Hillis family had re-created the Charley Umlang home, which they own and renovated, complete with charming gingerbread. Their banner read 1882-The Oldest Home in Utopia.

Rancho Chuparrosa carried not only a cocky papier-mache rooster, but a cow as well, advertising Robins Bowman's farm-fresh produce. She and her daughter were all smiles.

Quite a few families were represented in the parade, Gideon Thompson, Henry and June Fisher, Donohos, Murray Wentworth, and the Dukes. Was sort of jealous of the Dukes as they were all re-splendent in turquoise and white matching western shirts, and the Donohos were all color coordinated in yellow, and many in number.

Ranches represented were the Four Sisters, 7H Huebner Ranch, Ferrell Davis group, which proclaimed "We're Hog Wild About Utopia."

Other album images were of the Utopia Masonic Lodge, 984 AF AM, established 1908, the Baptist church brush arbor, Umlang Bros., am sure there were many more. But these provided a small bird's eye remembrance of that enjoyable day.

Driving up the Mill Creek road we stared in disbelief at the havoc left in wake of the torrential rains which fell in that area. Water marks must have been 30 and 40 feet high on some of the huge cypress trees. Other trees were broken half way up the trunk or uprooted completely. Hard to comprehend the force of nature.

Our remarks contained gratitude the 150th was so successful and well attended, and none of us knew what the week of July 4th, would bring.

The Green-ness of South Texas

Retracing my tracks from years gone by, I marveled at the lush green-ness of South Texas. Many other trips this direction have been painted in hues of drab greens and browns, but July 2002, the buffle grass covered the highway medians and waved its fluffy heads in greetings.

The live oaks (in Live Oak county), and the sandy land country, (Devine, Jourdanton), were heavy with foliage, clean and resplendent, reaching in new directions.

What was batch of blazing blue color I kept seeing at intervals? Had to stop the car to investigate as it was not easy to identify at 65 mph, turned out to be spiderwort in huge bunches, blooming away as

Rebecca Laurine Ware at Rancho de la Loma, 1979

if the calendar was proclaiming April or May instead of July.

Oranges and yellow entwined themselves in the fence lines, as native lantanas reached heights of 3 to 4 feet. This hardy Texas plant was lavishly covered by blooms, no hybrid could have been more glorious or colorful.

All along the route people were mowing weeds, pasture grass, roadsides, lawns, fighting back the riot of green growth.

Tanks were brimming full, and some ran around the spillways, creating wet lands of water in a land which had thirsted for moisture for the past three or four years.

And crossing the Nueces outside of Calallen was a large shock. The river lapped at the top of the bridge, and spread itself out over many surrounding acres on its journey to Corpus Christi Bay.

From my friend's home along the watercourse's south banks, we could gaze out and observe the magnitude of the July floods easing along, spreading its fingers over the low-lying acres. One of us remarked it would not have been possible to cross in the days of horses and wagons.

Do you have a life-long friend or relative whose company you've been able to enjoy over the span of your lifetime? In this time of mobile society, not many remain, but life has been generous to grant me several.

My cousin, college roommate, and friend is off the Harper family tree, and the next morning we entertained ourselves for several hours leafing through old photographs MT had inherited from her parents.

Here they were in remote West Texas, 40 miles south of Marfa on Uncle Rollie's Carrazal ranch. Tom was mounted on horseback, as Marty held the reins. The horse looked young and unsteady. A special shot of Aunt Bea Crane, wearing hat and gloves and riding among a herd of Herefords gave us much pleasure. It was tinted and had an "Old West" flavor. Aunt Bea and Marty were sisters, and MT explained her father, Tom, would gather all the available family manpower when it was time to gather cattle at the Carrazal; everyone would journey west, a long day's trip, and saddle up to help gather and brand the calves.

We launched into a discussion wondering how our beloved Fisher grandmother and aunt survived the isolation of that remote place without electricity, telephone, books, neighbors, family and very few conveniences. When the men rode away from the house pens at daylight, there was no way to know the time of their return, or if bad luck or an accident had befallen them. But this small, brave woman retained her happy and cheerful countenance to the end of her days. Her Bible was well worn and many passages memorized.

I recalled what a glad feeling swept over the Utopia relatives when Uncle Rollie and Aunt Ella returned to the Hill Country to pass their remaining days. The Wentworth sisters and cousin Gladys Fisher enjoyed many pleasant hours in their company.

And surprise! A photo in the pack surfaced and proved to be Annalee, Henry, and myself (age 2), on a Sunday afternoon visit to Marty and Tom's home outside Banquete. During the early '40s, Henry was employed with Humble oil and stationed at Ingleside, thus MT and I were introduced at an early age. The row of lantanas along the driveway had been dug up by Tom in the pasture and transplanted, these were the days of do-it-yourself landscaping

On an evening stroll around the neighborhood, we closely examined a crepe myrtle dripping lavender blooms. On the trip down to Corpus, the myrtles had been the most outstanding spots of color, and grabbed my attention at every turn. In Hondo, they seemed especially spectacular, and between Pleasanton and Jourdanton, a long row mixed shades of dark and light reds, creamy pinks, plus several shades of purples.

Driving over the Corpus Christi high bridge, the muddy Nueces mixed and mingled its brownish tinge with the blue salt water of the bay. Had read in the C C Caller-Times what great news the fresh water was for the shrimping and fishing industry. Fresh water pushes back the salt water and marine creatures have to move and migrate to other beds, making the catch more bountiful. Large numbers of brown pelicans were working the shores and grassy marshes for a tidbit of crab or sea life.

Arriving in Rockport, I was introduced to our godchild's new arrival, Jackson Lee Taylor. Is that a Southern name or what? Jackson was bright-eyed, alert, happy fellow, son of Rebecca Ware Taylor and Ashley Taylor. Naturally in the gathering of family, he was the center of attention.

Recalling back to Rebecca's arrival into the world, we wondered if it was possible for time to have sped by so very quickly. Do you harbor the feeling that years seem to scoot by similar to seconds?

And so, pleasant hours passed with friends and family brought back times when we'd all pile in the black, four-door Ford, minus AC, and travel to Corpus for our yearly July visit with Daddy's Mother and sister. Why was July the chosen month? School being out I suppose, and perhaps we may have celebrated a few July 4ths on the Padre Island beach.

Corpus is still the seaside jewel of a city it was then; yes, new buildings are on the horizon, but it is still small enough not to present traffic jams, or miles and miles of subdivisions. And on this July sojourn, the lushness of the tropical plantings, and the circling seagulls reminded me of days enjoyed in and near its environs.

Trail Ride Puts Life on Hold

Six weeks of the shingles put me in St. Luke's Baptist three different times and taught me how to sympathize with everyone who has lost their health and succumbed to hospitalization.

It's amazing how many people have been attacked by those sneaky mean shingles, and believe me, if you've ever fought them, you comprende as to the mighty foe they are.

Annalee held fast during the time I was unavailable, thanks to the special care and attention she received at Amistad, from friends, and from Mary Reyes and Beth Pringle.

Heartfelt thanks for all the cards, prayer letters, gifts, and calls. Believe me, it's a great morale booster to know friends and family will drop everything and come running to your rescue. Jeanne Burns did it for me, that's true sisterly love.

Mary Fisher Willis is in the process of returning to the roots of her childhood home. Jim and Mary are remodeling the Henry Fisher ranch house, northwest of Utopia. Thanks to both of them for caring enough to return to the canyon and especially for bringing that stately house under the oak trees to life again. All Fisher kin have warm wonderful memories of the hours we visited there.

Mary encouraged me to write of the time when she, Evelyn, and myself prevailed strongly upon over protective parents to let us join the trail ride which Happy Shahan was organizing from Brackettville to San Antonio publicizing "The Last Command Movie."

My mind is cloudy as to how in heaven we were ever able to persuade Henry Fisher, Annalee and Henry Burns to let two teen-age daughters and one college student out on such a wild adventure as riding from Sabinal to S.A. horseback?

One member of our group, Barbara Porter Mitchell, was not successful in persuading Bush Porter, her father, who was even more conservative minded than Henry F., to join us. Reports are Barbara took it hard and held the slight against dear Bush for many a day.

Even at a young age Ev Fisher had a persuasive personality, so I feel sure she deserves the credit for making the trail a reality for herself, Mary, and myself.

Ev relates she was "put out" at the very beginning because Henry decided she could not ride the steadfast Fisher horse, Champ. Reason being Champ was a small roan, and might not be up to the rigors of 20 miles daily.

So instead Champ was replaced with a tall paint, name unknown to me, which Ev needed a stepladder to mount. The switch paid off on the ride for her because the paint stepped out, hit a smooth gait, and led the rest of the group on the trail.

Another ace in the hole was Ben Cooper was also riding a paint. Can't say the same for my grulla mare, Chulita, who danced under me all the way from Sabinal to S.A. Remember Bush advising me, "Now, Annie, when you all hit the Kinchloe prairie, you stretch that little mare out and take the prance out of her." Which I never did because Chulita had a hard mouth, and I was afraid we'd be in front of the Alamo before I ever got her pulled up.

Mary was astride her sensible mare, Chula, who as I best remember was bay.

Now the year had to be 1955,and Ben Cooper and Maria Albergett had just wrapped up filming "The Last Command" at Alamo Village in Brackett. Happy Shahan family, movie people and local trail riders had progressed to the Sabinal City Park when we joined the group.

Ev reports that Henry was most impressed that Happy only had to issue a loud whistle and his daughters came running at the call, so he could introduce us to them and tell them to assist us in whatever manner we might need.

Henry was impressed with Shahan's girls' quick response to their Dad's call and for many years after he reminded his daughters of their lackadaisical response to his commands and requests. Why couldn't they shape up a bit and come a runnin' such as Tulisha and Jamie had?

A fourth partner joined our group at Sabinal, Patsy Nunley, friend of mine, and daughter of Roy and Latheal Nunley. Patsy was always a lover of horses.

Here Mary offers some interesting information. She relates that the Newton brothers, Willie and Jess (we think), were along on the ride. Henry, of course, knew them and requested the Newtons look after us. Apparently they did, because we had not one incident, knick, or bruise the entire ride.

So our first night on the trail we camped with the group at Sabinal City Park, slept on bedrolls, arose at the crack of dawn for a delicious breakfast provided from the Chuck Wagon. My remembrances include our ride across Kinchloe prairie, Henry and Bush driving slowly along side our group, making sure we were safe and sound and our second night in Hondo at the home of our cousins Orceneth and Willie Fly.

Willie, of course, provided all sorts of comforts, cozy beds and delicious refreshments for the four of us. We were sunburned and saddle sore after our first day on the trail. A question arose about the ride being such a great idea after all.

But come daylight, we were saddled up and ready to go toward Castroville, and at days end, we dismounted at Casa Mañana, a tourist court located between Castroville and S.A. Each evening Henry would appear and help us feed, brush, water and secure our horses for the night.

The last day was full of anticipation as we headed our horses down old Hwy. 90 and directly into the city of S.A. Rode right through the middle of town, via Houston Street. Memory fails me as to the fact of remembering a large crowd to greet us. Let's just suppose there was.

Faithful Henry Fisher was waiting for us when we reined in our horses in front of the Municipal Auditorium. He helped us unsaddle, toss our saddles and gear in the back of the truck and load the four horses. Naturally, he'd stop at the Nunley's and unload Patsy's for her.

Annalee and June Fisher were present to wisk us off to "Auntie (Gladys) Fisher's home so we could shower (or most probably bathe in those days, Auntie would not be modern enough to have installed a shower) dress, primp, and get ourselves ready for the showing of "The Last Command" at the Majestic Theater that evening.

Before the movie, we attended a reception for the riders at the St. Anthony; wish I could remember what we wore, but that was 47 years ago.

Do recall how striking beautiful Anna Maria Albergett was entering the theater. Ben Cooper was a nice guy, but not knock 'em dead handsome.

And so that event in our lives became a marvelous memory, enlivened by remembrances of people we know and loved, Henry and June Fisher, dear Bush Porter, and Gladys Fisher, Happy Shahan, Patsy Nunley, and Tulisha and Jamie.

Rounds in East Texas

Forty-nine calls on the answering machine from friends and family all questioned, "Anne, where are you? We've been calling and calling."

In fact, I'd spent the past several months touring Texas – East Texas that is, the part of the state with which I am least familiar. Taylor transported me to Tyler where he and Joan reside in a tranquil area near the small town of Whitehouse.

Tyler is the loveliest city I've ever visited in Texas. Old homes of southern architecture, built by old oil money lend a gracious air and a sense of gentility to the urban area. Plants flourish in the acid soil and 40-inch annual rainfall. Every place is attractively landscaped with azaleas, dogwood, pines, magnolias, and sweet gum trees.

In the evenings we took long walks, several times spotting deer and the family of red foxes who reside on the Burns acreage. How charming their faces and coats are to me. In all my years at the ranch, only once or twice did I ever spot any of these small creatures.

One weekend we traveled to Frisco, Texas, home of Larissa Brewton, Taylor and Joan's daughter, and her family.

The occasion was "Light the Night Walk," to honor cancer victims, and survivors. Larissa, who lost her daughter, Taylor Anne, age 4, to leukemia last fall, was the chairwoman for the event.

It was a bittersweet time for our family, but most inspiring to see 1,500 participants carrying lighted balloons on the 2.6 mile walk. Chris, Trystie, Tessa, and Taylor all participated, but Joan and I chose to sit on the sidelines and enjoy the spectacle.

Larissa and co-workers were elated to report the event raised over $135,000 for the Leukemia and Lymphoma society.

Later, I moved to Fulshear, outside of Houston, with Murray and Jeanne. During my stay, we drove to College Station to attend the Texas A&M-Texas Tech game. Loved all the fanfare of the Aggie corps, and the precision of the band. The game was a thriller, but A&M lost in overtime to the Red Raiders.

Also visited our cousins, Janice and Marion Stewart at their charming new abode in Sugarland. Accompanied Janice to M.D. Anderson on Tuesday where she weekly plays the baby grand piano in the lobby. People come and luxuriate in her music. One couple was especially touching. The wife had an arm missing, wore a turban, and had an IV pole. The husband was most helpful and attentive to her. They were both smiling and cheerful, and graciously thanked Janice for the music.

For Thanksgiving we gathered at Utopia and feasted on turkey and all the trimmings. It felt warm and welcoming to be in Burns-Bownds house with four small youngsters keeping the atmosphere lively.

When we traveled to Amistad to visit Annalee, Tessa, age 2, Trystie, 3, Wyatt, 3, and Max, 2, accompanied us. I worked getting everyone situated in the dayroom so Annalee could play "Rudolph the Red-Nosed Reindeer," "Frosty the Snowman," and "Jingle Bells" for the children. Soon their attention waned, and they were off on other ventures.

Suddenly, Mother stopped playing the piano, turned to me and stated, "These children are out of control. Whose are they, anyway?"

"They're ours, Mother," was my reply.

"Well, why don't you all discipline them, then?" she wanted to know.

"Mama, that's not the modern way, they don't do that anymore," was the only reply I could manage.

'Tis The Season to Remember the Past

Monday, Dec. 16, and the thermometer in the kitchen window registers 80 degrees, a picture perfect South Texas afternoon. Reminds me of a similar December day, my first Christmas season as a bride at Yucca Switch, Texas.

Had been reminding Mac for a week (make that 10 days) to come in early in the afternoon so he, Nacho, and Jose, could string the lights around the eaves of the red ranch house. Time went by, and it didn't seem to me as if Mac was responding seriously enough to my important project.

So, on an afternoon such as this, I grabbed the long ladder and by golly, set to hammering the colored lights in place myself. Took me three hours, but I got it accomplished.

Could just hear Mac saying when he drove in (after dark, of course), "Oh, Anne, you should not have worked so hard, we were going to put those up tomorrow."

Instead he made no comment until during supper when I questioned, "Well, how do you like the lights?"

"You did a great job, just as I knew you could," was the reply.

Decided I had two choices: pout, because I had to do it myself, or take the reply as a compliment. Chose the latter, which greatly helped my attitude for the next 32 years, when I tackled most of my projects alone.

But to give Mac his due, he was deeply involved one December when we struggled to erect the huge cedar Felix Real transported to La Loma for us. Is there any means of making a live 12-foot tree stand up straight?

Just about the time we had maneuvered the monster into place, it toppled over, pinning Mac to the floor. Never shall forget his cry, "Hurry up, Anne, this damn tree is eating me."

So those of us with a few years of wisdom and experi-

Allison Burns Noon, age 4, at Yucca Switch, Texas

ence in our banks can hark back to humorous incidents during past holidays and smile.

And naturally we chose the traditions of our childhoods when toys were not constructed of plastic, and stores did not display the Christmas merchandise until after Thanksgiving.

But it is fun to enter into the spirit of the season and string some lights outdoors, shop, and hopefully accomplish some baking and candy making.

Am preparing to tackle our aunt Georgic's Patience candy recipe, praying not to drop any caramelized sugar on my hand as I did one season.

Mac and Fred claimed Jane Mac made the most delicious Patience, which has been a tough act to duplicate over the years.

Was reading this paragraph penned by Annalee in the "Christmas Gift" book.

"Happiness at Christmas is lying awake at night listening to the house talk as only old houses do ... our old house says, "listen, I'm glad you did not ruin my character by pulling out walls and lowering ceilings ... I am not so young any more ... 60 years is getting on for a house ... that creaking sound is my bones settling ... I have sheltered many people during happy times at Christmas ... sadnesses too ... and it is good to gather your family under my roof and hear a child's laughter ... I know I am big and rambly and hard to clean, but please don't change me ... I like myself the way I am, which is old fashioned."

So if John Dale Chaney can lure the skunks out from under Bownds-Burns house, which is now nearing 100 years of age, we Burnses shall celebrate in it once again this holiday season of 2002.

And now our number is increased by the arrival of Wesley Sarah to Allison Burns Noon and Doug Noon. And soon we will be enlarged again by an addition to the Macieck family.

And surprise! A new member of the James Woodley family will arrive in April. I'm going to be a grandmother for the third time. Miracles never cease. Merry Christmas to each of you.

2003

Winter Days Bring Cooking Favorites

Even though the holidays are long past, food seems to be playing a leading role during these dark, damp days. Perhaps the lack of flowers and foliage out doors calls us indoors to savor the enticing tastes, smells, and colors of the delicious dishes we sometimes take for granted.

The vibrant movie, "Freida," set me to thinking "South of the Border," especially the scenes depicting all those savory dishes Freida whipped up for Diego. Will soon do some for myself, as Nell Capt promises to lend me her "Freida Kahlo Cookbook," after I left my copy of the artist's biography on Nell's doorstep.

And we discussed the new eating establishment on Uvalde's square where true Mexican dishes (from the interior) are served. Sampled the corn quesadillas con chorizo (so sinful, so delicious), enchiladas prepared with red corn tortillas and queso fresco, plus light, flaky rice cooked with vegetables, which could have come straight from Freida's kitchen.

Have become addicted to the cream of poblano soup served so expertly at another Uvalde square eatery. It is the most delectable sopa ever to cross my plate.

Amiga Suzie Groves got busy and prepared a batch, which I'd been too lazy to attempt. Hate roasting and peeling the peppers; is there any easy route to accomplish this task? If so, call me collect with your method.

But a recipe for crema de poblano is in my possession and I'll share it. Found it in Mary Sue Koontz's cookbook, "Stolen Recipes." Mary Sue is a friend who lives on the Koontz ranch at Placedo, Texas, there the Koontz family raises registered Brahama cattle. So I suppose if MS stole the recipe from a friend, she won't mind if I steal it from her.

Mary Sue is a personality who once you meet her, she'll forever remain in your memory. She will be a luncheon speaker when the Texas and Southwest Cattle Raisers convene in San Antonio last of March.

During a La Salle County sojourn, we enjoyed dining at the refurbished hotel in Catarina. It is operated both as a hotel and restaurant during the winter months (hunting season). Our meals of rib eyes, salads and scalloped potatoes could have easily held their own in any New Orleans eating establishment. And a friend's prime rib was cut and cooked to perfection, looked as if it came straight out of Adam's Rib in the Big Apple.

Over the last 40 years this historic hotel on Highway 83 has opened and closed innumerable times, hopefully the present operators are there to stay.

Quilting friends Jan Carter, Caroline Habermacher, and myself met on the Uvalde square to catch up on our holiday activities, celebrate January birthdays, and discuss the latest stitching projects. At yet another luncheon spot we feasted upon Italian stew, flavorfully seasoned with rosemary, baked potato soup, plus sandwiches put together with homemade bread.

Never have been able to concoct a beef broth to my satisfaction, and have worked to do it Julia Child's way, but this bowl was the example of beef bouillon perfection.

On to Austin where my order of spinach enchiladas accompanied by refried black beans, and rice was a complete surprise. The fresh corn tortillas were thin enough to see through, and wrapped around a mixture of sauted onions, garlic, mushrooms, and chopped, fresh spinach (not sauted), then covered with a light sauce of cheese (Velveeta) and cream, to die for – so completely different, light, and perfect combination of flavors.

Before leaving the capitol city shopped in a bounteous grocery, where it would have no trick at all to run up a $500 tab. But happily departed with a sack of garnet yams, introduced to me by our son and the brother from Tyler, plus a bottle of Rioja. Yes, the combination does sound a mite strange will let you know the results.

Roasted Poblano Soup

3 poblano chilies, roasted,
  peeled and seeded
3 tomatillos, cut in half
leaves from one bunch of cilantro
salt and pepper to taste
3 cups chicken stock
1 1/2 cups onion
2 cups half & half cream
crushed tortilla clips
grated monterrey jack cheese

Roast poblano peppers under the broiler, keep turning until black and bubbly on all sides. Place peppers in closed paper bag for 15 minutes. Remove seeds and skin peppers. Place stock, chilies, tomatillos, onions in a heavy pot, bring to a boil, reduce heat and cook 15-20 minutes. Remove, cool and puree in blender or cuisinart. Return to the pot and slowly add cream. Heat until hot but do not boil. To serve, place soup in bowls, add crushed tortillas chips and cheese.

All the Books and Movies

Drippy, foggy days have led to book reading in the middle of the mornings, and as many movies which one can manage when living in Sabinal.

Growing up, our Dad was a movie fan, and about once a week we'd all load in the black Ford sedan, swing by and pick up Biggie Wentworth so she could visit with the Arnims or Smiths and head toward Sabinal and the Ross Theater.

Both Annalee and Henry were avid readers, Daddy being a mystery and western sagas fan. Mama loved historical novels, biographies, and especially Texana pertaining to our area of the state.

So my brothers and myself spent many cold evenings before the dawn of T.V., reading in front of the fireplace, munching the popcorn or fudge Annalee usually whipped up after supper. It seemed natural for us to love books, movies, and the stories spun around our kitchen table when we were young.

During my sojourn at Fulshear, Jeanne picked up "John Adams," for Murray upon my recommendation. Although I have not read it (its length scared me), Caroline the librarian richly praised this account of Adam's life, indicating it was most readable.

Visiting our son in Austin seemed to present the opportunity for some movie going, so first we took in "About Schmidt," a Jack Nicholson film, depicting the void which retirement and later years can produce. Jack was perfect for the role, but for me, the plot was slow and a bit sad.

But not so for Steven Spielberg's "Catch Me If You Can." Tom Hanks gave one of his usual outstanding performances as an FBI agent trying to outwit con artist Leonardo Di Caprio. Everyone will enjoy this fast paced, quick-witted, true story.

Back in Sabinal, picked up my new purchase, "Breaking Clean," authored by Judy Blume. An autobiographical look into Judy's childhood on a Montana ranch, she expertly describes the experiences which confront ranching families. Am anxious to pass this volume along to Jan Carter who grew up on an Idaho ranch, 70 miles from the nearest town and school.

In Tyler, Taylor was just completing "Seabiscuit," one of my all time favorites. Have spread the news of its beautifully crafted story to as many friends and family who will listen. So was delighted when a preview appeared on the movie screen announcing the arrival of the film version. Look for it this coming summer. Do not miss the narrative of this small, brave thoroughbred in book form or film.

Over the telephone Murray related he had finally completed "John Adams," and was now into "Dauntless Courage," the account of Lewis and Clark's charting of the Missouri river country. It is also on film at IMAX in San Antonio. Cousin MT reported it to be most entertaining as well as educational.

Did not pass up the opportunity to meet Mary Tom in San Antonio, together we headed for "Chicago," the Broadway musical transformed into a movie. SENSATIONAL! And Houston's own Renee Zellweger received an academy award nomination for her performance.

Aware that the Lenten season is upon us, we shopped at Viva bookstore for a study guide to lead us through the six weeks preceding Easter. Chose to stick with my beloved author, Henri Nouwen's "Show Me The Way," while MT decided upon Joyce Rupp's "Fill My Cup."

Home again, late one night began the bestseller, "Forever," written by Pete Hamill. Had loved the story of his childhood, depicting the manner in which he came to love words and writing. Pete was the sports editor for The New York Times for many years, and squired Jackie Onassis about the Big Apple.

Thompson-Howard Barn

The Thompson-Howard barn

One morning, during the holidays we were in Utopia and checking on things at the Bownds-Burns place. Joe and I strolled through the old barn, finding all sorts of interesting relics, which Annalee would want saved and cataloged. We were astounded the flood of '02 did not take the barn away, but only undermined a small area of the foundation.

On the drive back to Crystal, began to enumerate in my mind the barns I had known over the years, and how very few are still standing today. So made a note to gather some information on the ones that have figured in my life, and also wanted to ask you to inform me of those I do not know, but are still standing.

Wrote my friend Barbara Howard; we were cheerleaders together at Sabinal High School, have the photos to prove it. Asked Barbara if she would mail me some facts and photos of the handsome, sturdy rock barn still standing on their Tom Howard ranch. Remember Annalee always loved what she referred to as "the old Thompson rock barn up on Anglin Creek."

Barbara quickly replied with excellent photos and a description of the barn. "The ground floor has two original rooms on the north wall that we use for storage. We built pens against the opposite wall, to use as birthing pens for the goats. Between the rooms is a stairway that leads to the second floor. The wooden floor is laid on large cedar posts and is supported by posts that stand in the center of the barn. I understand these were brought by wagon from the Frio canyon," Barbara related.

She also enclosed two of Annalee's columns, which refer to the history of the Thompson-Howard barn. "On Sunday, May 17, the Sabinal Canyon Museum members will conduct a tour to the historic Gideon Thompson home on Anglin Creek, now the home Of Lecil Howard. The rock house and big barn were built over 100 years ago by Joe Hastler, and another man of French descent.

"A milk house and rock fence were also built, and the fence around Thompson's pasture between his land and that of Henry Taylor. The rock for the fence was plowed up from the pasture with oxen and heavy plow. I have heard my father say Joe and his partner would take a load of deer hides to San Antonio, bring back a barrel of whiskey to set out with a cup hanging from the barrel so anyone was able to take a drink. Joe built many early day homes and lots of chimneys." (Interview, R. G. Thompson, 1960s).

"The rock fence went east to the Sterling Fisher place, halfway to the Kennedy place, north to the Henry Taylor place and south again. There were several miles of it.

"Gideon Thompson came October 10, 1852, with his family, consisting of wife Margaret and four children at that time. Aaron Anglin came later, and the Thompson, Anglin, Webster, and Kelly families went 6 miles north to what is now known as Anglin Creek or the West prong.

"In 1853 there was an Indian raid on this settlement. The Indians were followed south to Bear Creek and on down to the Leona. At least six Indians were killed."

From column the following week: "Groan! This Tuesday. I am not recovered from my climb up the stairs into the loft of the big rock barn on the Lecil Howard place. Built over a 100 years ago from rock quarried on the place, it has changed very little; Gideon Thompson the pioneer and rock mason Joe Hastler meant for the barn to endure."

As you can see by the photo the Howards maintain the barn in excellent, but working condition, as is their entire ranch. Someday soon I may call and request a visit to the house, which I have not entered since my childhood when the Bill Gross family was in residence.

One early spring afternoon 2003, Cousin Joy Davenport accompanied me on a ride up Anglin Creek road to check the Hindes property. As we passed the Howard ranch, I stopped and snapped a photo of one of their nannies that had two fresh born twin kids.

Traveling to Mexico

Several years had slipped away since Mary and myself jumped in the car and headed west for a day across the Rio Grande to look, touch, taste, at either Piedras or Acuña.

On this viaje we had a legitimate pursuit, furniture for the Casa Blanca at Crystal; being Spanish in design, the house calls for pieces from across the border.

Setting out from Sabinal, our first stop was La Paloma so Mary could visit the new residence. Naturally, I was pleased when she responded to the bougainvilleas dripping from the kitchen patio, "It's beautiful."

Since Eagle Pass is only 41 miles from Crystal City, we parked the blue Explorer at the ranch, and turned the red one past the imposing entrance of the Farias ranch (would Mr. Halsell have approved? I doubt it.) and were soon paying the fee to cross the bridge.

First stop was the modernistic building that belonged to the government and in the past housed the cream of Mexican arts and crafts. Now it is a store selling original designs of handcarved furniture, in the style only Mexican artists can fashion.

Spotted the perfect piece right away, a large coffee table, the carved top with the standby Mexican design of the fellow taking a siesta under a tall cactus, and it fit perfectly into the back of the red Explorer.

Cooking ware at the Piedras Market

Next door at Benavides drugs we purchased Flonase ($33 bucks compared to $78 in the US), amoxiciflin, and Retin-A. Why are our American drugs so pricey?

Being August, the temperatures were beginning to soar, so we parked in front of the Moderno, with the blessings of a policeman, and ducked into the dark, cool, interior of that special restaurant. Coke Colas and the delicious peanuts hit the spot for a snack.

"You like the peanuts?" our waiter inquired.

"Mucho, mucho," we replied.

"You stay here 10 minutes, while I go to the store to buy more for you," he offered. Okay, after we handed him $5, he took off.

Refreshed, and well supplied with peanuts, we stepped across the street to the market. OH, The Mercado. Nothing sets my senses in such a swirl as a Mexican market. The smells, colors, sounds, sights, people and piñatas blend into an exotic experience. But the best is the hope of finding that one special item you never knew existed or that you needed or wanted until the moment you see it.

Bean pots, properly seasoned to cook the perfect pot of frijoles, pronto, are my Christmas gifts to friends and family this year. "Four please, plus two of the square serving dishes of the same design."

By now, the madama of the booth and I were becoming fast friends and prices were falling by the moment.

By chance, I gazed upward, and there on the top shelf, covered with five or six years of dust, was my surprise. A marvelous clay cooking pot, large enough to hold a three-chicken sopa was calling my name.

Soon all the clay pieces in Mexico will be made by molds, not hand shaped as they have been in the past. Realistically, we had no need of this exquisitely stained piece of pottery. "How much?" I questioned. "Fifty – U.S." "No, no necisito." "How about $35?" How could I resist?

Meanwhile, Mary was busy at the next stall purchasing lovely, deep green avocados for us to transport home. This involves having the seeds removed, and a half a lime placed in the centers.

"We'll return when the pots are packed," we informed our new best friend, the madama.

Through the market, past the taco-man's delicious smelling stall, we came onto the grocery market special to Mary. Delightfully clean, attractively arranged, we began to work the store, sacking tomatoes, potatoes, lime. "No, No limes cross." "Oh, okay," forget the limes.

On the floor lay a huge plastic bag of the freshest, most inviting chicharrones I'd ever encountered. "Must have some of those for the cornbread and the turkey dressing," I muttered to Mary.

"Okay," she answered while gathering up cans of jalapenos.

Passing through the market, we gathered up two teenage boys to transport our purchases. After loading up the packages, my marvelous pot, and the groceries, we agreed, it is lunchtime.

Cast my vote for the Palapas (not the current name) on the street approaching the bullring; knew it was now a buffet, serving delectable Mexican dishes.

Sure enough, they were open at 4 p.m., and happy to greet us. Settling at our table, it was welcoming and comforting to notice the original decor and the authentic Mexican kitchen where two small madamas patted out fresh corn tortillas, and cooked them on the griddle. Yes, we had found heaven.

First trip pass the buffet, we had liberal helpings of guacamole and other salads, which we sat to the side. Next trip we filled our dinner plates from the many main course offerings – beans boracho or refried, Spanish rice; chiles rellenos, enchiladas, carne guisada, chicken sopa, chicken mole, menudo, pork guisada, and more which escape my memory.

Covered my chile relleno with lovely white créme-cheese sauce, and added rice and beans on the side. Mary branched out into chicken mole and menudo.

Neither one of us spoke except for "Delicious!" "Perfecto," "Ummm," for the next 20 minutes. The two of us just feasted, sighed, inhaled, and took in the satisfaction of experiencing a perfect Mexican meal on Mexican soil. Ideal ending to our time in Piedras. We shall return.

So Many Things To Do

March whizzed past in a flurry of weather, wildflowers, wind, cold, and activities. Attended the charming out-of-doors wedding of Kristi Kay Hindes and John Schulte at the small settlement of Coughran Hall, located near Pleasanton. The couple exchanged vows under a huge oak, the evening weather was perfect, and a meadow of pink phlox colored the background.

Middle of the month, Larissa, Trystie, and Tessa arrived to celebrate spring break. We began at Sea World, slowly the fog and drizzle lifted about 12, and we hit the walks of the water wonderland along with hundreds of other spring breakers.

Two-year-old Tessa clung to Aunt Anne while Shamu leaped high and handsome. Later Tess decided the beautiful animal was one of her beloved friends, so naturally the aunt had to purchase a stuffed Shamu for her collection.

All of us loved the seal performance with Willy the water weasel sneaking in and out to wreck havoc for the performers.

During the day as the four of us sat in sand boxes, feasted on fries and chicken nuggets, and sipped sodas. I was delighted by the charm, health, and innocence of all the beautiful children around us. How totally blessed we are in America for our children to have opportunities to be perfectly nourished, clothed, and educated, so easy for us to forget this is not true in most of the world.

Then the USA went to war, so I had to pass some hours in front of the set, plus more hours praying for our troops, the President, and the poor children of the Iraqi people.

My first war memories are of WWII, coupon rations, no rubber doll for Christmas, and Daddy working graveyard shifts at Humble Oil refinery. Later on in life came Korea, then Vietnam, the Gulf War, and the Iraqi conflict, world peace still eludes us.

Speaking at the kick-off luncheon of the Texas Cattle Raisers Association, Robert M. Gates, president of Texas A&M University, and a former 30 year veteran of CIA service made some clarifying remarks: "September 11 completely changed our secure American way of life. Our country will never be completely safe again.

"We need to take greater note of the success of American law enforcement and military in preventing subsequent attacks."

"Three regimes in the world must be overcome, Iraq, Iran, and North Korea."

"France double-crossed us when push came to shove. Many Americans will not forget their actions."

"Washington D.C. is the home of inflated egos, the only city in the world where you can meet a politician strolling along holding his own hand."

"The CIA hires more graduates from Texas A&M University than any other university in America."

Saw many friends at the convention in SA: Robin and Peggy Clark, both progressing nicely with their medical treatments, Becky and King Terry of Alpine, Becky always sports a flower in her hair the color of her outfit, Bob Nunley from home, Chip and Jill Briscoe, reporting both sons are now at Baylor, and Beth McNutt of Junction, sporting a pin stating, "I've survived damn near everything."

Was present in Plano for the christening of Wesley Sarah Noon, who played her part most admirably. Wesley is the daughter of Allison and Doug Noon, grandmother Mary Jo and great-grandmother Elsie would have been proud.

All of us had to reach deep in the closets for wool coats Sunday morn. Freezing in the metroplex, as well as Sabinal, which I found out after arriving home and rushing out to check the tomato plants, whose leaves were burned off, but pinched out the tops, watered, and gave 'em a pep talk. After all, we're facing a large contest among friendly tomato growers, and I do not wish to be embarrassed.

Do you have family and/or friends involved in the war? At Amistad, Margaret informed me her grandson would be shipping out this week. I promised to pray for him.

And so March 2003 was a time of great contrast, our country at war on foreign soil, while we are safe, warm, and have full stomachs. Our Texas hillsides are covered in colorful sweeps of wildflowers, but there is anxiety among our people, protests against the war and demonstrations of support for our troops, giving voice once again to Dicken's memorable quote, "It was the best of times. It was the worst of times."

Spring Brings New Life

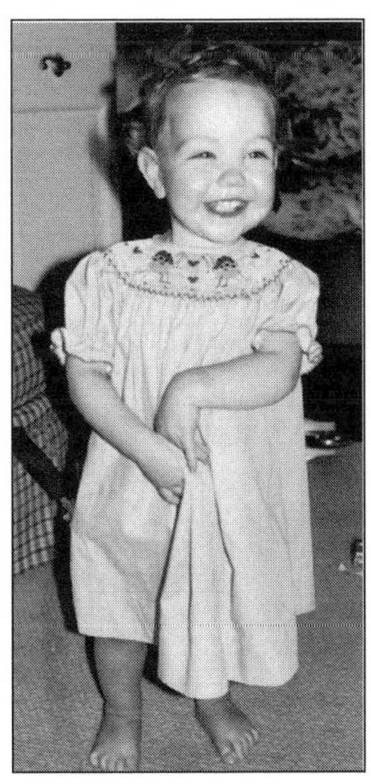

Elizabeth Woodley, age 2

Southwest Flight No. 125 touched down bumpily at Love Field, the wind whipping mightily from the southeast, not many people on planes these days, and much security at the airports. Hurrying to get out of the house, did not give much thought to my footwear, and subsequently found myself stepping barefoot through the security check.

Shortly after arrival Jamie and I headed toward Plano for Mason's baseball game. Our tall, smiling boy plays first base and third, plus pitches, after battling the 40 mile-per-hour winds, the seventh-inning score wound up 6-6.

Wednesday, April 16, both boys and myself bounded out of bed before 6 a.m., tossed on our duds and headed for

Baylor hospital, and by 8:30 Elizabeth Monroe Woodley had arrived. Found Mom Lisa was serene and elated to have a girl in the family.

Easter week heralds time for new life, worship, flowers, church services blessings and springtime, and now the gift of a new life has been placed in our family care.

Walking down the Woodley's street, Hanover, I spent much time admiring the bountiful plantings enchanting the handsome homes. Azaleas were in full bloom. I used to know the names of some varieties, but could only come up with rose, pink, and white, and single and double. Too bad these exquisite, care-intensive plants do not also bloom in the fall.

And an added bonus is tulip season, and they were magnificent, although the winds were giving them quite a beating. My favorite planting, lining the front of a New England style home, was a mixture of pink, white, yellow, red, and wine colors. Further down every hue of pansy imaginable, plus camellias, azaleas. and alyssum provided perfect nesting places for huge Easter eggs in front of an imaginatively styled residence.

And then, unexpectedly in the midst of this huge city, I stumble upon a garden that made me smile and feel at home. It contained a charming, round herb garden, blooming yellow and white Banksias roses intertwined along rail fences, and inventive lawn sculptures fashioned from old tractor parts. "Must be a retired farmer," crossed my mind.

Saw a big, bossy blue jay perched upon a tile rooftop. Cardinals were preoccupied building in the fotina bushes and mockingbirds were singing lustily. At Mesquite we cheered as Luke's team squeaked by their opponents, 6-5. Luke filled the center base spot, and connected for two nice hits.

The Burns girls, Larissa and Allie, Al's Wesley and I dined alfresco on quesadillas and fish tacos while Tessa and Trystie were hunting eggs at their school. Seems to me that half of the state of Guanajuato is employed in Big D, and more than a few of them have opened their own excellent eating establishments.

Nights while the boys studied I read Queen Noor's autobiography, "An Unexpected Life." She leads one throughout the journey of an American young woman who married Jordan's King Hussein and bore him five children.

Searched the bookstore shelves for Kinky Friedman's mystery, "Meanwhile Back At The Ranch," but could not find a copy. Friends told me Utopia, Friedman's Animal Rescue shelter, and local citizens were incorporated into the tale. Hear by the Utopia news line the Rescue Ranch pulled up stakes and relocated near Medina, so some canyon folks are smiling.

Get your hands on a copy of Texas Monthly's April issue, which proclaims on the cover, "Hill Country Forever." Turn to the back page to Kinky's column where he states, "If I could, I would surround this magic kingdom (Texas Hill Country) with the fragile, freckled arms of childhood and keep it the way I remembered it." Love that sentence, and if it were with in my power, Kinky, I too would do the same. But, as John Graves states in same issue, I'm grateful that I came to know the Hill Country before it was overrun. Happy to be back in my part of Texas, to have a darling new child to love, find Annalee okay, know Utopia Methodist will soon be renovated, and to witness the yellow wildflowers while driving home. This thought of Rabbi Abraham Herschel fit my mood perfectly. "Just to be is a blessing. Just to live is holy."

Vacation Out West

Julie Douglas

Our plane dropped down low over its Columbia River approach, giving passengers on the right side a bird's eye view of the Dalles, the Columbia River gorge, and the "greenness" of Oregon. Ironic that the settlers coming to this productive area over a hundred years ago entered the Willamette Valley along the same route.

The legacy of the Valley's fertileness drew first settlers over the Oregon Trail. Still one of the most productive agricultural regions in the world, this is an area of many diversified crops, and ag-related businesses.

Portland is a lovely city situated on both sides of the Willamette River, climbing up the verdant, green hills and affording spectacular views for its residents. The rose test gardens in its Washington Park were calling my name, so early morning hours found us gazing at literally thousands of rose bushes; floribundas, climbers, miniatures, hybrid teas, grand floras and native old-fashioned.

I'm always drawn to the showy hybrid teas – Mr. Lincoln (deep red), Peace (yellow with pink edges), Queen Elizabeth (porcelain pink) and South Pacific (showy coral). But an archway of rosy-pink climbers spilling out onto the lawn below drew our attention to its perfusion of blooms, hard to make a decision of one favorite among such an immense display of color and beauty.

Difficult for us Texans to realize other states are not the size of ours, so in only several hours driving time, we were headed west, exploring the Pacific coastline, in hopes of finding the perfect seafood restaurant.

And, sure enough, in Newport we indulged in Halibut (cold-water flounder), clam chowder and oysters at Moe's Famous Chowder House.

Watched the fishing boats unloading their catch, which was being carried by conveyer bells into the cannery. Colorful lobster traps were carefully stacked waiting to be loaded onto boats.

Couldn't resist the bountiful display of fresh seafood in the window of the cannery market. It seemed the perfect place to purchase king salmon and red snapper for the friends we planned to visit later in the afternoon.

Driving from the coast, we again crossed the wonderfully picturesque Willamette. Rye grass and alfalfa lay windrowed in the fields, the cherry harvest was in full swing, saw farms producing all sorts of flower bulbs, Christmas trees, oil seed rape, soybeans, wheat barley and many vineyards.

Made some new best friends when we stopped to ask directions of a farmer towing an automatic hay bale stacker. Turned out the couple ranches on both sides of the Cascades, so naturally we fell to discussing the ups and downs of our agricultural businesses. And, in the end the four of us all agreed it is the very best way of life for us.

Friends Lea and Bill, plus their grandson, Will, greeted us at the Rick Lane home between Sisters and Bend, Oregon. A landscaping project was in progress in the front lawn area, while Kim's

Bill, Will, and Lea Lane, Bend Oregon

four horses grazed in the adjoining meadow – perfect afternoon for enjoying the cool, crisp outdoors.

Bend is the perfectly planned small town of 50,000, built along the Descutes River, many of the businesses open out to a lakeside setting in the city park. So fun to lunch outdoors and watch the large Canadian geese swim by, then tip over in search of a meal, with only their tail sides protruding.

We took advantage of the hospitality of Debbie and Bob Lane. The perfectly centered window in their hall provides a framed view of Mount Bachelor, the Three Sisters and Mount Jefferson, more perfectly than any painting could capture.

Down through eastern Oregon we viewed many black cows and calves along the creeks, they were obviously thriving. During this Fourth of July week, many farmers were thinking only of bailing their hay and properly stacking it for the winter months.

Below Reno at Yarington, we caught the early morning workout Julie and Doug White pour into their powerfully bred jumping horses.

Paco, a 17-hands high, dark brown bay, was balking at the low water jump, but in the end, Julie gracefully coaxed him over, and we all agreed he would soon forget his hang-up with that certain obstacle.

Doug gave us a tour of the area ranches and cattle being backgrounded for the Harris feedlots in Arizona and California. Their aged beef has no equal.

Lots of onions are being grown in this Walker Valley area and much alfalfa. Later that evening we dined upon prime beef and Julie's fresh garden peas, while discussing the many personalities we had known and encountered in the cattle business. Is there a more colorful group of characters?

My favorite story concerned Mr. Gus Miers of Del Rio and northern Mexico, and his huge ranching operation in Coahuila and the thousands of head of horses he ran there.

In the month before the revolt, one of Villa's colonel's rode into the ranch headquarters prepared to purchase a thousand head for the rebel's troops. When the colonel made his offer, the rancher's only response was, "What color do you want?" All bays, all grays, all sorrels, or all blacks?"

But the very best aspect of the trip was sharing the scenery and experiences with someone who is in the cattle business, and completely understands its life of ups and downs. So when I have referred to "us" in this column, notice the name

Joe and Anne Hargrove

change at the start of the column and you'll realize, Joe was my traveling partner as well as my new life partner.

Library, Church Are Inspirational

June already. How can it be? Recall the days of childhood dragging, creeping, crawling by. Now in modern maturity they race, run, and skip away, sometimes several at a time.

Couldn't seem to come up with great thoughts on a certain subject, seems as if hot weather and watering keep the mind unfocused, so just penned a few bits and pieces.

Stopped by for a quick look at the new Utopia Library building, how grand to have such a comprehensive, attractive facility now open to all in our community. Connie gave us a tour and visions of what is still to come. Heartfelt thanks to everyone inside and outside the community who worked together to make this dream a reality.

And also the Utopia United Methodist reopened its doors this past Sunday for services. Reverend Kent Kepler delivered his last message June 2, before retiring during the annual Methodist conference in Corpus Christi.

Visit the new version of our stately church. It sparkles with the grace and light emitted through the intricate, colorful art windows, which were previously blocked by the balcony and downstairs rooms.

These stain glass proclamations of faith were given by the Porter, Fisher, Harper, Redden, Jones, and Wentworth clans in honor of certain family members. The other windows were a gift years ago from

Utopia Methodist Church

the John Wheelers and Frank Jones. Now visible together for the first time they illuminate the old frame structure with a renewed brilliance.

Memorial weekend Saturday my guests, Wesley, Allie, and Doug Noon were most agreeable to dining at Neal's; there we visited with Merrill, Janet, and Phil Hughes.

Merrill was in Uvalde for a coffee given in her honor Saturday morning at the Willoughby home. She will marry this June in the Washington D.C. area where she has been working and residing. Merrill, you'll be a storybook bride.

Received graduation notices from several of my favorite young people. Kristi Sloan received a scholarship upon her graduation from SHS. Visited with her grandmother in H-E-B, whose eyes sparkled when I complimented Kristi's high record.

Mrs. Sloan has raised her two small granddaughters from childhood, and she remarked, "Oh, Mrs. Woodley, I'm so proud, I so want those girls to have a better life than I did." They will, Mrs. Sloan, thanks to the efforts of their grandmother.

Diane Causey and I discussed over lunch how each year we envision our gardening efforts producing such bountiful results we'll have to can, preserve, freeze, and beg folks to take away part of the harvest, but it never happens.

Certainly didn't occur with my great potted tomato project of 2003. The plants are as tall as I am, perhaps to date I've pulled four or five scrawny tomatoes and probably invested 50 bucks on the entire production. As I've been reminded, you can purchase a lot of tomatoes for that amount. But OH – think of the fun of planting, planning, don't forget dreaming, and there's always next year.

Visiting Amistad was saddened to learn of the loss of Mildred Patton. Joe Glen and Mildred resided in Utopia during our childhood days; think their daughter Barbara was a member of Taylor's class.

Heartfelt sympathy to Joe and Lois Elaine, as we used to know her. The two of us visit while caring for our parents.

Loaned my copy of "The Purpose Driven Life" to a friend. Sensibly written, easy to read, it brings one back to the fact the God creates each of us with a definite purpose in mind. Finding and fulfilling that purpose is our life's work.

Father Einer Ochoa and I had a visit before he departed our community for a new parish at St. Agnes in San Antonio.

Personable and articulate, Father did much to bring the denominations of Sabinal together to work for community good. Thanksgiving services at St. Patrick were a special time, the sanctuary packed, and the delicious meal of gratitude served afterwards.

Einer Ochoa grew up in a small village of the Yucatan, north of Merida. His family emigrated to California seeking to improve their fives and educate their children.

Together we extolled the merits of America where a person can become whatever they dream with hard work, education, and time.

Failed to mention my other graduation notifications were Justin Dean, Bobbi Kay Smithson, and Stacy Littleton.

Justin's family has been friends since Utopia days when his grandfather, Austin Dean, worked with Henry at Utopia Telephone.

Bobbi Kay graduated with honors from Texas Tech, she visited us at the ranch in her younger days. Her Dad, John Smithson, provided help when Mac was running steers.

Stacy Littleton is Fred and Joan Woodley's granddaughter and fresh out of Baylor, summa cum laude.

Jack Woodley used to joke he graduated from Baylor, "Laudy, how cum?" So he'd be especially proud of you, Stacy.

Congratulations to all graduates, never forget in America you can become whatever you dream.

South Texas Summers

Driving south these days the countryside has reflected hundreds of different variations on the color green. The rains in early July, and the moisture from Claudette brought the brush country into full flower.

Roy Hindes, III and Bob Hindes, 1940s

The wildflower season is behind us and now it is the season of grass, klein, cottontop, sideoats, blue panic, needle or purple three-awn, field grass and buffel.

Last weekend we had the pleasure of meeting Gary Pogue, Pogue Seed Co., to tour their company's grass plots near Fowlerton. That area is as green and lush as we'll ever view it. On the old O'Connor ranch, now the Hindes-Eustace estate, the Pogues are growing a sensational crop of Japanese Guinea grass. As we drove through the stand, the lacy, wispy seed heads waved and shook themselves free of millions of tiny grain seeds. Gary described the headaches involved in trying to harvest the seed crop. Easy to see this could be a dream crop of cattle forage in our part of the country once you established a stand.

Next we saw a plot of bundle flower, a huajillo-type plant with a small, lacy leaf which is very high in nutrient value for cattle as well as wildlife. A boost to any brush ranch trying to increase its profitability through the diversities of its forage.

But the one that truly caught my attention was the stand of cold-tolerant buffel, which had been established for several years. It was a cattleman's dream, waving its dark maroon heads in the morning breezes. Buffel has always struck a chord in my heart, and we all agreed this was one of the most outstanding grass plantings we'd seen in ages.

Was pleased to at last visit the O'Connor ranch, had heard Mac and Bob and Roy discuss it years ago when the Hindes Brothers were in the heavy equipment business and clearing the Albright pasture across from Yucca for Mac. Here in the middle of the brush ranching country they have carved out a piece of productive land and irrigated it over the past 30 years; easy to imagine the work and effort poured into the project.

Enjoyed our conversation with Gary Pogue, whom I had not seen in years. He described his enthusiasm for his work with plants and plant research. "There is no greater, thrill to me than to see plants grow, and to play a part in improving farms and rangelands."

We gardeners understand the lure of the outside world and the science of plant propagating, it is a study to intrigue the mind for a lifetime.

Speaking of people who love plants, planting, working with growing and improving production, Eddie Falkenburg spent his life in the farming business, and I daresay if we could question him now he'd proclaim he enjoyed every minute of his labors.

Our friendship with the Falkenburgs, Sophie and Eddie, goes back a generation to our parents. Henry taught Sophie at Tay-

Prince Domino, Hiler-Woodley Ranch, 1940's

lor school above Utopia, when her parents lived on the Harper ranch. Later the Mergles moved to Sabinal and Mr. Mergle worked for Big Mac Sr. for years. Some of Mac's favorite memories were of the times he stayed at the Hiler ranch with them. Can't resist adding this wonderful little incident. Mr. Woodley traveled to Fort Worth Stock Show one year and purchased a prize Hereford bull, Prince Domino. The Prince was transported to the Hiler for Oscar Merle to care for, and the next trip Big Mac made to the ranch Mrs. Mergle had the bull in the front yard, giving him a proper bath and combing.

Eddie also worked for Mr. Woodley after the war, so when I moved to Yucca as a bride the Falkenburgs were our closest, and over the years, dearest neighbors.

I believe others teach us much more by their actions than by all the words they speak. Eddie Falkenburg was a gentleman of the highest degree; I never heard him utter an oath, saw him lose his temper, or heard him speak an unkind word about any person. He was completely capable in his chosen business, a master farmer, a steadfast friend.

Together Mac and Eddie spent many hours, checking equipment, hunting, looking for insects on the crops, discussing their childhoods, and just enjoying each other's company. Still quote this saying from Eddie's father to his many sons when discipline broke down among them, "Now if you boys can't hear it, you'll just have to feel it."

When June and roasting ear season would roll round the Falkenburg-Woodley families would set aside a certain day to put up corn. Early in the morning Eddie, Mac, Cuco, Ben Amein, Edwardo, Jamie, T.M., would pull eight to 10 tow sacks of corn. Mac and Eddie were the judges of when it was "just right."

Behind the house they would begin the shucking process while inside Sophie and I were readying our equipment, (Did we have enough ice on hand?) and beginning preparations for lunch.

Soon the first ears would arrive in the kitchen via Jamie or perhaps Cuco, and we'd begin blanching them, and cooling 'em down in ice water, then slicing the corn off the cob.

At noontime we'd cease corn proceedings, serve a huge meal consisting of fried steak, homegrown fresh tomatoes, scalloped potatoes, fresh green beans, corn on the cob, Sophie's homemade bread, and most certainly a pie or two she'd prepared the day before. Then Jamie, Eddie, Leland, Mac, Deanie, T.M. and probably an extra boy or two gathered round the table and we'd feast. After dinner, Sophie and I would return to the corn process and clean-up duty.

Eddie Falkenberg and Chessie, San Antonio Stock Show, 1984

Remembering those times provides me the greatest of joy and pleasure, all built upon simple sweet good times of our two families working together to enjoy the fruits of our labors.

There is no other possible profession that would have suited Erich "Eddie" Falkenburg. He was born to the land, loved its secrets and plantings and was proud of the product it produced.

Everyone loved and respected him. Sharing Eddie and Sophie's friendship enriched our lives and Deloris and Rodney's, Felix and Lillian's, and many, many others whose lives he touched.

Meet the Machens

Walking into Barbara Machen's kitchen envelopes you in the warm feeling of "coming home." Good smells are everywhere. Backstraps frying in the pan, and lunch (actually dinner is what we called it in Utopia) is hot, homecooked, tasty and filling. The conversation is Texas ranch subjects, my type of talk.

For reasons unknown to myself (perhaps a few illnesses intervened), I had never visited Gary and Barbara Machen's comfortable, inviting, hilltop

Mr. Big - Los Cazadores Logo Buck, Machen Ranch

home until this week. We have been ranching neighbors for years, the Machen ranch being south of the Hiler ranch on the banks of the Frio. Occasionally Gary, or in earlier times, his Dad, Cap, would call to report some of our cattle had wandered down the Frio onto their place. Other times I remember hearing Fred and Mac discussing, what an excellent farmer Cap Machen was, and they were always interested in which crops he was growing and his fertilizing practices. After his dad's death, Gary turned from the cattle business to high fences and growing trophy bucks. Sunday, March 31, Paul Duggan of the Washington Post published a most interesting article, "Making Big Bucks on a Texas Ranch," discussing Gary's intensive breeding and hunting program.

Quoting Duggan: "Machen, 56, is a burly Texan with short brown hair and an old belt buckle almost the size of a bread dish. He works at the supply end of Texas's $2 billion-a-year hunting economy. Thousands of ranchers and farmers, unable to make ends meet through agriculture alone, allow hunters to roam on their fenced-in lands, for a price. The bigger the deer, the bigger the fee. And if a property owner's deer happen to be scrawny, he can turn to a breeder such as Machen, who sells bucks that are born for wall mounting. "It's improving the quality of our deer overall," Machen says of breeding operations, which are common in many states. In Texas, about 3000 people are licensed

126

to raise deer for hunting. "I don't see one thing wrong with it," he says. "God gave everyone what they've got, and if we don't try to make it better, then we're being remiss."

At the time of my visit water was standing in the bar ditches, but I know moisture has been in short supply. This area has missed many more rains than they've caught in the past 10 years, making ranching and farming a non-profitable enterprise.

Back to the Washington Post article: "Like many other Texas ranchers," Machen says, "I couldn't afford to retain ownership of this land without hunting." His property, 60 miles southwest of San Antonio, has been in his family for generations. Hunting for his deer isn't cheap.

"I cater to a clientele that's mostly big executives," he says. In winters, during hunting season, "they'll fly in here from all over the country. Now, they enjoy the experience, being out in the wild and everything, but they can't stay for long. They want to come out and kill the best buck they can in the shortest time possible."

Last summer season, Barbara and two helpers bottle-fed (five to six times daily for newborns) 47 fawns until they were able to be placed in the pens and digest dry feed.

Barbara Machen's wide, ready smile defines her happy nature. She is quick to tell you, "I'm doing what I love. I'm a happy person." Her day begins in the early morning hours, and during hunting season can last until late at night. She cooks for the hunters and keeps all the many details of their operation pulled together for Gary.

Loved her wonderful horn trees out doors, which she has accented with lights. Also she constructs crosses, wreaths, table bottoms out of shed horns she finds around the ranch.

Had to chuckle over the comments Duggan recorded in his Post piece; "Machen, who began his operation in 1995 with a few dozen deer bought from other breeders, has 150 larger-than-normal whitetails prancing in his pens. He knows what hunting opponents think of his business but he doesn't care. "Bunny-huggers," he scoffs.

The Machens display Texas spirit. They were not afraid of hard work and dedication.

September Days

Soaking September rains fell on much of our area Thursday the 11th, and more on Sunday the 14th, giving promise of a fall season of abundance and the moisture to begin planting oats, wheat, rye, and other fall crops. But the cotton farmers are still picking and nervous, hopefully they'll soon complete what appears to be a bountiful harvest.

Can't recall many Septembers as cool and delightful as this one of '03, but of course we've enjoyed an exceptionally delightful and moist summer. On my morning outings one or two Monarchs drift by, already on their trip south. And the huge, brilliant yellow and black butterflies linger on the bright bougainvillea blossoms, while the solid yellow and pure white ones flit around searching for other flowers or milkweed.

Here at Crystal, Andy Armadillo makes a morning visit to my bird bath on the ground. He's too blind to see me, so I chuckle as he drinks happily and freely, then (every time) sits up, holds his front paws together as in a prayer of Thanksgiving, then wanders blindly off.

Could murder him, as he excavates daily around the plants, but here on the banks of the Nueces there is an armadillo family as large as the Wentworths or the Sutherlands, so it seems futile to dispatch one member knowing two more will take his place.

The first batch of chili pequin jelly was a flop, the Certo jell must have been five years old, plus these chilies in Zavala county are fuerte. So my next attempt, cut the amount of chilies in half purchased new Certo and presto! The jelly jelled, tasted exactly as it should, and had the rich, red hue of the autumn season. Success after failure is sooo rewarding.

Looking out the kitchen window, can follow the progress of the oat seeding, done by a sophisticated computerized rig. It properly measures the exact amount of seed to be planted to the acre, can be set to calculate the area covered, and also operated on automatic pilot. What ever would Homer, Henry, and Vic Niemeyer think of such an invention?

Also am having fun anticipating the planting of green beans and cabbage here by the house. Jimmy Speer and David Jones are doing the farming, and it's fun to be part of a vegetable operation – all new to me. But I'm ready to prepare green beans and coleslaw for Thanksgiving dinner.

And did any of you in the cattle business think you'd ever live to see the day of 90-cent fat steers? And aren't you glad you did? Being on the top instead of the bottom for a change is a grand feeling for people who expect adversity each time they purchase a set of cattle.

Not that I want beef priced out of the limits of the consumer, but it is enjoyable to see a group of business people come into some prosperity, after the low markets cattle people have dealt with the past few years.

Saw a large flight of bluebirds, (eastern) on my visit to the 4-H ranch last week. Dee built four or five birdhouses suited to the blues, then placed them in strategic places such as described in a magazine article, entitled The Bluebird Trail. And his efforts paid off magnificently, as the second season the entire families returned to the nesting places.

Here's the recent reading list we've been working on: "The Secret Life of Bees," If you haven't read it, you must. "The Da Vinci Code," so intricately detailed and fascinating, you'll not be able to put it aside, "Man 'O War," a follow up on the coat tails of "Seabiscuit's" popularity, "Daughter of Fortune," by Chile's Isabelle Allenede, excellent fiction, "The Purpose Driven Life," now being taught in courses in church classes, and book groups. And am most pleased with my new Smithsonian edition of "The Birds of Texas" so many new birds here along the banks of the Nueces, saw my first pair of orchard orioles here several mornings ago. Annalee would be delighted.

One South Texas rancher spoke of September range and price conditions in the following manner, "the table is set." Indeed it is, let's busy ourselves drinking in the bounty of these golden days.

Memories Move Writer

Wanted to share the accompanying photograph if you missed Jeff Parker's radiant field of sunflowers on Highway 90 west of Uvalde.

Driving into Uvalde one August a.m., the sun was at a perfect angle and the golden heads were facing its warmth and glow, couldn't resist snapping some shots of the magical flowers.

While tossing a half dozen milk bottles of "Promised Land" in the trash, decided to check the label to note if returning them was an option. It wasn't. Surprised to find the label boasted a biblical quotation, "He brought us to this place and gave us land: a land flowing with milk and honey." - Deuteronomy 26:9

Now I'm more enamored than ever with the superior Floresville product produced from those loveable Jersey cows.

When Edwardo Sandoval was in residence at the ranch, he requested a cow for himself to milk. Mac dispatched Henry to pick up two on his next trip to the auc-

Jeff Parker's sunflowers

tion. Daddy delivered the two charming girls to Yucca Switch, one was dark colored, the other light, and Edwardo was smiling proudly from to ear.

A short period later, the dark cow succumbed to milk fever. Then events developed which moved Edwardo to a new location below La Loma, and ChaCha, the light colored Jersey, accompanied him. She produced buckets of rich, creamy milk, which Edwardo would skim and then deliver the cream to me.

After pouring the cream in my food processor, I'd give it a few whirrs, and presto! We'd be rich in homemade butter.

Cha-Cha ran with the Beefmaster cows who bullied and bossed her, and would fight her away from the cubes when I'd cake them. But she had her day in glory. Once Gary, the big bull wandered, pushed, jumped, by some means managed to cross the neighbor's south fence. He had a mind of his own, there were no pens which he could be driven to, and how to get him home without a lot of hassle and heartbreak?

Mac decided to cut our fence, then coaxed Cha-cha through the hole, and directed her to bring Gary home. Which she did nicely and easily that very evening when it was milking time. Still picture that huge bull tagging along behind a tiny boned Jersey like an admonished schoolboy.

Never see a Jersey cow or a photo of one without Cha-Cha darlin' coming to mind.

Had two marvelous meals during my Utopia weekend, one at the Masonic supper honoring Frank Jones Jr. and Sid Mauldin with 50-year pins. Mary and Jim Willis were in charge of the affair, featuring tasty brisket.

Sunday morning after worshipping at the newly renovated Utopia Methodist, how splendid and spiritual it is, joined members for the monthly luncheon. Church dinners are as savory as ever, as Utopia is blessed with many capable cooks.

The kitchen at Southwest Livestock seems to be a depository for all types of culinary goodies. Frieda, I knew her as Rucker, Bain shared seasoned sugared pecans from her '03 crop, so fresh, so special.

Jon Taylor transported a stalk of bananas plus two large bags of limes, and pickled okra from Carrizo for everyone to taste. The bananas were sweeter, slightly different taste from storebought.

I made lime, not lemon square cookies, and the change in flavor was light, and not tart.

Brother Taylor arrived for a weekend of South Texas dove hunting and bequeathed us with enough birds for dove dumplings. If you do not have a recipe, use your chicken and dumplin' one, but split the bird breasts and then brown them before adding to the broth, simmer 20-30 minutes, add dumplings. Another way to enjoy birds if you are not overly fond of dove.

Beth Pringle treated me to a lunch of gorditos, prepared and sold in Sabinal. So you no savvy gorditos? You've missed much. Large, handmade corn tortillas, fried and then split halfway to hold a filling of either beef or chicken, lettuce, tomatoes, avocado, and hot sauce, combine to create a taste tough to surpass.

Was reading a questionnaire asking you to name your 10 favorite meals. My number one was easy, Grandmother Burns's fried chicken, mashed potatoes, green beans (fresh), corn on the cob, green salad, and peach cobbler.

Bet yours will hark back to childhood also, and include some special dish that your mother, grandmother, or relative prepared.

Perhaps we'll peruse this topic during the upcoming Sabinal Homecoming, Oct. 11-12. Our class of 1958 will mark 45 years since graduation from SHS. How can it be? See you there and bring a covered dish!

Nature Offers Solace

"We who were born in country places
Far from cities and shifting faces
We have a birthright no man can sell
And a Secret joy no man can tell."

Pepe prowled while I sat quietly on the large steel pipe running from the river to the irrigation pivots. Here in Zavala County, the riverbanks of the Nueces becomes a natural habitat in which live oaks, pecans, cedar elms, native cherry, willows, and redbuds grow to immense heights. The leaf mold creates a cushy, mottled carpet softer and more interesting than any Brinkmans could weave.

Gave myself the gift of an afternoon watching the turtles sunning themselves on a willow branch, which stretched over the green depths of the water. Sunlight glinted off their wet shells, and they seemed to soak up its warmth. Cardinals called "Sweet, sweet" to each other and flitted through the vines and underbrush while a garden spider weaving an intricate web entertained me.

A small boat motored by, and I envied its mobility carrying the person to other secrets which the river might reveal.

These are but a small handful of the daily joys given to me exploring the riverbanks, putting out corn for the cardinals, green jays, woodpeckers, and believe it or no, a huge blue jay.

Christmas season is upon us bringing its bustle, shopping (seems to be much this 2003), plans, travels, special programs, and family gatherings.

Our ranch gals gang convened at the Moderno, Piedras, to celebrate and congratulate amiga Fannie Hindes, gifts were in order for the December birthday lady, who will hear wedding bells in 2004.

Pam Hindes and Fannie Grace Hindes
at the Hindes Ranch

Guacamole at the Moderno it is in a class alone, so it was necessary to order several extra dishes for the center of the table. And my frog legs were just as I had anticipated, delicate and delicious.

Established in 1938 by the de los Santos family, this distinguished Mexican restaurant has a dignity and atmosphere difficult to find in today's casual world.

Starched and crisply ironed white tablecloths, presided over by dignified, polite waiters, exceptional cuisine, and live music make it a destination to be appreciated and enjoyed.

Pleased my three cousins, Betty, Diane, and Evie could join our group and visit our casa at Crystal. While trying to keep the Explorer on the highway (high winds last Tuesday), we discussed the Christmas story Mama recorded of uncle Harper Simpson and aunt Fannie coming from "over on the Murlo," their wagon loaded down with gifts and food for our great grandmother Fisher's fatherless family. Where is the Murlo (a creek) located we wondered? Annalee and Henry Fisher always referred to it as "the other side of Uvalde."

Joe's sweet sister Charlotte provided a tin of delicious pralines for friends at the sale Thursday. Must make sure to have copy of the recipe.

While attending the festive Christmas party hosted in part by John and Patti Driskill, my mind returned to the rough road their family has traveled, and how I admire the poise and composure this couple has maintained, "grace under pressure" Hemmingway called it.

Their son Robert will be moved to a nursing facility at Hondo next week where he will continue to receive physical therapy.

For those who have lost a loved one, are struggling with injuries, diseases, or pain, the holidays can stab the heart easily and deeply. Our Grandmother Wentworth could never listen easily to "White Christmas" after the loss of her darling Murray on Dec. 27. "There are few sensations more painful, than in the midst of deep grief, to know that the season which we have always associated with mirth and merriment is at hand." Sarah Hale.

The altar at Sacred Heart Church was literally covered with hundreds of red long stem roses for the Dia de la Lady of Guadalupe celebration, making it sufficient to sit and drink in their intoxicating color and magnificence. They were a sermon in themselves.

The scripture struck the true heart of Christmas, John answered, "The man with two tunics should share with him who has none, and the one who has food should do the same." - John 3: 11

Homecoming Review

"There is no old age. There is, as there always was, only you."
-Carol Mattheu

Like that quotation by Carol Mattheu, Walter's literary wife. And it held true for a handful of Sabinal High School graduates, as we huddled together on Glen and Beth Pringle's front porch to view the SHS Homecoming parade while rain fell freely.

Graduates present were Glen, Mary Jean Farr Lillie, Wanda Redden Neely, Bill Soyars (Big Bill), Artie Ballew, Eddie Perkins, myself and Gene Perkins.

Surprised to see Mr. Otis Fowler looking spry and enjoying the festivities in spite of the elements. He was always kind and soft spoken when helping customers at Fowler Lumber Company, and he supervised the building of quite a few homes in the Sabinal, Knippa and Utopia area.

The EX-Student Association did an excellent job of producing a super-duper parade. Two of the Rose Bowl class entries were constructed in my barn. "The Land of Oz, or The Yellow Brick Road" and "Willie Wonka and the Chocolate Factory." Could see parents and teachers had poured tons of time and efforts into those imaginative moveable fantasies.

A favorite participant was Cameron Moore riding a small Shetland pony. Her radiant red hair shown brightly through the wet weather, as she waved gaily to the onlookers. Her mom is Barbara Jane Clary Creech, daughter of Nell and Ott Clary. Her great-grandfather, Sam Henderson, taught Annalee Spanish at SHS.

A clown, who I perceived to be Charley Jack Woodley, ran up to our steps and cheerfully showered the group with candy. Charley is one of my favorites, and now serves in the U.S. Navy on the USS Kitty Hawk, and has seen action in the Persian Gulf. His grandfathers, Charley Colvin and Jack Woodley, both Sabinal Exes, would be most proud.

Just as the past week held many bright moments sparking with happiness, it was also peppered with sadness when word came of the loss of Dovey Knowles. She had endured a long and difficult illness, gracefully under pressure. For all of us who knew and loved Dovey, she was the picture perfect expression of grace, style, and Christian virtues.

The hours we were together over the years she never failed to discuss how dearly she loved her church, husband, sons, grandchildren, parents, and siblings.

In the Knowles playroom hung a photo of Dovey the year she was chosen Queen of the May fete. Dressed in a pink tulle gown, and wearing a flower halo, she epitomizes the natural beauty, which the month of May bring us. I shall always think of her as Queen of the May.

Never heard it worded so adeptly as Rev. Jerry Scott expressed the present day situation during Dovey's services. He was recognizing the fact she prepared, on time, three nutritious and tasty meals daily for Pete and the boys, and or grandsons. The he asked, "Isn't it terrible that all these women who could and would cook are dying off?" Admittedly there are not large numbers of us left.

On one of my sojourns in Dallas, it boggled the mind to learn of a drive-thru deli where you pick up a completely prepared casserole, ready to pop in the oven.

But Dallas was glorious this past weekend when Larissa, Trystie, Tessa, Allison, Wesley, Taylor, Joan, and Aunt Anne walked through the turnstiles at Fair Park. We could not have ordered a more picture perfect day from Sears-Roebuck and Company, sunny with a delightful south breeze. Being a senior citizen was sweetened by the fact that Thursday was free admission day for seniors.

After a tour through the petting zoo, the white sows and their pink piglets were the chosen favorites of the younger group, we set about indulging in sausage rolls, slurpees, lemonade, tacos, shrimp sticks, and corny dogs.

Trystie and Tess voted the flying Dumbo carts favorite among the rides, but personally I held a warm, special feeling in my heart when seeing our three small ones seated upon the beautifully crafted carousel horses, which moved gracefully to the music of the Beautiful Blue Danube. Secretly I wished for Mary Jo and Annalee to be peeping upon these darling children, savoring a day at the fair.

Topped off my visit by cheering when grandson Mason crossed the goal line, and ultimately led the ninth-grade Scots to a nice victory. His grandfather would be as pleased as punch.

Returning to our part of the country, we were elated to hear the Coyotes had brought home a victory, naturally we felt Cline Speer had a large part in securing the win.

Joe turned out some steers on dry land wheat pasture Friday, Oct. 17, the earliest date ever in his cattle business career. And still the market continued to spiral upward, cattle market as well as the Dow. God has been extremely gracious October 2003.

★

Reverie Can Be Fun

Shuffling around in my copious amount of posted material, yes, like Annalee, I still possess almost every letter sent my way, came across an interesting packet received several years ago.

It was postmarked Abilene, Texas, and bore the return address of Cowboy Smith, who resides in the big country of West Texas, and dotes on the history, music, and love of Texas. He was born and raised in Dundee, and became fast friends with Mac during their days at TCU, when they were members of the rodeo club together.

Cowboy writes: "Regarding the enclosed newspaper clipping about the selling of the Baca ranch to the federal government, the owner was from Abilene, Pat Dunigan, a nice guy.

"I have dreamed of owning the Baca. As a fellow said to me once when we were touring an exceptionally beautiful ranch, but light years away from being as exhilarating as the Baca, quote, 'If I owned this place, I would send out for food' ah, never leave.

"Do you suppose Mac and I could have ridden out the entire 95,000 acres in one summer, horseback of course? You and Helen would have been able to enjoy some cool days, bringing picnics to us in the high country. Reverie can be fun."

Glen (Cowboy) and Helen Smith at Western Swing Festival, Wichita Falls

The Baca ranch to which Cowboy refers is a 95,000-acre tract lying within the Jemez Mountains of northern New Mexico. It is home to one of the largest elk herds in America, estimated to number as many 65,000.

Bill Clinton signed the law enabling the federal government to purchase this spectacular privately owned acreage. Now it is known as the Valles Caldera National Preserve, a unit of the National Forest System.

Last hunting season Bob Mauldin received the opportunity of a hunter's lifetime when his name was drawn to hunt elk on the Valles Caldera. Bob explained there are four different times when hunts are available, and individuals who have paid a $25 fee to post their names are chosen by the lottery system.

Once chosen, each hunter is allowed to bring a guide along with him, so Bob chose brother Tom. No one is allowed to camp on the federal lands, so the Mauldin brothers headquartered at La Cueva, 10 miles away.

The time allowed for each individual hunt is five days, and here Bob's story becomes extraordinary. After two days searching for the choice elk, Bob and Tom received a call; cellphone of course, from Cindy Mauldin stating their Dad, Sid Sr., had serious medical problems and was hospitalized in San Antonio.

The brothers caught a flight out of Albuquerque, arrived at the Alamo City, and after waiting for assurance from the medical team their Dad was stable, they returned to New Mexico for their remaining hunt time (one day).

And fate smiled on that morning as Bob sighted a huge bull elk, downed him, and found himself the proud possessor of a set of horns scoring 319 on the Boone and Crockett scale. Not having access to scales, they estimated the weight of the prize to be between 800 and 900 pounds, and the points measure 6 x 6.

So the brothers Mauldin did experience a hunting dream out on the Baca, and have the horns to prove it. But the best part of the exciting story concerns their dad, Sid Sr., who recovered nicely and has now returned to his golf game.

Halloween came my way early at the Dick Kinzer residence. Stepping out onto the colorfully decorated patio, I was greeted by a most authentic witch, who was presenting treats to the youngsters. Later, without attire, the witch proved to be the same as longtime friend,

Pepper Kincaid Kinzer, grandmother of Ellie and Hannah, Taylor and Jennifer, and Riley, all present to celebrate Halloween.

Had been years since I last saw the three Riley Maner sisters together, and each one is a version of Pepper, in her own unique manner.

Attending the Uvalde Homecoming Queen presentation was exciting with all the handsome students in formal attire. The attractive honoree was Katelyn Huffstutler, wearing a stunning toffee-colored gown. When congratulating her mom, Kerry, I learned Katelyn had solicited Kerry's assistance in making the dress choice. What a thrill for a mother, to be asked to play a large role in her daughter's special occasion.

Memorable Quotes

Listening to Ray Melton deliver the eulogy for Joe Gulley, a phrase lingered in my mind. Ray was referring to his conversations with Joe and noted often he would quote his Dad, "My ole' Daddy said 'Son. don't spend all your time chasing dollars, there's too many out there to catch, Do some living between.'"

Sincere sympathy to the entire family, who endured tragedy and trials at a time when they had planned to be enjoying the Thanksgiving season.

Betty, in my book of quotes I came upon these lines from Cormac McCarthy's "All the Pretty Horses." For me this observation has proved true. "Gustavo said to me that those who have suffered great pain or injury or loss are joined to one another with bonds of a special authority and it has proved to be. The closest bonds we will ever know are bonds of grief."

May God keep his hand upon your shoulder in the days and weeks to come.

Thinking of quotes, Annalee had (still does) a large book of "Bartlett's Quotations" which is well worn. She consulted it from time to time and would weave the ones she loved into her writings.

So I suppose it came naturally for me to latch on to "sayings" or certain expressions, which I have collected in a large book over the years, thought it would be fun to share a few.

In the stage show "Patsy Cline," the gal narrating describes her first meeting with Patsy, "She wuz more like we wuz than we wuz ourselves."

Have read faithfully Monte Noekle's column in the "Livestock Weekly" for as many years as he has been writing it. A favorite, "I was working so short-handed my shadow was my only companion."

Larry McMurtry has penned many memorable lines in his numerous books concerned with Texans and our way of life. Admired McMurtry's observation of his own father, a lifetime rancher, "I read the countryside casually, in great contrast to my father, for whom land, grass, and sky composed a great, ever varying text whose interest he could never exhaust. He was a countryman, lifelong, and had a countryman's eye for the small variables of landscape that occurred even along a road he had driven many hundreds of times. Here a water gap might be out, a stretch of fence beginning to sag, a patch of grass ruined by a saltwater leak from some improperly tended oil well. When our well-to-do neighbor, Mr. Bridwell, let his Beefmaster bulls into the bull pasture next to our land, my father would always slow when we approached a group of bulls. Sometimes, because of the magnificence of some of these great animals, he would come to full stop, just looking, arrested by admiration as a stroller in an art museum might be when brought face-to-face with a great picture, a Rembrandt, a Matisse.

"I have looked at many places quickly, my father looked at one place deeply. Most of the citizens of Itliers just saw the path that led to Swann's house as a path; it took Proust to see it as a world which, on a homey scale was how my father looked at Sam Cowan road or the other country roads he rode or drove along for some seventy years."

Our beloved aunt, Lola Arnim, was most astute in telling incidents, bits of history, and stories gleaned from her husband Cecil. One afternoon as we sat on her screened porch discussing how deeply we had enjoyed being the wives of cattlemen she stated, "Annie, the Arnims and Woodleys originated in Moulton, La Vaca County. They saw life in the same light, breathed the same air."

During our visits with the Falkenbergs, the conversation would usually roll around to statements that our parents had made. Eddie remembered if any of his Dad's sons expressed an interest in a girl of which he did not approve Mr. Falkenberg would speak up, "Why that gal couldn't even bake you a loaf of homemade bread."

Dwain Turner and Joe Hargrove at the San Miguel Ranch

Annalee has always loved brightly colored clothes, especially red. No gray, brown, or taupe for her. During a coffee break one afternoon she remarked, "Looks as if she's trying to punish herself with those drab colors she wears."

One day a fellow applied for a job at Southwest Livestock, stating he would be willing to work a full 40 hour week, to which Joe replied, "Hell, we don't need any part-time help around here."

Discussing our childhood homes, friend Dwain Turner out did me with a remark–comparing how cold the houses would be during winter: "Why Annie, that ole' frame ranch house at Evant was so drafty when a norther blew up out of Amarillo, you'd have to walk the rugs down."

2004

Country Show Kindles Memories

Wanted to share with you what's happening at Crystal, and to show off the handsome work of Ron Baker, who conceived the design and construction of our handsome and functional fire screen for the ranch house.

Ron is married to Joe's sweet niece Mary Lou, and it is great to

Ashley, Rhona, Jessica, Mary Lou and Ron Baker at Rancho La Paloma

have him in the family as here we possess two end tables, a coffee table overlaid with Joe's cattle brands, the fire screen, and lamps. Horseshoes and rasps figure prominently in Ron's use of materials, and fit perfectly in ranch and country style homes. Am encouraging him to place some of his pieces where the public can have access o viewing and purchasing them.

Had a special day attending the Real County Junior Livestock sale. Fun to visit with my lifelong friends Karolen Hart Baugh, Allyene Patterson Crider. Karolyn and I were cheerleaders together at Sabinal High School, and I served as one of her bridesmaids, when she wed Gary Baugh, still remember the lovely dusty pink dresses we wore.

Ruth and Alton Hart, Karolyn's parents, were two of the kindest, sweetest people you'd ever hope to know. Many nights I bunked under their roof during those high school years. Ruth would always prepare exactly what we preferred for breakfast, she seemed to take pleasure in pleasing Karolyn and Gary plus their friends. And when Karolen graduated Fuzzy (as we fondly referred to Ruth) surprised her with a pajama breakfast. All the friends arrived at 9 a.m. in sleeping attire and Fuzzy served us up a most delicious meal.

Delighted to see Allyene Crider's darling granddaughter with her grand champion lamb at the show. Madison is the daughter of Mr. and Mrs. Mark Crider and great granddaughter of Tela Patterson. All five reside on the Patterson-Crider ranch at Mountain Home, Texas. When I complimented Mark upon his bravery of being the only male in the ranch operation, he gallantly replied he felt himself blessed to have four such capable and talented women in his family.

It does my heart good to see Tela attending every function in and out of Real county and making the most of life. My fond memory of a visit in the Patterson home during Allyene and my high school days is when one evening Tela announced she was going to butcher a goat the next morning.

Come the a.m., I accompanied Allyene (it wasn't anywhere close to daylight when we left the house) on her ranch rounds to check water troughs, fences, salt, goats, etc. Returning to the house, Tela had advanced the butchering project to the meat wrapping stage. I was flabbergasted to learn she had handled the entire procedure herself. I had assumed Jack would do the butchering and Tela the wrapping, that's the way it went in our household, but not on the Patterson ranch.

At the Livestock sale Tela was sitting by her friend Helen Chisum. The announcer informed the crowd that Helen had never missed a Real County junior show and sale since its inception, and Tela had only missed one.

While we were discussing life changes, I questioned Allyene if their move to the Divide had been a change for her family. She assured me it had, remarking Tela's only requirements regarding the move were: "Get a place where we won't be able to see any other houses or any vapor lights or highways." Naturally Allyene accomplished those wishes.

Tela Patterson is a Texas original, an octogenarian of true grit who has lived through the depression, the '50s drouth, and the loss of her husband, Jack and still lives her life with great gusto.

She and Annalee have been amigos since the years when Mama taught school at Rio Frio, also our grandmother Burns, and Irene Patterson, were dear friends.

So Tela was delighted to learn Joe had moved me to a ranch where we can't see security lights, houses, or highways.

Next day lunch time found us at the Zavala County Junior Livestock show, eating brisket lunch and visiting with Barbara and Danny Parker, Margie and Curtis Bourn, and Jack and Evelyn Kingsbery.

Learned from Jack this was the 47th consecutive year he had weighed animals for the show. He was proud of the new metal barn erected on the show grounds, and the hard work of the youngsters involved in the show.

"I'm 82 and Evelyn's and my calendar is full everyday," Jack told me. "After I wrote my first book, 'Rattlesnakes and Horse Wrecks,' people who had read the book would call and remark, 'Well, I was just wondering if you were still alive,' so entitled my second volume 'Yes, I'm Still Alive.'"

Terry Reagan was kind enough to come and auctioneer the show in the absence of Dan Haby.

 ★

Stock Show Fun

It's Ground Hog Day as I attempt to pen this, but find it difficult with the distraction of five to six male cardinals in the oak trees, along with seven green jays, inca doves, mockingbirds, woodpeckers, and one small ruby crown kinglet. The jays hastily gulp whole corn, cardinals prefer sunflower seeds, but the kinglet and mockingbirds have an addiction to peanut butter (crunchy). A most pleasant aspect here in our bird preserve is the absence of any sparrow population, cannot believe it. but find life fun not to have that riffraff munching up half the seeds.

Cline Speer, Miguel Chariez and Justin Speer with Cline's prize winning steer at Uvalde Junior Livestock Show

One juvenile vermilion flycatcher stayed behind these winter months while his family traveled south. He stays near by the house and we chat when Peppy and I are out and about. Haven't seen anymore of the Kiskadee or the blue jay. Plan to put up a thistle feeder in hopes of attracting a group of gold and house finches.

Stock Show time has been busy and enjoyable. So fun to see all the youngsters outfitted in their finest jeans, latest style western shirts, and silver buckles. Seems as if several of the small tykes weighed only a pound or so more than their trophy clasps. And I was happy to discover braids are high style for girls. It looked as if some of the more elaborate ones were time consuming for moms or hairdressers to accomplish. Bows and/or beads, a step up style-wise from our childhood, enhanced many of the braids, which we called pigtails in my younger days.

Those of us with experience (plus years) behind us know it is grand to be greeted cordially by young people. My friend Jerod Hawkes of Sabinal never fails to seek me out and shake my hand and, sure enough, he came by to say "Hello" during the Uvalde Junior Show. And it was a pleasure to shake hands and exchange greetings with Muffy Marmion, a charming blonde version of her mother Janey.

Muffy's grandfather Dolph Briscoe was most generous and kind in purchasing Cline Speer's grand champion steer. Dolph and the First State Bank have been major supporters of the Uvalde County Junior Livestock Show for many years, investing in the area youth involved with FFA and 4-H projects. Remember when you were showing a lamb, calf or pig? You never forget the person who bought your animal.

Heard many compliments on how efficiently and quickly the Uvalde sale was managed. It was evident the committees had labored diligently to produce and coordinate an exceptional show and sale for the youth involved.

Martha and Chris Griffith's enthusiasm over their new Hill Country home was easy to understand. They are a couple who enjoy dogs, horses, hunting, and most aspects of outdoor living, so everyday, they pass on the banks of the Frio will be heaven for them.

Struck me we had been present at Retama Downs when Martha's parents honored her with an extraordinary deb party. And, Martha has not changed in looks or manner since those days. The two of us share an affection for yellow Labs and Welsh Corgis.

Martha, did you see the National Dog show last Saturday, when Wesley, a Welsh Pembroke, was named the champion of the working breeds?

Dudley Ilse stopped at the auction to chat, and I asked if he and Kimberly were installed in their new Kinney County residence. He assured me they were and now he has a vantage point similar to ours at La Loma, which provides a vista of five miles or more. Am proud of Dudley and his accomplishments; he spent many hours at the ranch during his and Jamie's eighth-grade year at Sabinal Junior High. Whenever Dudley's band is playing and I am in attendance, he always sings "Faded Love," knowing it is my favorite Bob Wills tune.

Last week was perfect timing to celebrate Caroline Habermacher's birthday at Francisco's in Kerrville. Along with Jan Carter, we ordered "The Special," our favorite.

If you've never sampled "The Special," make a point to do so on your next Kerrville outing. It is freshly prepared chicken salad served on a crisp tortilla, topped with lettuce and tomato, grated white cheese (perhaps asadero or Monterry Jack), sliced ripe olives, and garnished with pico de gallo. On the side is a delicious cup of black bean soup, completing the entree.

Joan Woodley introduced me to a new product on the supermarket shelves, which has an interesting story. Our friends Wister and George Kampmann's daughter, Ann, married Johan Steenkamp some years ago. Johan's parent's family purchased the Las Campanas ranch at Vanderpool during the '70s, and continued to retain their property in South Eastern Africa. Ann and Johan now divide their time between the two ranches.

Several years ago Johan began cultivating the seeds of a plant growing near his African home. It produced small peppers of a rare and exotic taste. Deciding he had hit upon some thing really new, Johan set about developing a secret recipe to process the fruit, and gave it the name, Peppadew, which are peppery, but as sweet and tantalizing as the dew. Worldwide research, global registration of the trademarks, international sole rights to grow the plant, commercially, the establishment of commercial sweet picante pepper farms in the bountiful farmlands of the Tzaneen area, and the building of a special processing, bottling and packing factory followed and Peppadew is now being savored around the world.

You can find them next to the pimentos in the supermarket. During the holidays I stuffed Peppadews with soft cream cheese and topped them with an olive slice. Everyone loved their sweet, delicate, peppery flavor. Johan and Ann are now involved with marketing their product worldwide. And to think we can enjoy a South African pepper in Utopia, Sabinal, and Crystal.

Came upon "An American Original, The Life of Frank J. Dobie" in the Texana section of Market Square Antiques. Purchased it for our Texana library, and am enjoying it, as Dobie is one of my Texas heroes. Imagine my surprise this a.m. as I read, "He accepted an invitation to make the commencement address at Sabinal High School on May 22, 1915, choosing as the title for his speech, "The Practicability of the Beautiful." He took as his text "Mahomet's beautiful dictum: 'If I had only two loaves of bread, I should exchange one for a lily.'...I wish to elevate my hearers to a thirst for the beautiful; I wish to make the beautiful come to them as something needed every day."

Possibly Dobie spoke to the Sabinal graduates because of the family ties his wife had to the Edgar Kincaid family, must check with Betty Kincaid Mathis to discuss this bit of Texana.

Violence Enough Without 'Passion' Movie

Willie Edwards approached the subject of offering his opinion on Mel Gibson's "The Passion of the Christ" in his column, but decided not to jump into the controversy surrounding the film.

Last week my dear cousin, spiritual mentor, and college roommate, Mary Tom Harper Hefte and I passed a quiet, delightful evening together. In our conversation we discussed the pros and cons of Mel's movie, and reached the decision we were of like minds. As there's more then enough violence available to all of us in today's world, not necessary for the two of us to pay money to line Mel's pockets. And as MT noted, the film is only one man's version, and she felt no need to see it in order to enrich her faith, or to form an opinion, or because it is the hot topic of the hour.

She is not stranger to violence, as her own life has been touched by tragedy and family illnesses. These experiences have called her to labor daily in many endeavors dedicated to eliminating poverty and illnesses through the channels her church offers.

Both of us agreed that any type of violence ("Jaws" "The Exorcist") taken willing into our own psyches can never be fully flushed from the soul. To this day neither of us allow ourselves to view most of the trash on television.

For myself I decided no immediately after the first article I read describing the details of "The Passion." Years ago, 20 perhaps, I read an in depth description of Christ's suffering which scholars were able to assess by studying the imprint on the Shroud of Turin. The agony of his suffering was stated so vividly, it struck my heart and still lies embedded in its recesses today.

The past 22 years of my life have placed me in countless emergency rooms, hospitals, nursing homes, therapy hospitals, and funeral parlors (Annalee's nomenclature). I have witnessed enough violent suffering at work in the bodies of those I loved most dearly and deeply to cover the spans of three or four lifetimes. You need not enumerate for me ravages of paralysis, strokes, breast cancer, lung cancer, ovarian cancer, Alzheimer's, leukemia, cervical cancer, or heart disease. I have seen them all attack family and friends. The toughest of all was watching a beautiful, vibrant 3-year-old child die with leukemia, that was true life, realistic suffering, no movie version involved.

And what did I learn from all those hours passed in Cancer Treatment and Research Center, Dallas Children's Methodist, St. Luke's University of Texas, Uvalde, Tyler, M.D. Anderson hospitals, Warm Spring Rehabilitation center, and am still continuing to learn at Amistad nursing facility?

My conclusion is we must help and love others. We must offer people out time, our attention, our financial aid if possible, our acceptance, our hospitality, encouragement, smiles, hugs, compliments, and gifts of agape. I am only one, but my interpretation of Christianity stands on the belief Christ's grace was offered to save our souls, and that we, in turn teach others by the love and. compassion we offer them.

Christ's grace is free to all who have learned and studied his teachings. We have only to respond by the simple act of taking him into our hearts and minds. Then we make use of his example by reaching out to others in order that they too may learn of Jesus, his love, life and the path and the path to salvation.

Mel's movie is not free and for many it will extract the huge price of placing great guilt upon their hearts and in their heads. And guilt has the capacity to hurt and to cripple and maim people. God needs strong, whole, happy, willing workers in the many fields of his kingdom. Not sad, dejected, weary guilt-laden souls, who do not and cannot reflect the brilliance of the love of Christ in words and actions.

Sorry, Mel, your version of Jesus' suffering is not my cup of tea, but fortunately in America we are all entitled to our own choice.

Personally, I chose the image of the risen Christ calling us each and everyone to the glorious gift of his freely offered grace. The grace which radiates from the presence of those who truly reflect his love (you know the ones), and who are out laboring to decrease the violence, sickness, and suffering, in the world. Who are offering their hand to others in order that they, too, may experience God's glorious, forgiving grace made available through his lovely son, Jesus.

We now find ourselves in the meditative season of Lent. So I ask you, my dear, beloved family and friends to take it few minutes daily to invite God into your own mind and soul to reflect on the deep impact of his love sent to us in the form of the living Christ.

Enjoying Pleasures Of Spring

Easter Weekend outdid itself in terms of stormy, turbulent weather, not at all conducive to hunting colored eggs. At Crystal one of the rain gauges registered 1.7 inches. The other had not been dumped since the weekend before, but from a distance seemed to hover around the 5-inch mark.

Here at La Paloma we were fortunate to come through the hailstorm without roof damage, and the tomato plants are still standing. Verdict is still out on the status of the corn and cotton near by the house. The corn looks to be recovering, but the true damage will be tallied in the bushel count,

Was not in residence during the actual storm, but the huge oaks bear testament to the severe beating they withstood. Crystal itself shows many signs of missing roofs, smashed windows, tattered trees and shrubs, reports of ice 2 to 3 feet deep were common. Fortunately, no loss of human life was incurred, but on the outskirts of Piedras it is another story.

Visiting Utopia this past week, was thrilled by the clarity and swiftness of the Sabinal.

Below our red barn, water rushed by and perch seemed delighted by its depth and clearness.

Passing by the Fisher camp, I noted the tremendous flow over the newly renovated dam. Was grateful to all the individuals involved in its repair. Glen Pepper and his crew did an excellent job in reconstructing it after the 100-year flood.

Along I-10 toward Houston, the vibrant display of wildflowers thrilled and inspired us. Pink primrose, bluebonnets, Indian paintbrush, stiff-stem flax, red flax, Indian blankets (gaillardia), wild phlox, and wild delphimuim all competed for attention as we sped by. Wanted to stop and wallow in their spring glory, but did not wish to dismay my traveling partner.

Even an appointment at M.D. Anderson can be softened, enriched and made enjoyable by residing in a serene comfortable home, which for us was the Marion Stewart residence in Sugarland. And we caught up on family visiting as Jeanne and Murray hosted our group to a delicious meal of snapper enhanced with pecan sauce.

Next morning, I drank in Janice's elegant touch on the baby grand piano in Anderson's lobby. Here you are confronted with the magnitude of suffering cancer brings to the world. No age group is spared, but patients gravitate toward the music and many radiate hope and love despite their physical adversities.

Enjoyed an unexpected treat at Grady Spear's new "Burning Pear" restaurant in the Sugarland Marriott. Grady, you may remember, opened his first business in Alpine and has gone on to receive much culinary fame.

My two compadres ordered meat loaf served over mashed potatoes, while I indulged in chicken and dumplings, not an item you find everyday on restaurant menus. These were the slick, rolled out, Grandmother Burns type, most tasty.

Glanced through Grady's newest, the fourth, cookbook, which was prominently displayed, "The Texas Cowboy Kitchen." It's a showy, coffeetable treat of a cookbook combined with historic, western photographs by Edwin Smith. Contained tales of chuck wagon cooks and cattle drives, as well culinary tips such as Grady's use of piloncillo, the dark, coneshaped Mexican sugar.

Returning from Houston, our hearts were prepared for the Easter season of rejoicing, after receiving an excellent report from the Anderson doctors. We stopped to stock on Easter essentials – ham, fresh asparagus, and cascarones. God is so generous during these springtime April days.

If These Old Barns Could Talk

Passing by the Brushy Hill Ranch, known to me as the Rehm ranch, it came to mind there stood a wealth of barns with interesting stories to tell. So early One morning, planning to travel north, called Pete Denny to ask if it would be convenient to show me around and provide some pertinent facts about the barns.

Pete, being the Southern gentleman he is, graciously assured me it would be a pleasure to provide whatever assistance possible. My amiga, Suze Groves, joined me, as she and Pete had grown up together in San Marcos, and I knew she'd love seeing the place.

Al Rehm, Pete's uncle was one of the first people in South Texas to purchase heavy equipment, bulldozers, plows, rakes, road graders for the purpose of clearing brush from South Texas ranches.

In order to maintain and manage all the machines involved Al constructed two huge barns behind the rock Rehm ranch house located on Highway 187, approximately five miles south of Sabinal.

The first barn has two pitched roofs and was the repair headquarters where much welding took place. It is sturdily constructed of red D'Hanis tile and rafters (beams) from an old railroad bridge given to Al when the structure was replaced by Southern Pacific.

Entering the cool darkness of the repair barn, you are struck

Bell Tower at Brush Hill Ranch

by an object you'd least expect in this setting. A mirrored ball, such as the ones in dance pavilions, hangs gleaming from the bridge beams, and is accented by strings of blue Christmas lights. A jaunty touch as the barn now serves as a home for Pete's musical band, which gathers annually in September and stages a celebration in recognition of Pete's birthday, and the opening of bird season.

To the right a sign over the door proclaims, "Pete's Pickin' Palace." Entering you find musical instruments, drums, electric guitars, sound boxes, etc., set up amid many rows of wooden bins, each compartment numbered and some still containing Caterpillar parts. Here Pete and pals have cut two CD's, labeled Barn Jam I and Barn Jam H.

Originally this was the domain of Slim Clements as he oversaw equipment repairs, handed out the proper parts, and kept welding moving along. Others who worked for years with Al were Joe Shane, John Putman, Juan Musquiz, Bill Nunley and John Muvicka. Pete was sure of there were many more, but off the top of his hat could not provide names.

Picnic tables provide ample areas for refreshments or a snack. The tremendous building has a second story where furniture is stored. Also much equipment from bygone days is still stashed around, plus a few jeeps and other ranch vehicles, all adding ambiance to the barn where we also dance.

Directly behind the repair barn is yet another D'Hanis brick structure used to store bulldozers and other expensive equipment, passing by the ranch you do not notice its location.

South of the house stands the ranch's original wooden barn sheltered by tall hackberries. The ranch house itself was constructed of red sandstone rock in 1938, and remodeled by Wiley Dallas, originator of Dallas furniture, in 1950. The original picket and rock walls compose the fence surrounding the home.

Inside the yard, nearby the north gate entrance, stands an impressive bell tower constructed of the same red rock. Now home to the original Sabinal fire bell, which was given to Al when the old fire station was dismantled.

Across the highway stands yet another impressive barn-type building, also constructed of D'Hanis tile. It was built as a grain storage facility, 35 percent of the building being underground. Pete noted it never satisfactorily served its purpose as the concrete maintained too high a level of moisture for storing corn, Milo, or other grain crops.

Pete and his sister, George Ann, the only two children in the Rehm family, grew up in San Marcos but spent their summers at the ranch. Eight years ago Pete moved to the ranch and took over the hunting operation. Have pleasant memories of a New Year's Day Open House there hosted by Pete's mother, Pete, and George Ann.

The two have inherited a place of beauty and historical interest in Uvalde County. The interesting old ranch house maintains its '40s flavor, and the massive barns attest to the years when Al and his Caterpillar tractors labored to make South Texas ranches more grass productive, and clear away the mesquite menace. Thanks, Pete and George Ann, for maintaining this valuable and interesting part of Texas heritage.

Bright Colors After The Rain

Monday a.m., the sun made a welcome appearance, after three-four days of moisture, north winds are cool on this 26th of April, and the saga of this exceptionally wet, verdant spring continues.

Had a wildflower experience par excellence this past week, which made me wish for Quentin, my native plant expert and amiga, and for all who crave blooming native plants. On an errand to Carrizo, Rosa and I explored an outlying road in hopes of discovering flowers.

And did we hit pay dirt! On the outskirts of town were several acres of the vine variety of wine cups in prolific profusion. And mixed among the vibrant fuchsia flowers were all these other varieties – prairie phlox (purple), creeping sweet pea vine (deep pink), yellow popping weed, white horsemint, sandy land sunflowers, yellow Mexican hats, stiff-stem flax (orange), prickly-pear (yellow and orange), wild honeysuckle, gaillardia, yellow butter cups, burridge green thread, orange lantana, yellow plains wallflowers, Texas yellow star, white bull nettle (dangerous), plus several species I could not identify.

Have Rosa and hopefully some excellent photographs as my witness to this huge display of flourishing native flowers. The soil was sandy and well drained, which the natives seem to prefer.

Pleased to receive an Easter greeting with a photo of two handsome fellows, Jackson and Grant Taylor. These two potential athletes are sons of my godchild, Rebecca Ware Taylor, and Ashley Taylor. Looks as if Becca and Ashley have a full time job boy sitting.

Annalee would be delighted to know the summer tanager has been sighted on three occasions at our birdbath. They are small birds, completely scarlet, who love to nest in oaks, and which visited Mama summers at Bownds-Burns house, and Jones cemetery.

Also the painted bunting dropped by to pay his respects, and I was delighted to come upon two different nests of bobwhites. Bird land is busy repairing and rebuilding after the horrific hail.

Joe enjoyed "The Truth and Then Some," Tom DuBose's stories compiled into book form. Reading it took me back to the days of my youth when Tommy and his distinguished and gentlemanly father, Winn, would participate in the calf roping at the Utopia rodeos.

And his description of how he would load his saddle and shotgun on the school bus, then entrust the driver to deliver them to Billy Winn's bus for a weekend hunt at the Winn ranch caused me deep nostalgia for those carefree, simpler days gone by.

Avail yourself of a copy of Tom's tales, you'll greatly enjoy the recollections, especially if you grew up in our part of Texas and knew the cast of characters involved. They are written with clarity and humor.

How's your garden progressing? Ours is slow due to hailstones and cold nights. Friend Freida Bain treated us at Southwest Livestock to a sample of her fresh garden lettuce. She reported the tomato plants, which she placed in holes with a banana peel, are twice as large and vigorous as the others. Must make a mental note to remember this trick next planting season. From the looks of the photos of their perfectly planted vegetable garden, Freida and Curtis are master gardeners.

Habermacher-Kennedy home, oldest house in Uvalde County

Friends who enjoy the same endeavors are jewels in life's crown. Jan Carter and Caroline Habermacher drove down and helped me properly christen the sewing area Oscar Contreras designed and constructed.

In one afternoon's time we transformed the Italian cotton "fat squares" into a rhapsody of green, gold, reds, thus creating a quilt of special significance. Now whenever I gaze upon it, my mind shall return to the special day we spent together.

Baxter Black has been compiling some columns lately that cause me great jealousy for not having composed them myself. The last one I clipped from "The Weekly" concerned the marvelous calving season at his ranch. None of the cows needed help delivering. In two paragraphs Baxter summed up the essence of spring:

"When the new baby sniffs, or blinks, or wiggles an ear, at that moment it feels is though a burden has been lifted from our shoulders. We did it. We did it again. Just regular common people like us, engaged in that age-old profession of stockman, have participated in a miracle: life being passed from one generation to the next.

"It is no small thing to be a part of, and every time it happens, it renews us. The miracle never diminishes. As urbanization inexorably isolates people from the land, fewer and fewer humans are able to participate in this ancient experience. It is our loss."

★

Weeks Whirl By

Sitting on the porch in the cool of the morning, the chimes of Sacred Heart pealed out 10 a.m. The two house wrens nesting in the red begonia are not pleased with my presence, and the babies are cheeping for the bugs and worms the parents provide.

Weeks of 2004 have whizzed past, and now suddenly we find ourselves in the season of Mother's Day and graduations. Annalee, Georgie Smith, Larissa and Trystie Brewton celebrate birthdays during the merry month. Still find myself thinking I should pull together a party for Mama and Georgie.

The handsome fellow in the photo is Word Sherrill, class of 1936, Texas A&M University. His children, Word Jr., Linda, and Martha, printed the invitations with this photo on front, sent them to many friends, and a grand get together took place to celebrate Word's 89th year. Naturally the honoree loved every minute of the occasion.

Word Sherrill

Joyce related the fact they had enjoyed 66 years of married life, a mark not many meet. The two still reside in their own home and are out and about Uvalde. What full, interesting lives they have lived here in this part of Texas.

Saw faces of friends I'd been missing for too long a time. Kay and Bill Cauthorn reported Juno to be as green as Ireland, and the Devil's river running full.

A treat to see Wave Thompson dressed in her lime green suit, bright handbag to match. What an inspiration she is to us all, always ready to go, smiling, glad to be among friends.

Tela Patterson drove down from the divide for an overnight visit with friends. All of us were smiling and comparing notes on this incredible spring in our own areas. Wave and Tela are two of my heroines, living life to its hilt, involved in what's happening.

Mary Tom Buchanan and daughters, Helen, Susan, and Mary Anna brought me up to date on happenings at Neal's Lodge. A remodeled dining room is in place for the 2004 season, complete with a new roof which Mary Tom claimed the structure had not had since it was built in 1929 – add MT to my heroine list.

Glad to shake Governor Briscoe's hand and see him looking so well. Dolph's generous gift to the Utopia Library touched my heart as well, as his many other civic donations.

Friend Elaine Bracy was her perky self in a lovely blue jacket. The two of us shared a room together at Santa Fe La Fonda one year, and our time there lingers in my mind as a fun and happy sojourn.

Have wanted to share with you the pleasure we've received from responding to the television appeal from Christian Children's Fund. Called the number 800-776-6767, made arrangements to adopt a boy, and have the $25 month fee placed on the credit card. This allows a child to attend the Christian school in their area; you are free to send monetary gifts to the fund for aid to the family, and also to correspond with the child.

My most favorite Christmas card was a letter from our Aldi, Jakarta, Indonesia, with his yellow bike he had purchased after receiving our Christmas gift. The smile on his face revealed a changed child from the dejected one in the first photo we received.

Aldi writes, "I hope, to braiding friendship with you, please write the letter for me if your time is enable. I am facing my general test in school, because of your help now I am more excited to go to school and

I promise to study hard so I can get good grades and never let you down. I'll more diligent to school and study hard, I will not make you disappoint."

The 8-year-old always includes drawings of himself, family, and friends. Touches my heart to receive outpourings of gratitude and affection from a child; thank you letters are tough to come by in the modern American mode of life.

If you are wondering what small step you might make to alleviate the suffering of one child halfway around the world, you may enjoy adopting a Christian Children's Fund child. So many children need a glimpse of hope to light their lives. Call me if you want the information, 374-5208.

A window in the wet weather provided the opportunity to load 11 trucks with 735# steers bound for Barrett & Crowfoot feedyards, Hereford. Seemed to be the culmination of all the factors us in the cattle business have spent years hoping to experience, adequate moisture conditions, cattle gaining nicely, a strong and rewarding market.

The handsome gray gelding Ron Baker rode to push the cattle on to the scales and trailer performed admirably, and I thought how rarely we witness men working horseback these days and times. So it topped off a grand day when Joe told me the gray was a 15-year-old out of Mac's old mare, Fanny Badger, who Mac had given to Joe years ago when he no longer had anyone to break colts for him. Sometimes it's surprising how far over distances in time the bonds of friendship reach.

Week of Traveling

Green was the ornamentation Mother Nature had chosen for Texas as I set out on travels this past week. Needed a driver in order to be free to stare at a landscape so resplendent with lush foliage and decorated with wildflowers.

First destination was Lakeway, situated on Lake Travis, new home of son T.M. The area is booming with new construction and homes surrounding the lake. So pleasant to sit at sunset and watch the sailboats glide over the sapphire waters of the lake, which is at a high level due to all the wonderful rains.

T.M. was kind enough to accompany me to the National Wildflower Center, located near Austin. Begun in 1982 under the inspiration of Lady Bird, the center offers many excellent programs of study and research as well as inspiration for visitors.

The buildings are so environmentally sensitive; each one is designed for collection of run-off rainwater. A wonderfully designed aqueduct is constructed of red-brown sandstone brought from the Lampasas area. Drew me back to memories of the inspiring Roman aqueduct we witnessed in Segovia, Spain. The observation tower serves as a cistern, as well as an overlook, giving one a perspective of Spanish mission architecture in Texas.

More than 400 species of native plants are cultivated on the center's acreage, and many were in bloom. You could invest several days studying the flora, green houses, nature trails, plantings, and library all incorporated into this excellent facility for the propagation and encouragement of use of native plants in our state.

Had to renew my membership in order to keep abreast of the many activities, workshops, and educational advantages available through the center.

Returning home by the time the laundry was completed, it was time to travel to College Station for the graduation ceremonies of Justin Speer.

An unexpected highlight to the program was to see Norman Borgland presented with a lifetime achievement from Texas A&M University. The "Father of the Green Revolution," Borgland in 1970 was the first agriculturalist to be presented with Nobel Peace Prize.

At age 90, he remains active in his pursuits of teaching and research, dividing his time between the A&M classrooms and the maize improvement center in central Mexico.

I remember what a boon it was to area farmers when his genetically engineered wheat, Natadores, became available for cultivation.

Fred McClure, past president of the board of regents of Texas A&M, presented an inspiring commencement address. These were his six points: 1) There is always an obligation beyond self, 2) With blessings come expectations and responsibilities, 3) Have no fear of failure, there is no progress without failure, 4) You must learn to face the future unafraid of change, 5) Ain't nobody gonna give you nothing, commit yourself to a lifelong struggle toward excellence, and 6) It's not you're aptitude, but your attitude which will determine you altitude in life.

Wise words not only for graduates, but also for all of us enrolled in the big ole university of life.

Was pleased to see Nylon Falkenburg receive a master's degree in agronomy, his granddad, Eddie, would be oh so proud.

And Laura Jane McGehee of Uvalde was granted a degree in education and Roy Reid Redden, of Utopia, a diploma in animal science.

Am sure there were others from our area receiving degrees, but there were five different graduations in order to accommodate the 5,000 or more graduates, ours was the last ceremony.

Stopped by to visit Jamie and Elizabeth, Murray and Jeanne Burns before departing Aggie land. Jamie is headed for an A&M work-study program in Costa Rica. Elizabeth received her diploma August 2003, and has been involved in graduate study. She enters M.D. Anderson this week to begin treatment for bone cancer. Our family asks for your prayers that she may be healed and continue to lead a normal life.

Sifting Through the Memories

So many layers of life to pass through and peel off, clean, and investigate. Looking backward, remember wondering why Mother and Jane Mac did not love to shop.

Now it is easy to realize, they'd already done that, and shopping was not their cup of tea anyway.

Am in the slow, slow process of sifting through my third house. First Mrs. Woodley's, which was easy as she was not a collector.

Then my own, which was a nightmare, as AW was (notice the was) a collector with enough dishes to start a cafe, and enough books to stock a small library.

Now it's time to sort and sift at Bownds house. Annalee was a collector of the written word. Stashed in every drawer, closet, and desk are letters, newspaper

Sid Maudlin and our Dad, Henry Burns at Ingleside, 1941

clippings, cards and her diaries. Some of the letters date back to 1880s. Much history of the Sabinal Canyon and its inhabitants are involved.

Decided to lighten the task by enticing two Fisher girls, Betty Leighton and Evie LeBouf to lunch. Later I lured them to Bownds house, promising, "this will only take an hour so, no longer."

What an afternoon of enjoyment, plowing through a small portion of letters, columns, clippings provided us.

From Munich Germany, dated Nov. 29, 1945:

"Dearest Ann, Henry, and Kids.

"I am at the German Georging Air Base now. It is an AAF Replacement depot for this part of Europe. We live in big steam heated dormitories with private baths. This place is where all the big boy Nazi pilots went to school.

"We left Newport News, Va., on the 8th, and got to Le Harve on the 17th. We came across on the USS Montecello. It is a former Italian luxury liner.

"The train ride from Le Harve to here took 5 days and nights. You have no idea how things are torn up over here, lots of towns are completely destroyed. All the people are cold and hungry.

"Ann, everything here is so different from home.

"Well, today is Thanksgiving at home. I would have liked to have been there to furnish the turkey. Henry, have you got your buck yet?

"Kiss the kids for me, and write back soon. All My Love, Sid Mauldin Sr."

Had to wipe a few tears from my eyes, thinking of Siddy (our fond family name for him), probably 18 or 19, across the Atlantic, his first time away from Utopia, wishing to be out providing the turkey for the family table.

Later we came across these remembrances which Annalee had penned after morning coffee with her sister, Mariella Wentworth Mauldin, and her beloved cousin, Henry Fisher.

Mariella remembered:

"I cut my hair for the first time a short while before Horace and I were married in 1922. Just before the big day, I decided it needed cutting a little more. Horace could do anything, including barbering, and he offered to cut it for me.

"Somehow or other he cut one side a lot shorter than the other. When I looked in the mirror, I thought I was ruined.

"Now, I had kept my long hair put away and made me some puffs to put over my ears. This was the style in those days. I pinned the puffs on securely, and no one knew the difference."

Have not come across a wedding photo of Auntie and Horace. Am anxious to find one so we can check out the hair-do. Do any of you Mauldin cousins have one?

And in the same writings from 1988, Annalee relates this encounter from Henry Fisher's childhood:

"One muddy day when I was about ten, Papa asked me to saddle up and go to Utopia to get the mail. This wasn't hard for me; I was just about born on a horse, and have been riding ever since.

"So I struck off, going down the old road that went through the Schweinfurt place (now owned by Laurie Baumer), and came up Donnelly Hill (now owned by the Burns boys). Then I got down about where the Boswell ranch is now, remember this is just a narrow lane in those days, and muddy!

"My horse bogged up and when he lifted his feet, the suction would just about pull him under.

"Pretty soon I came upon a real sight. Here was old Judge Koerner and some other man, in a wagon. They had a jug of whiskey along, and were already pretty drunk. They had un-hitched their horses, but didn't know what to do next, were just muddlin' around, asking me to catch their horses, and hitch 'em up for them.

"Now I was a timid little kid, and didn't know what to do. You must bear in mind that kids had a healthy respect for their elders in those days; they were taught to obey them, not to sass and to mind their manners in every way.

"Well, these men and their rig had the road blocked. Rather than try to get around them, I just turned my horse around and headed for home. I was pretty sure what Papa would want me to do."

Naturally, we girls of Fisher blood (and raising) fell to discussing how we absolutely adored our own fathers, and wanted to do their bidding in every situation. Just as Henry's first thought was what papa would want him to do. When did we lose that mindset in America? Think it was an ill wind that blew in during the '60s.

Dear Mac lived his life stating in certain circumstances or business situations ,"That's the way daddy would want me to handle it."

How impoverished are today's children who have lost this rule of thumb for their lives.

Weekend Travels Provide Writer With Rich Experience

Two weekends in a row provided us different but similar entertainment in the art of rodeo, horsemanship, riding broncs, and western ways of competition among Mexican and American cowboys.

A large crowd of horse lovers, ranch families and second and third generation competitors gathered at one of the arenas outside Villa Acuña for the contest among members of the Charros del Norte. That last, lovely week of May, we enjoyed the benefits of a cool breeze. Occurred to me how well designed the grandstands were, facing directly east, thus protecting the audience from the 4 p.m. western sun.

At some point in time I'd attended a charriada, perhaps on a visit to Guadalajara years ago, and it was easy to recall the costumes, beauty, and precision involved in the different events. Charriada is an old Mexican tradition where the riders display their skills with ropes, horsemanship, handling cattle, and riding unbroken horses. They are clad in exceptionally beautiful, detailed outfits, which must adhere to the standards of the charro association.

These costumes consist of the traditional Mexican sombrero, (Pancho Villa style), which are elaborately decorated with embroidered insignias. The shirts and pants are likewise embroidered with a design across the shoulders and down the leg and accented with a floppy silk tie, decorated suede chaps are worn during the events, plus suede boots, and personalized silver spurs. Garbed in these age-old costumes, the charros cut a handsome figure. My personal choice was a gray felt sombrero accented with red embroidered roses, and worn with gray shirt and trousers.

Miguel and his 6 year old, Mikey, joined our group. Mikey wore the de rigueur of the young charro generation, Wranglers, plaid shirt, concho belt and straw hat. The children of the families involved in the competitions were beautiful with their dark, liquid eyes, and sweet smiles.

Wished for Annalee when the loud speaker played las Golondrias and Cieto Lindo, two Mexican tunes she always played and sang to on the piano.

The horses were magnificent, wonderfully bred and trained, responding quickly and quietly to their rider's commands. One owner described his elegant chestnut mount to Joe as "muy tranquilo."

We were distressed when an eye-catching powerful gray stud was injured in the steerthrowing event. At first it appeared as if he had broken a leg, but the next day, a report circulated the horse would recover.

Charriada in Villa Acuña

Loved the eight young girls from Saltillo, riding sidesaddle, in unison and gowned in ivory dresses trimmed in green and purple braid. The riding demonstration they presented was one of great skill and beauty. Their horses passed each other quickly and competently while completing certain intricate patterns.

Later we drove to the small town of Zaragosa, which I had never visited, was taken by its huge pecan trees and the charming irrigation ditches formed by springs. Joe explained this area of Mexico has a very shallow water table, and this wet spring the plant growth was verdant, as was the ranch. High-horned, crossbred cows were sleek and fat; their stout calves peered out at the gringos from huisache and guarjillo brush. The tanks were full, and we enjoyed a merendaro by a huge cement water tank.

Perfect finale to pleasant hours passed in Mexico.

Memorial Day weekend found us attending a similar event, but this time located in my beloved hometown, Utopia. New to Utopia, the 2nd Annual Ranch Rodeo, provided thrills and entertainment for the audience, while the cowboys involved worked very hard, as the members of the 11 teams participated in every event.

Events were: bronc riding, one member of each team must ride a bronc for 8 seconds, stock saddle and two hands allowed; wild cow milking, each team must rope a cow out of the herd, milk her, and cross the finish line with a least a drop of milk in the bottle; penning and mugging, each team sorts the numbered cow they drew from the herd, pens her at the end of the arena, ropes and mugs her, then ties three legs; branding, team must head and heel numbered cow, brand her (paint), run back to the fire.

These different set of rodeo events presented formidable problems to the teams involved, which came from far and near. Fast paced and lots of action provided an interesting and different type of horsemanship from which we witnessed at the charriada, but enjoyed equally.

Always uplifting to return to Utopia and especially to find the canyon looking spectacular with the river's sparkling waters, and a mantel of green covering the countryside.

Writer Reminded of July 2002

Tuesday preceding July 4th holiday, and the skies are pouring out water. Viper is showing large red clumps all over the radar screen, and local rivers and creeks are beyond flood stage. Is this a replay of July, 2002? All of us in our area of Texas are loath to cry ENOUGH! But the wet weather is beginning to damage crops in some parts, and we would love to avoid the destruction and the loss of life and property that follow the paths of too much water coursing down streams and low lying areas.

Time in its flight brings many faces and events into focus. Last week a group of amigas assembled to pick green beans. Naturally among four women the discussion ensued describing how we'd prepare and keep them fresh. Years ago Sophie and I used to wash, snap, and can them in the pressure canner. Then we'd have attractive jars of green beans lining our pantries, much labor involved.

A daughter of one of our group provided us with new green bags that keep produce fresh longer; great point about the bags is they really work. A consensus among us brought agreement we'd only boil the beans 7 minutes, drain, and add seasoning. But I did not promise to forego frying bacon first and browning the beans, and adding the bacon as Biggie Wentworth did. Growing up with that taste in your memory bank makes all other recipes pale in comparison.

Attended Sabinal Methodist Sunday and enjoyed the service presided over by new pastor Walter Hoke, who mentioned he had been

Furniture designed and constructed by Rob and Carolyn Ridout

an accountant and also served in the military. The Hokes come from a part-time pastorate at Sentiss, Texas, and Carol is attending seminary in Austin several times weekly. Hopefully they'll find the parsonage satisfactory and settle into the swing of Sabinal – welcome and Godspeed.

Am anticipating the opening of the West Main Library Archives and Museum in July. Took a sneak preview tour several weeks ago and was overwhelmed by the scope and vision of those involved in planning and designing the facility.

Driving by last week almost crashed while staring at the grand improvement of the grounds. The trees are sensational, and with grass cover and plantings, the entire repository will be spectacular, a library for- all of Uvalde and visitors to use explore, and enjoy. Plus an edifice signifying the patronage and support of many Uvalde County citizens.

Visited the recently remodeled Neal's Lodge for Sunday lunch and found it to be spacious and in keeping with the feeling of the original structure. Was especially enchanted by the new deck where one can dine outdoors, as well as enjoy the view of the crystal clear waters of the Frio flowing by.

Need to check with Mary-Anna to learn the date when her grandparents began to operate this resort to which families return season after season due to its warm and easygoing atmosphere.

My friend, Marylana Driskill, took charge and guided me to a table and gave me an update on her Dad, Robert.

Marylana was one of my star Sunday school students in days past, and in August she will enter Texas A&M University. Along with her sister Robin, she has devoted many hours and support to Robert's recovery. May your days at Aggieland be productive and pleasant, friend.

Rob and Carolyn Ridout have labored to construct a desk and set of bookcases for my office here on the banks of the Nueces. Saturday they were installed and it is difficult to get much accomplished for staring at the Chinese red and aqua shelves, which I love, home now to my many books. The Ridouts put a special Western touch with nail heads and a handsome pine top on the desk.

Shall enjoy every minute I pass working with the unique furniture.

Healing Power of Lavender

"With immediacy and intensity smell activates memory, allowing our minds to travel freely in time." -Tom Robbins

Did not purchase the Texas Monthly issue for the cover of Kinky Freidman dressed as "the Queen," but rather for the article entitled, "Is This Texas or Provence?" And it proved worth the price, as it provided information of a lavender farm open to the public near Blanco. Now myself plus several amigas are nuts for lavender, and most of the products, which incorporate the plant with its lovely, soothing scent.

So early one July morn, we set out to find the fields of lavender touted in TM. At the Blanco courthouse we found friends Fannie and Joe who had motored over from Driftwood to meet us. Joe is familiar with eastern Hill Country terrain as he has homesteaded in that part of Texas many years now.

Turning down River Run road paralleling the crystal clear Blanco River, we veered right into a picture perfect landscape, oak trees shading a stucco farmhouse and lavender fields blooming in the back of the structures.

Out to greet us was Charley, the owner, retired from Beaumont into a state of lavender bliss in the Hill Country. First he apologized for the poor production of blooms on the plants. But being ranch and farm wives, we understood completely when he explained the wet weather had played havoc with the flowering season. There were flowers enough for us and soon we set to snipping our own bouquets.

This was my first experience to see lavender growing, with its rounded perfectly shaped dome plants in straight rows presenting a pretty picture, and the aroma is, of course, heavenly. Next Charlie explained the mechanics of his new distillery, which transforms the plant heads into super smelling oil. And then, of course, he could tell we'd be most interested in the gift shop, and he was correct.

Native to the Mediterranean, lavender has been grown since Roman times and valued for its healing and relaxation powers. Science is now looking at it as an original source of compounds that could kill cancer cells. And it loves to grow in hot, dry climes, on limey, well-drained soils such as we have in the Hill Country, thus creating in Texas a touch of Provence.

After being treated to delicious chicken fried steaks at Blanco's Bowling Alley, we set out in search of Fredericksburg peaches, which we found just down the way on 281. Imbibed in tasty homemade peach ice cream, and enjoyed the cool breezes while we visited and updated each other on events in our own little areas of South Texas.

Back at Crystal, I put the peaches in to cook for preserves, hoping I'd added enough sugar as Biggie Wentworth would deem proper. Our grandmother wanted her culinary products plenty sweet, no sparing the sugar. Toyed with the idea of adding a few lavender heads to the preserves, but decided no, perhaps we were not ready for that new step.

But made plans to try some lavender lemonade, even the name sounds inviting, by tossing a few flower heads into the boiling water meant to melt the sugar. And perhaps I may follow my book's suggestion and concoct a lavender bundt cake, which is basically a pound cake with chopped flower heads added, and then coated with lavender sugar. And in October, perhaps a few plants in the garden will produce enough flowers to enjoy, vamos a ver.

El Rincon de Viejo

Perhaps 35 or 40 years have passed since, my first visit to the Rincon de Viejo located on the outskirts of Nuevo Laredo, where we would travel as Mac and Louis Wardlaw were involved in bringing cattle across from Mexico. Louis headquartered at the old Hamilton Hotel in those days, so we'd take the boys and check into the hotel in downtown Laredo.

Mac was always hungry for cabrito, the Rincon was one of the few places where young kid goats were cooked al pastor, over an open pit. Actually, the small café was just an outdoor area whose main attraction was a small shabby bear chained to a tree. T.M. and Jamie thought he was a great grizzly, and entertained themselves throughout the meal checking on the bear's behavior.

Over time we ate many paltillas of cabrito, guacamole, pico de gallo, corn and flour tortillas, refried beans and other house specialties at this out-of-the way café.

So an article in "Saveur" magazine about the marvelous cabrito of northern Mexico set my mind in motion and my mouth watering for cabrito al pastor, different from the method of baking it in the oven.

Called up friends, Rosina and Blas Martinez, true gourmets when it comes to Mexican cuisine, and made arrangements for an evening at the Rincon, and we were not disappointed. The shoulder was light golden brown, and the meat white and tender, falling off the bone. Guacamole had the special distinctive flavor which comes only from Mexican avocados, the small hand-patted corn gorditos were hot and delicious, all combining together to create a memorable meal.

New from the olden days is an ingeniously constructed oven with an open fire ring inside, lined with blue tiles and about 10 to 12 feet high with a decorated tile chimney. The maestro told Joe each day 14 kid goats weighing from 10 to 14 pounds are spread open, placed on poles to stand them up, and slowly cooked above the open coals, never touching the flame.

If you have a yen for cabrito cooked in this manner, treat yourself to a trip to the Rincon, but seek directions as it is off the main route.

Several people have asked me about the article in "The Livestock Weekly" on Ted and Frances Harper, and at the Fisher reunion Mary Tom Harper Hefte and husband, Kenneth, provided copies. Colleen Schreiber wrote an excellent account of Ted and Frances' life in the deep West Texas country between Marfa and Presido.

Ted is the last surviving child of Ella Fisher Harper and Rollie Harper, first cousins to the Wentworth girls and Fishers. I came to know Ted and Frances well the year I attended Sul Ross. They are true individuals who have carved a marvelous life out of tough country, optimists always, ascribing to philosophy, "We can do that. Nothing's impossible." Ted, is 89, Frances, 86, and they still saddle up. A pair of Texas originals.

And the Fisher reunion was a perfect Sunday, cool breeze blowing over the Sabinal River, flushed from the rain on Saturday night. A nice, sturdy roof had been constructed over the slab, cousin Suzanne Bradley, minister at Menard Methodist, delivered a most fitting sermon on our cloud of witnesses, and the, meal spread with Wayne

Elizabeth Burns showing her heifer at Livestock Show

Boyce's brisket as main course was homecooked reunion fare.

Weren't the Reagan services some of the most inspiring and dignified programming to be aired over television in many a day?

What a guy he was, what a gal she was, a class act. Together they gave America their best, and we are richer for the picture they painted of how marriage can be.

Friends and family ask of Elizabeth Burns' condition. It has been a tough situation, after the first chemotherapy treatment at M.D. Anderson, she developed several complications. As of this date, June 15, she is improved and able to take several hours out of hospital daily. Our family asks for your continued prayers in her behalf.

★

Pleasant West Texas Weekend

Had heard reports of green pastures and a wet spring in far West Texas, but we had not traveled in that direction until last week. Heading west, first stop was Memo's restaurant, on the banks of the San Felipe creek. Memos was completely destroyed in the flood, but the family pooled their resources and resolve to rebuild this inviting place on the banks of the creek. Wanted to purchase a cassette of Ray Price's "Los Dos" for friend Fannie, an admirer of Price, but none were available. Had to a settle for a CD of Blondie Calderon's piano renditions playing country and Mexican favorites. One of the Calderon family was a member of Ray Price's band for years, and music is still available on the weekends at this talented family's restaurant.

Stopped at the Pecos high bridge to marvel and exclaim at the tremendous amount of water being carried by the Pecos River; years have passed since it ran so full. Joe pulled off and drove to the impressive rock ledges at Langtry, and the big river Rio Grande was still flushed and muggy from recent rains. We wished this had been the weekend for the cabrito fry at Comstock, but we were a week or so two out of time sync.

The government spent big dollars in building the huge dams after Sanderson was flooded, situated as it is, in a natural bowl shaped basin. Passed the Downy ranch, Longfellow, and nearing Marathon, the country took on a greenish hue, and fat cattle lounged around water tanks full to the brim.

Felt fortunate to have the refurbished Gage Hotel as our destination, and its green lawns, lovely pool area, plus quiet comfortable adobe brick quarters did not disappoint us. Constructed by successful businessman Alfred Gage, the original hotel opened its doors in 1927. In 1978, J.P. and Mary Joe Bryan of Houston purchased the hotel, and now it is a destination for many visitors to the area.

Marathon sports an excellent bookstore, which I did not want to miss. Purchased Sandra Day O'Connor's "Lazy B," an account of her childhood days on an Arizona ranch, John Steinbeck's screenplay for the great movie "Zapata," and "Beneath the Window," Early Ranch Life in the Big Bend Country" by Patricia Wilson Clothier. You will enjoy any of these stories, but the Big Bend memoir is especially poignant.

Since we still had a large amount of daylight to burn, headed the vehicle toward Alpine, and the scenic loop through Fort Davis and the Marfa area. Passing by Sul Ross, was surprised to see my old dormitory Lawrence Hall is now the Museum of the Big Bend, and was astounded at the huge additions to the once Spartan campus. Kokernot Field is still in existence and use, but the appearance of Alpine is vastly altered by many expensive new homes hanging from nearby hillsides, a small Sante Fe.

North of town we continued to marvel at the green gamma grasses waving in the breeze. Found Fort Davis to be a bustling place, many tourists around, and parking spaces around the Observatory were almost full. Two new observation towers had been constructed since my Sul Ross days, and feel sure it would be possible to spend several days exploring the area.

Paisano Hotel, Marfa, Texas

The Indian Lodge seemed to be doing a bustling business, and many horses stood in the pens at the historic Prude Guest Ranch. Wished for extra hours to explore the renovated Olympia Hotel, the Fort, and the Blue Mountain Winery, hopefully next time.

Between Ft. Davis and Marfa stood several of the high tech greenhouses, which produce the marvelous tomatoes available in our supermarkets. The plants are grown in water, by the hydroponics method and the labor is bussed daily between the operations and points in Mexico. Would also be interesting to visit this space-age method of producing food.

Stopped at Marfa to inspect the newly renovated Paisano Hotel, headquarters to the crew and cast of the film "Giant," filmed in the area more years ago than any of us care to admit. The pink facade of the hotel was inviting, the halls held many photos of the famous filming, but the kitchen was out of order – so much for having a meal.

Back to Alpine, sighting several herds of antelope along the way, and dinner at Grady Spear's renowned Reata restaurant. We opted for patio dining, such cool and pleasant high, dry air. My order of chili rellenos was super sensational, stuffed with cream cheese instead of the traditional beef of a Mexican method. Other entrees, strip steak, raspberry and pecan coated chicken were delicious, but the calf fries and gravy were some of the most mouth watering I've tasted, including my own recipe.

Next a.m. the men drove out to deliver the steers, so we gals wandered down and had breakfast at the local drugstore, checked out the shops, which were open and passed a pleasant hour in the hotel's patio. The steers weighed nicely, the ride home was enjoyable, and West Texas provided a pleasant western week-end for those of us who haven't been able to get to Santa Fe in several years.

Cowboy Cooking

In the introduction of his "Cow People," J. Frank Dobie speaks of cowboys, cattlemen, and states, "they represent vanished ways and a vanished tempo." He also writes, "A good cook drew higher wages than anybody else connected with a cow outfit except the boss. No matter how friendly he might be with the hands, the cook, like an army officer, found avoidance of familiarity helpful to authority. A servitor, he nevertheless dominated."

Years ago I gave up riding horses, too much work involved, and no horse pens close by the house, and if you can't take care of them properly, like many other endeavors, best to set it on the shelf. But I was always interested and wanted to be involved whenever it was time to deliver the steers. So decided the fastest and easiest route to a cattleman's heart, plus the way of being included in the action was to become the camp cook. Over time it has given me great pleasure to feed hungry hands and boys and men engaged in the serious business of working or shipping cattle. My red enamel cast iron pots have held many beans, much chili, and literally thousands of tortillas, and they were most always empty after the crew had a second helping.

My first cooking location was at Yucca Switch; Mac had Nacho and then in later years, Cuco dig a hole out behind their casa in which to place a calf's head. I'd go to the packinghouse the day before and purchase several heads, depending on how many days we'd be delivering steers. Come home wash, and season the thing, and wrap it securely in heavy aluminum foil. Then I'd deliver it to the man in charge of the fire in the pit, and make sure he had all the proper equipment needed.

Cuco Sandoval with beef head at Yucca Switch

In my kitchen I'd put a large amount of pinto beans into soak, and when I was younger and more energetic, throw enough flour, lard, and warm water into my food processor to make several dozen flour tortillas. Rolling them out was always the challenge, could never get 'em perfectly round as many cooks with more practice than myself could accomplish easily. Then I'd brown five to seven pound of ground chuck (for my standards nothing else will do), add flour, several tablespoons of chili powder, Knorr's Caldo de Tomate (coupla of Tbsp), boiling water and Viola!, beef chili was ready.

Cuco Salazar, Will Sieckenius, Leroy White, John Smithson, Mason Woodley

When Woody Angermiller was weighing steers for Mac, I could not disappoint him, so had to throw together a peach cobbler, because we usually delivered in June, peach season. But other times cookies would have to suffice, mostly my refrigerator ones, which could be made in advance and stored in the freezer, then pulled out and baked the morning of the round up.

In her marvelous memoir, "This I Can Leave You,"Margie Burns whose husband was the foreman of the Pitchfork Ranch near Gutherie, states, "Good food is the basis for contented cowboys; at the chuck house we had hearty, no-fooling meals. We averaged one beef a week; anything beyond beef, red beans, and potatoes was considered fancy."

So I never strove for fancy, but for flavor. You can concoct quite a few delicious fillings for a tortilla with ground beef, fideo, tomatoes, onions, garlic, green chilies, and asadero cheese. If you're out of fideo, refried beans will do nicely. Baking was never my specialty, so the crew never received hot homemade bread or biscuits, but always tortillas, and plenty to wrap 'em around.

And for us shipping weekends were always festive, as all our hard work and expenses, and time plus worry had gone in this certain set of steers, and now we were hopeful for the weights to pay off. So I'd get on the phone and invite friends and family to join us for lunch, since I'd be cooking for a crowd anyway. Annalee and Henry Fisher and Aunt Lola joined us one year at Yucca, Father James Dudley blessed our meal one season at La Loma, Margaret Kennedy loved being included, as well as Haldydene and Jerry Aaron, Sophie & Eddie. Over the years Sam & Ross Horton arrived to help, as did Leroy White, Bill Kennedy, Kenny

Spence, John Smithson, always Will Sieckenius, Mark Vanham, TM, Jamie, Woody plus the boys receiving the cattle and perhaps some truck drivers.

So this past week it felt as old times when I loaded the red pot and pans into the red Explorer and headed toward the Chaparral pens with lunch for the crew. One day I chose chicken fried steak as the basis for the grub, and carne guisada the next day. It's fun to see the faces light up and everyone take a break when the cookie arrives. And best of all your efforts are appreciated, and received with smiles, thanks, and you're left with clean pans.

Service Proves Meaningful

July 12, 83 degrees at Crystal, cool breezes blowing in off the Gulf, shower clouds hanging low on the horizon. Crepe myrtles dripping lavender, rosy pink, watermelon blooms onto the St Augustine. Can this be South Texas?

Sunday afternoon we drove through a Bermuda grass pasture home to the crossbred cows. Some had recently been transplanted from the vicinity of Freer, and by the contented gaze on their faces, and the size of their body weight (approx 1,200 pounds) they must feel as if they've fallen into paradise. New calves were sleek and sassy; there has been no shortage in their mother's milk supply. Life somehow seems more fulfilling with cows and calves in it.

Got an early start in order to attend the 100th year celebration at Knippa's Emmanuel Lutheran Church Sunday. I felt it would be a meaningful, memorable service, not to be missed, and I was correct.

The sanctuary was packed with members, people returning to their childhood church, visitors, and those of us whose lives had been touched by its outreach.

The service was led by the presiding minister, Bill Snooks. Former pastors Walter Hildebrandt, Daryl Knox, and Robert Schlortt participated as lectors. Bishop Ray Tieman, who presides over the Southwestern Texas Synod, delivered the message centered on the scripture of the Good Samaritan.

And in his closing the Bishop reminded us, "We are the pioneers on the Frontiers of Faith for the next generations."

Sitting in my pew, easy to see names and faces, which had touched our lives while farming in the Knippa area. Steady, hard working, God-fearing people of the land: Niemeyers, Falkenburgs, Dornbusches, Schawes, Mueckes, Kellings, Sanderlins, Langners, Knippas, Edes, Meyers, Reagans, and oh, so many more. A huge flow of gratitude poured over my head and ran down upon my shoulders for the opportunity God afforded us by being able to pass many years living and working among such enterprising friends.

Shook Reverend Walter Hildebrandt's hand and remembered the many visits he paid and prayers he offered for Mac during our days of difficulties. Those are the acts of compassion which live on forever in your mind.

Eva Sanderlin sent Annalee and myself a copy of her recently completed book, "Faith on the Frontier," the history of Emmanuel Lutheran, which was founded in 1904. In her preface Eva states, "Now we have a record of the accomplishments of our ancestors who first conceived the idea of a church on the edge of the frontier of Texas."

Congratulations to members of Emmanuel Lutheran and to Eva; you celebrated the accomplishments of your congregation in a gracious and spiritual manner.

July's long afternoons provide perfect time frames for reading new volumes, or re-reading old ones which we particularly enjoy. Here by the Nueces we've just completed "Funny Cide," the engrossing story of a group of friends who purchased a race horse which ultimately won the Kentucky Derby and the Preekness.

A friend sent Joe "Dark Star Safari, Overland from Cairo to Capetown." Since Africa was the theme, I handed him "Out of Africa," one of my all time favorites, plus "Land of A Thousand Hills, My Life In Rwanda," and now he's in the middle of "West with the Night." Think I'll also suggest "The Heart of Darkness," one of the greatest adventure stories of all times. And we can't leave the subject of Africa without mentioning "The Poisonwood Bible," a spell-binder story of a missionary from Georgia who moved his wife and four daughters to the depths of the Congo.

Arranging my favorites on the red shelves, reminded myself to re-read, "Death Comes to the Archbishop," "Lake Wobegon Summer 1956," "The Five People You Meet In Heaven," and "Mother Teresa, A Simple Faith." Aren't books fabulous friends?

A World Full of Color

"Color is the language of light; it adorns the earth with beauty. Through color light brings its passion, kindness and imagination to all things: pink to granite, green to leaves, blue to ocean, yellow to dawn. In a world without color, it would be impossible to imagine beauty; for colour and beauty are sisters. As Goethe said: the eye needs colour as much as it needs light." – John O'Donohue

Several months ago, April to be exact, when in Houston with my amiga, picked up the book, "Beauty," by author John O'Donohue. It was excellent, and expressed many sentiments which I held in my heart and head, but was not able to place on paper. The above are a few many of phrases that I felt compelled to underline.

My first few months in Crystal, I used the library facilities to compose my columns for the paper. There I met a charming and outgoing woman, Carmen Garcia. Somehow our conversation led toward gardening, and she expressed regret concerning not having more property upon which to expand their garden at home. And Carmen invited me to drive by and view her husband's handiwork manifested in colorful and unique birdhouses, which are displayed among the flowers. I was instantly charmed the first time I drove past 409 East Maverick Street.

Birdhouses and bird ladder

Pride of Barbados, lined the property fence interspersed with espranza blooms in all of their golden glory, and periwinkles danced across the front and spilled gaily and haphazardly out into the street. A golden candlestick was huge, proclaiming itself to be the main focus of the front area. Blue, yellow, red, turquoise, and many other hues of color gave the birdhouses constructed by Juan a festive feeling.

On my next visit to the library, told Carmen I must have several of the birdhouses for the lodging of feathered friends at La Paloma, and she issued an invitation for me to visit at my convenience.

So one morning in August I could not resist the colors radiating from the freshly painted Garcia home, a soft avocado green, combined with barn red roof parked the red Explorer in front of the residence, and rang the bell. Carmen was preparing to depart for her job at the library, but assured me Jesus would show me around, which he kindly did.

The backyard held as many surprises as the front, several spaces fenced off to contain the grandchildren's turtles, each with its own pond and many more birdhouses, plus Jesus' workshop. He assured me he enjoyed staying busy, which was easy to see.

Under protection, he raises white quail – taking the eggs, placing them in an incubator, and then caring for the baby chicks in another hutch. The small eggs were beautifully marked, Jesus carefully lays them in a foam rubber nest. The baby chicks are not much larger than a big bumblebee.

Behind the chick house was an area for tomato plants, citrus trees, and the pots containing new plants that Carmen pots and sells to interested gardeners. Naturally I had to purchase several espranzas, and a pride of Barbados, being how mine were still planted in Sabinal.

Driving back to the ranch, I reflected upon the wonderful manner in which Jesus, who is disabled, and Carmen have enriched their lives, those of their children, and their grandchildren, in the pursuit of providing beauty inside and outside of their home. How wonderful our small towns and cities would be if all of the citizens would pursue similar objectives. All of us hold within our own hands – remember Jesus' hands have been impaired – minds and dedication to greatly improve the beauty and quality of our own lives right where we live, and in doing so we make the world around us a happier, more beautiful, better place.

Thanks, Carmen and Jesus, for sharing your handiwork and accomplishments.

Catching up with family and friends

Many interesting people and items occur daily, and give spice and zest to life. Nice to know what is transpiring in the lives of others, and what going out in the big ole' world outside of Crystal.

Cuarto Hindes and Roy Hindes III at the Hindes Ranch

At La Moca we enjoyed a visit with a few members of the Cravey family – fun to catch up on their activities. The sisters, Margaret Davis, Jackie Baker, Shirley Greenwalt, Jamie Harris and Joyce Herndon had recently returned from a sojourn in Ruidoso where Shirley maintains a summer residence. They were joined by the Patterson group, Tela, Allyene, and Rena Jo, and it sounded as if a domino tournament may have been in progress the entire trip.

My memories of the Cravey girls hark back to the basketball games of the 1950's when Shirley and Margaret were Leakey's HS's stars of the court. Can't remember if Jackie was a basketball person, which she may well have, being a member of the Cravey family. Margaret's daughter, Dana graduated from St. Mary's Law School in the same class with our Jamie Woodley. Our Dad loved doing business at PCA with Joyce Herndon; he always remarked what an astute business mind she possessed.

So I was pleased to receive a lovely cookbook in the mail from Margaret entitled, "Recipes to Remember, Cravey Family Favorites II." The dedication states the sisters put together a selection recipes every five years to distribute among friend and family. Am anxious to try Jackie Baker's Cauliflower Salad, Lauren Baker's Ground Beef Stew with Cornmeal Dumplings, Donna Schuster's Southwest Chicken Lasagna, and Joyce Herndon's Peppermint Cloud Cookies plus Leo Lane's Pesto Sauce.

Took a peek at Shirley's marvelous Texas Animals quilt top when I visited Jan Podrovitz's home to pick up my quilts which she had so beautifully machine quilted for me. Shirley's hand appliqued top is a masterpiece of Native flora and fauna, an heirloom. Margaret assured me she was working on a similar one, just had not quite completed it yet.

While speaking of families, had a joyous visit with my Smith (Wentworth) cousins this past week. Invited Doris and Bob Kruger, Janice and Marion Stewart, and Dan and Madis Keath, plus Pattiand John Driskill (almost kin), down to La Paloma for a look around. After the gals inspected the casa, and the men Joe's oat planting operation we headed the vehicles toward Eagle Pass; destination – the Moderno Restaurant in Piedras.

Over the years the Moderno has been a pleasant place to meet friends and dine on white tablecloths, while listening to enjoyable live (never loud) music, and consume delicious dishes produced in the restaurant kitchen. Imagine our group's surprise when we encountered Mac's cousin and long time friend of the Smith girls, Beverly Sullivan George at a nearby table. Beverly's Dad, Hermann taught school at Sabinal in the dim, distant past, and Beverly's Mom was Louise Woodley, so visiting with Bev enriched our day. She promises to pick me up and take me to her home between Crystal and Carrizo.

So dining at the Moderno set me to thinking back to Richard Bennett's interesting and informative article in the South Texas Newsletter concerning the invention of the Nacho. Seems as if the de los Santos family opened the Moderno during the Depression and Prohibition years, the sign states, "Moderno, Since 1928."Don Rudolfo, the owner persuaded five waiters from Mrs. Crosby's in Acuña to join his staff in Piedras, one of those waiters being Nacho Anaya. Quoting Richard, "Because Nacho always aimed to please his customers; he began to serve a toasted tortilla with Wisconsin cheddar cheese (melted) and a jalapeno pepper on top of a toasted tortilla. As the patrons requested the concoction, they realized it needed a name and they began to call it Nacho's special, and from that it was shortened to 'Nachos.'"

Friend Fannie sent a clipping of the Pleasanton newspaper containing the article about Roy Hindes III being named the "Cowboy of the Year" in Atascosa County. Roy and wife Pam live on the Hindes ranch as do their children, Cuarto and Kelly, and Kristi and John Schulte. Kelly and Cuarto are the proud parents of Leroy Hindes IV, and Kristi has her bags packed waiting for the Schulte baby (boy) to arrive. Little Roy and Pam have assumed a leadership role in the organization of the Cowboy Fellowship Church at the show barn in Pleasanton. Roy is only one of the musical members of the Hindes family who provide music for the Sunday services. Congratulations, Roy; your Dad and Compadre (Leroy Sr.) would be proud.

Received a notice from Main Street Utopia that the Laurel Tree restaurant three miles below Utopia would be opening in October. Have taken advantage of the gate being opened as I passed by, and visited the building during its construction. Handsome and attractive, the feature which captured my imagination was the wonderful rock wall encircling the aged oak tree on the property. This will provide an area for outdoor dining, complete with a fireplace. We are fortunate to have such an attractive dining facility in our area.

And WOW! Happened to flip on Dr. Phil (yes, I admire his hard hitting tactics), and found he had taken on the entire town of Elgin to reform. Good for Phil! He states our American values have shifted and cities and towns across the country families are in crisis, which all of us know, but do not know how to tackle the problems. Children are the losers in all of these situations involving divorce, child abuse, drug use, gang shooting, and a complete displacement of family moral values. Almost every family you know is involved in trying to cope with a stressful heart-breaking situation where young children involved. Annalee used to say "It's the children who fall through the cracks." So my best wishes to Dr. Phil on his quest to heal the hurts which families are encountering in Elgin and everywhere U.S.A.

Splendid October Days

"We are in many respects too adaptable for our own good. We can survive in a concrete jungle, even fool ourselves that we are enjoying the amusements and material comforts they provide, and yet deep down we know that something is lacking. We miss our contact with the natural world." Donald Norfolk in "The Soul Garden"

As Pepe and I made our early morning stroll, we discovered several surprises, while drinking in the glorious cool air of an October morn. Monarch butterflies are migrating through our country, and they were just being roused by the warm rays of ole man sol when we were out and about. Suddenly near the house a covey of quail flushed, giving us a start as always – most grateful to have "house" quail again, must remember to scatter some milo for them.

Sunday services were made special at Crystal Methodist by the presence of the New Creation and Chancel choirs from the First Methodist Church in Uvalde. Their rendition of "The Wonderful Songs of Grace," was such a sizeable blessing, I expect it to carry me through several weeks. Afterwards a delicious lunch was served in the church hall, and it was pleasant to renew friendships.

Our kitchen sports a new welcome addition – a handy, handmade cedar stool with Joe's cattle brands burned in the top. Crafted by Larry Crider, it is a perfect perch for a few minutes of bird watching or an additional seat at the ice cream table. And a new San Pasquale tile gift from Barbara and Don McLaughlin is happily satisfied in the Mexican Mayan blue setting. Am an admirer of San Pasquale, but had to leave the one Mary and I constructed of hand painted tiles I had purchased in Dolores Hidalgo years ago in Casa Anita. So now have two saints in the blue kitchen, the tile one joins a needlepoint version stitched especially for me by amiga, Lea Lane.

As I tap this out on the Dell, I pause to ask blessings upon our Elizabeth Burns, age 22, who reenters M.D. Anderson this morning (Monday the 11th) to begin an intensive round of chemo slated for the next 12 months. Our family again asks for your prayers in behalf of this brave, determined sweetie who is recovering from knee replacement surgery. Other friends on my mind are Lea Lane, Frank Dunkle, Curtis Bourn, Milton Harper, Farris Bennett, and Jan Phillips. One of my most major ambitions is to live long enough to witness the defeat of cancer.

Journeyed to Dallas then on to Tyler for the wedding of Taylor and Joan's beautiful daughter, Nacole. An overnight in Dallas provided an opportunity to visit my granddaughter, Elizabeth, who is a year and a half, darling, mild-mannered charmer. Mason, age 16, had broken his leg while quarterbacking for the junior varsity of Highland Park HS. Luke gave us a rendition of a few tunes he is mastering on the guitar. Amazing how quickly children grow; you can almost see them sprouting skyward.

The main question at the wedding was, would our Wesley Noon, age 20 months, go down the aisle with her cousins Trystie and Tessa Brewton? She had all the perfect trappings, a lovely white organza dress, a crown of interwoven roses and daises, a small bouquet, kid ballet slippers, a winning smile, dark curls, and an entire family, (both sets of grandparents) to cheer her on, but would she chose to walk the walk? Why certainly, and she was proud of herself after completing the accomplishment.

The stain glass windows of Marvin Methodist in Tyler are a sermon in themselves, no words needed, so they added to the grace and beauty of the wedding ceremony. And our family enjoyed gathering with Taylor and Joan's friends and family at a time of celebration. Those brave two united five children into a family and have labored to educate each one, the bride being a graduate of the Nursing School at the University of Texas, congratulations to both the bride and groom and the parents.

Have you ever experienced an October of greater splendor? Here at La Paloma, Joe's oats are up and growing, but the usual combat again army worms must be waged. My bougainvilleas are struggling to flower, but some dirty sneaking little worm is chewing the buds; I've been cursing them, but that hasn't helped one iota, so suppose now must march on to spraying.

Sending best hopes you are able to get out and about and pass a few golden hours outdoors these October days.

Utopia Trip Revives Memories

Fresh and invigorating outdoors this a.m. (Monday Nov. 1), after high temperatures obtained a slot in the record books for October 2004. Now if only a few cool puffs of Canadian air will filter as far down as Crystal.

But October was busy even though it seemed to be shorts and T-shirt time. Here at La Paloma we hosted the meeting of the Texas Agri-Women. Everyone arrived bearing their own special salads, and when combined, we set forth a feast such as I have not seen the likes of since the last Fisher reunion. It was heart warming to realize some women out there who still and will cook. No food purchased with money can afford the comfort and satisfaction derived from sitting down to a meal prepared by capable, willing, loving hands.

LD Bownds in front of milking shed at Bownds Ranch, 1907

Then one day I slipped away to Utopia and Bownds-Burns house to tackle a few projects and pass a few pleasant hours in the Hill Country. Took an inventory of some of the items stashed in our barn: a pressure cooker which only Arnold Shwarzenager could lift, a very early type of wheel chair, with three wheels and a cane back and bottom, Taylor and Murray's

181

bikes, nesting boxes for the hens still upon the walls, old implements, and several other "finds."

Still a marvel to me, the old structure (it is fast becoming a centurion) withstood the violent power and force of the 2001 flood. A testament to its solid construction and the durable quality of the cedar posts standing strongly in their places.

Among Annalee's papers, found this excellent photo of Mr. L.D. Bownds in front of the milking barn. Feel sure it came to Mama from Robert Bownds as he kept her updated on the history of the family home and farm.

Called up my cousin, Sid Mauldin Sr. and made a date to meet him at the site of our mutual grandfather Murray Wentworth's barn on the now Bub Mauldin property. In my dim distant childhood memory I envision being out and about the barn with our grandmother "Biggie" Wentworth. Annalee used to tell of the many hours (about 8) she passed in the barn "keeping an eye upon" Bub Mauldin age 2 or 3 at the time), while he rode one of Poppa Wentworth's saddles.

Sid showed me how Murray would store his oat crop in the granary section of the barn, and how he had hand carved a small porthole through which the oats could flow out into his hand held bucket.

Forgot to ask Sid if he had clue as to the whereabouts of the grindstone, which had stood in Biggie's back yard. As a child, I was fascinated with the tool, which we turned with a handle to sharpen knives and other instruments.

Later in the day, I toured "the loop," passing the most of an hour sitting on the small bench in our Jones cemetery plot. A few "naked lady" lilies were showing bright red color, and the "wandering Jew" produced purple blooms after the recent rains. And I felt at home with the hearts and spirits of our family hovering around about me.

We were pleased to travel to the Barden ranch for a gathering of Bebe and Jim's friends and family. Medina county judge Jim tied the knot between Joe and me, so he holds a special place in our affections.

Bebe is involved in the care and raising of a herd of Longhorn cattle, and a few of the wonderfully marked fellows kept an eye on the party proceedings from a nearby pasture. The ranch house was constructed six years ago close to the 100 year-old Donoho barn. And now a convenient guesthouse has been added to the ranch headquarters. Bebe has furnished both houses with special Texas pieces, which put the icing on this extraordinary Hill Country setting. My personal favorite was the boot pattern quilt in a guest room.

And on Friday the 29th, I drove to the picturesque Baptist Mission at Concan for the Jack Graves funeral services. It was fitting they were held in this inspirational country church of Jack's design. I found friends Judy and Jimmy Cavendar in the annex, as the sanctuary was full to overflowing with friends and family. Jim Graves and Dolph Briscoe gave fitting testimonials as to the sort of friend and brother Jack had been.

The family graciously provided the perfect setting for people to gather and greet each other at Neal's Restaurant. I had a visit with Janeille, Gail and Jodie. Gail had moved back to their Concan residence the past few months to be with her Dad, after getting her last Korbel daughter settled at Texas University.

On the drive home, I was meditating on how deeply I loved both Billie and Jack, and my reflections played upon the point that the Graves and Buchanan clans are the "almost" perfect families which we all dream of establishing for ourselves. And they have flourished in that magical setting, Concan, which Mr. and Mrs. Tom Neal endowed upon them.

The Music of Bob Wills

Preparing for Thanksgiving festivities and houseguests was effortless and breezy last week. The chores whizzed by as I hummed "Twilight falls, evening shadows find, there beneath the stars a maiden so fair, divine. Lonely there she kneels to tell the stars above her song of undying love."

Reason for my cheerful demeanor was due to our outing the Saturday before to hear the original Texas Playboys with Leon Rausch. The minute my amiga, Suse Groves, informed me The Playboys would fill the Quihi bandstand, made a vow to be in the crowd. Only once, many Novembers past, had I been present in person to hear the now famous Bob Wills music played by the original band, and never before had set foot in Quihi dance hall. My heart told me I did not wish to die without having heard Leon sing "Faded Love" within those walls.

So when the Playboys struck up "Big Balls in Cowtown," we knew we were in the right place at the right time. Bob Will's inimitable

Western Swing struck a chord in my heart, and deepened the conviction that dancin' on a hardwood floor with your fella to Bob's tunes is about as close to heaven that a girl from Utopia could hope to come in her lifetime.

Ray Benson's "Asleep at the Wheel" band expresses for me the status of Bob's

Leon Rausch and the Texas Playboys

original music in their tribute, "I grew up in Texas, the home of country music, the home of western swing, don't matter who's in Nashville, Bob Wills is still the king.

"If you ain't never been there, then I guess you ain't been told, that to live in Texas, takes a lota soul. It's the home of Willie Nelson, it's the home of western swing, he'd be the first to tell ya, Bob Wills is still the king."

"Everything I Need to Know I Learned in Kindergarten" author Robert Fulghum adeptly describes one evening at the Buffalo Tavern: "The Indian could dance. I mean he had the moves. Nothing wild, just effortless action. Subtle rhythm, the cool of a master. Looking at the band, and then at the crowd, the Indian said, "Let's Dance!"

And dance we did over time. One of the first memories I hold is being 4 years old, and in downtown San Antonio on VE, Victory in Europe Day. Annalee and Henry joining the crowd dancing in the streets.

Everyone was dancing, people were on the edge, filled with raw emotions and they expressed themselves by dancing, and it spilled over and touched me even at that tender age.

Annalee always entertained me with stories of her and Henry's courtship at the Rio Frio dances, which left romantic impressions in her mind. Our Methodist grandmother Wentworth did not entirely condone dancing for her daughters. But they managed to slip past the rules as they all had rhythm in their heads. No one ever danced a meaner Charleston than Georgie Smith.

First dancing efforts for me began at the Utopia Rodeo pavilion, with Adolph Hoffner providing the music, and Henry as my partner.

I struggled to follow him because he had a trick turn and step which I never mastered, but Mama had it down pat.

High School weekend evenings were passed at Garner Park dance floor, the place where every teenager in the area gathered to meet and greet each other. We girls sat in eager anticipation, praying the guy of our choice would ask us to dance when "A White Sports Coat and A Pink Carnation, I'm All Dressed Up For the Dance," came over the jukebox. So many memories of the happy hours we experienced there, every once in a while I considered having my ashes scattered over the dance floor.

On to Sul Ross where I must admit the proper dancing partner was a subject of greater interest than studying Civics, or English 101. All classes would break at 10:30 a.m., giving us the opportunity to gather in SUB and dance on the hardwood floor. At Christmas the big question was would we have a date to the Hoyle Nix dance in the Holland Hotel?

Those of us fortunate enough to attend were heartbroken when we turned into Cinderellas at 12 p.m. while the music was still playin'. But we knew our cranky old dorm Mother would lock us out at 12:01. I was convinced no one ever had asked her to dance, so she had out her revenge on us.

At Texas A&I we danced every Thursday night upstairs (hardwood floor) in the Student Union building. Many romances began and flourished there while Ray Price's peerless voice sang out, "Crazy Arms."

And we kept on dancing at Crider's Rodeo and dance pavilion, the Divide Country Club, Tilden rodeos, Rocksprings 4th of July rodeo, Uvalde Country Club, the Ranch House, D'Hanis, Hondo Armory, Mrs. Crosby's, the Civic Center, Pete Denny's barn, our garage, the Roaring 20s, Cowtown, the Moderno, La Posada on New Year's Eve, and wherever we found a hardwood floor and an excellent band.

Two grand experiences stand out in my mind, one when we traveled to Vegas for a Glen Miller weekend and danced ourselves silly to "In the Mood," "Tuxedo Junction," and "A String of Pearls." And a Cattle Baron's Gala in SA, staged in front of the Alamo, where we kept dance

The Rio Frio School

time to Willie Nelson (in person) singing his classic "Blue Eyes Cryin' in the Rain."

In my volume where I keep favorite quotes, have penned the lines I heard Ross Snodgrass utter when we were all assembled at a dance during the Sheep and Goat Raiser's convention.

The men were all huddled together discussing cattle prices, weather, and politics, but when Jody Nix's band struck up "The Wildwood Flower," Ross rose from the group and announced, "Well, I don't know about the rest of you boys, but I came to dance." And off he and Clarabelle waltzed, leaving troubles behind, glorying in the music they had danced together for some 50 or more years.

So my suggestion to the male population is to tell your gal, "Honey, why don't you buy yourself a new outfit for the Holidays?"

Then search out the location where a western swing band is playing, and take that gal out dancing for her Christmas gift. She'll be in the best of spirits for days to come, and you'll probably feast upon fresh biscuits for weeks.

For the festive season let's everybody adhere to the song, "Put on your new shoes, put on your gown, Big Balls in Cowtown, we'll dance around. Shake off the sad blues, the big balls in town!"

Prime Rib for Feast

Shuffling through my paper cache, came upon this photo which to be timely for November, Thanksgiving, and hunting season. The best count I can come up with is 20 bucks, and five or six turkey gobblers. Mike Marks gave me the photograph, which his dad took inside the Sabinal icehouse sometime during the '40s or '50s.

Mike has a treasure trove of prints his dad made during the years the Marks resided in Sabinal. Someday I hope to take my

20 bucks, and five or six turkey gobblers inside the Sabinal icehouse

Smith cousins to Austin and we'll visit Mike and dig through the photos, making copies for ourselves.

Wednesday a.m. here at the Paloma and finally the sun is breaking through the water-laden, indigo clouds, and is providing a respite from the heavy rainfall.

The project in progress at the moment is pulling the irrigation pumps out of the river, as the Nueces is on a large rise and rollin' our way.

Thanksgiving week is upon us so all the papers and magazines are featuring favorite recipes to prepare for the family feast. We are opting for prime rib as turkey doesn't play well with the beef eaters who'll be present around our table. Purchased a meat thermometer as to be prepared while seeking to brown the roast to the perfect temperature of medium rare.

Hopefully, I'll be able to pull together a Yorkshire puddin' to serve along with the roast. Have memories of dining at Simpson's on the Strand, London's premier beef establishment.

There large racks of beef are served to individual diners from an ingenious cart bearing a large silver dome shaped lid, which slides back, so the waiter can slice the perfect serving of your choice – well-done, medium rare, or rare prime rib. The entire apparatus is heated by sterno, and Yorkshire pudding accompanies the roast.

Simpson's is the restaurant made famous by Ernie Pyle and the many American correspondents who dined there regularly while covering World War 11. At the time of our visit, it had changed little since war days; the large room with very high ceilings was unadorned, the visual eye catchers being the gleaming silver domes on wheels holding mouth-watering prime roasts.

Perhaps you are, perhaps you aren't a Ray Charles fan. But when Ray came out with his version of "I Can't Stop Lovin' You," I was hooked as an admirer of his music. So while in SA last week, slipped away for several hours to see "Ray," starring Jamie Foxx. And sure enough as the reviews predicted, I was not disappointed.

The movie brilliantly captures the harsh poverty of Ray's childhood, his loss of sight, his mama's struggle to prepare him for a life of blindness, Ray's rapture as a small child with the piano and the music it could create, and the public's overwhelming response to his talent. My only regret was that Annalee was not able to attend with me; she loved Ray's version of "America."

What's on your list of thanks this year of 2004? A few items on mine: God's Grace, Jesus Christ, the church universal, America, family, amigos, the right to work and pursue our own dreams, the abundant moisture of 2004, living in the country, a fire in the fireplace, tamales, good health, community Thanksgiving services, books, corn bread dressing, homemade yeast rolls, our President, and being a Texan.

Beefeaters: Jimmy Speer, Melody Hargrove Speer, Anne Hargrove, Joe Hargrove, Justin and Cline Speer, Rancho La Paloma

Recuerdos of Friendship

"Hand grasps at hand, eye lights eye in good friendship, and great hearts expand, and grow in the sense of this world's light." – Emerson

Again we find ourselves forced into the holiday season, before Thanksgiving this year by merchants, Madison Avenue, and the ever-present uninvited visitor in our homes, television. Much hoopla is being made over the fact consumers may spend more of their hard earned dollars in 2004, searching for things which may or may not make the receiver joyful.

Here at the ranch, the festive season is experiencing a slow start shifting into gear. The flu bug bit Mrs. Christmas planner and laid me low on days when I'd planned to address cards, stir up some pecan pralines, and perhaps put some packages in the mail.

All I could accomplish was moaning, groaning, tossing, turning, praying for the antibiotics to kick in quickly, and feebly counting my blessings.

At some hour between 2 and 6 a.m., when pains and aches were nibbling on my bones, and playing rock and roll in my head, comfort descended as I began to review the day before when my friend and I had taken time to polish, shine, and update our vintage friendship.

Ah, the harmony of brotherly love, how rare is a friendship among the same two participants which has aged to 60 years of perfection,

188

Anne Burns Woodley Hargrove and Mary Tom Harper Hefte, Harper Ranch, 1941

flourished and flowered, all the time enduring the ups and downs which the road of life inevitably brings to each of us. Rare, indeed, I should suppose. In his new autobiography, William Buckley states 40-year friendships are jewels in the crown of one's life.

Family was the bond which brought us together early and formed the framework of shared confidences, adventures, establishing homes, raising children, caring for parents, sadness, travel, rejoicing in each other's triumphs and tragedies.

Time has not tarnished the communication between us, or lessened our determination to visit, whenever situations and circumstances permit.

Our latest meeting was planned as a celebration of sorts in observance of our approaching birthdays.

Although the day was dreary and damp, our destination proved to be sparkling and bright, providing the perfect launching spot for instilling holiday spirit. The Christmas tree in a foyer was covered in Mexican papier-maché fruits and vegetables, exploding with gaiety and color.

Turning a corner revealed a nativity, fashioned entirely in clay, cleverly and imaginatively executed by some Mexican artist whose name shall remain ever hidden from us. But its artistry spoke boldly of the reverence the Holy Night holds in his heart.

Together the two of us explored the Earth Store, I chose a colorful set of cards proclaiming peace. She would like a set also, "Sorry, that is the last one." Sad to report I was too greedy to relinquish mine.

Onto our favorite bookstore, must have a copy of Lance Armstrong's "Every Second Counts." We stared at the art exhibit, marveled at the construction of jeweled crosses, wished we had space for one more nativity set.

Driving past our favorite nursery, we tried not to stop, but the vehicle automatically swung into the driveway. There we found an orchid tree, same variety as the one I planted in Crystal, blooming profusely. Admired the marvelous blue flowerpots, MT knew they were made in Vietnam. "Only Mexican pots will work at La Paloma," was my reply.

Strolling under the colored lights draped in the trees lining the river walk we were surprised and delighted by river barges filled of children singing Christmas carols.

Dining under the myriad of piñatas, Christmas lights, and tin ornaments at Mi Tierra, we found all the color and warmth one could want. The coffee was steaming and fresh, and the migas covered with a perfect ranchera sauce. The place was filled with a festive feeling.

Shopping in the Mexican market, we discovered tin tree ornaments fashioned in the shape of the Alamo. Couldn't resist the purchase of several handmade nativity scenes for the tree, and I needed two of the corn shuck poinsettias to complete my mantle.

Took time out to share the recent family photos, a grandson's first buck, Thanksgiving family groups, and the venerable aunt and uncle with a passel of their great-grandchildren.

Also we explored the possibility of launching our trip to see the tulips blooming in the spring, delayed now for several años. Will we ever get off?

Naturally we exchanged books, "Creativity" for me; my offering to her, "The Soul of the Garden."

And as always we discussed the status of our hometown churches, and concluded "struggling" in each situation, but also came to the conclusion, it has ever been so.

Parting time found us energized and invigorated by our mutual enjoyment of being together, and the exchange of ideas and experiences with another who "gets" your slant on situations, and is receptive to your thoughts and ideas.

The most generous of any gift we could present to another during the holidays is love and acceptance in the form of friendship. After all, Christ-

Anne Hargrove and Mary Tom Hefte, Rancho La Paloma, 2003

190

mas is the story of God's gift of his son, Jesus, who gave of himmself to us and others, thus enriching our lives.

"When I am with my friend, I need nothing more. All my desperate strivings recede into insignificance." – Arnold Beisser

Decorations Add Spice to Season

Christmas seasons are always enriched by the many ingenious decorations devised by families; businesses, churches and communities; each has their own originality and spontaneity making them delightful to the reviewer.

A standout in our minds was the personalized nativity scene constructed by Alma and John Ellisor in front of their home on Highway 83.

It was convenient for us to drive by one evening as the Ellisors live on the Mike Pryor ranch located between Crystal City and La Pryor.

Several years ago Alma began conceiving plans for an outdoor nativity, which would convey the deep significance of the Christmas season and impart a setting of peace and tranquility to travelers passing by the ranch.

First she searched for a photograph or painting of a horse to use as a pattern and eventually found one of a pony with its head lowered in a moment of repose.

Nativity set on the Mike Pryor Ranch; designed and constructed by Alma and John Ellesor

This set her husband, John, in motion to do some sketching (he had tried his hand at drawing before), and presto, he came up with a pattern for constructing a horse, then another pattern depicting his favorite cow dog, Patch, and last, one of a cowboy resembling himself.

John's son and son-in-law pitched in and helped cut the silhouettes from plywood and secure them upright. Then John painted the figures himself, and constructed the stable from cedar stays and palm branches found at Hargrove's working pens, so inadvertently, Joe contributed. Alma was responsible for the doll wrapped in swaddling clothes, and much of the labor. The family's combined efforts produced their goal of creating a peaceful Christmas scene in ranch country offering praise for the gift of the baby Jesus.

Warm weather during the holidays made travel easier, hunting not so profitable and tricked a few plants into thinking spring was imminent. Here I congratulated myself for breaking with tradition and putting up an artificial tree. Pay off time came when we disassembled the blue spruce, or whatever the manufacturer claimed it emulated. No needles all over the floor and carpet, no spilled water from the container, no red hands full of pine or cedar needles.

Yes, the mad cow hooked her path into our holiday season and trampled roughshod over the merriment we'd been enjoying from excellent cattle prices. My, how the media loves to create an uproar over any setback in the agricultural industry. Wonder how the food supply would continue if any of these crisis seekers had to operate a dairy or feedlot, grow corn, or run a hog farm for a year.

So many, perhaps most, of the people in agriculture today stay in the extremely volatile business strictly because they love the life and are willing to endure its many risks and hardships, and we get tired of being trounced upon. American citizens have never been hungry; perhaps if so the media and consumer would be more farmer-rancher friendly.

Smile each time I attend Crystal Methodist Church. Greeting the parishioners is an odd pair, an old yellow Labrador, who makes a lazy effort to growl while vigorously wagging his tail, and his buddy, a beagle whose enthusiasm and good will is not dampened by the fact he only has three legs. Considered their presence a sermon as the dogs are at church every Sunday, they help each other, and the beagle is not defeated by his defect in any manner.

A true surprise gift arrived in my name from Jay and Lynn Evans, Austin. Eagerly unwrapping it Christmas morn, I was thrilled to receive "Waiting for Daylight" photographs complied by Janell Kleberg while working alongside los Kiñeos, King Ranch cowboys. Easy for me to relate to Janell's love and fascination of being involved in the everyday work and management of a cattle ranch. She has deftly documented the men, horses, cattle, land, and the method of work involved in running a business.

2005

Christmas Holidays With Our Friends in Argentina

Approaching Buenos Aires from the north, the muddy Rio de Plata cut an impressive course through the Pampas, and formed a huge harbor which encompasses the port of BA on the south of the river's mouth and Uruguay's capital Montevideo's port on the north bank.

Twenty or more years had passed since my feet last stood on Argentine soil, when Kinsels, Lanes and Woodleys traveled south together in search of the fabled land of the gaucho.

B.K. Johnson had graciously obtained for us an introduction to the King Ranch operations in the Santa Fe providence. After much negocios, the men were able to charter a flight out to the estancia, and tour the property. But at that point in life our budgets did not permit another plane for the ladies, so we waited at the hotel in BA. Before they flew away, Bill Lane hung a sign around Lea's neck stating, "No Moleste."

Now return to the land of beefeaters would provide us the opportunity to reacquaint ourselves with the bounty of the land. One of Joe's life ambitions has been to travel to Argentina to view its ranches (estanicas), horses (crillos), cattle and meet the people.

Christmas Holidays caused Buenos Aires to be rather devoid of people, and it seemed strange for Dec. 25 to be warm summer weather. Difficult to adjust to the

Steaks at La Nazarenas

195

reverse of seasons, December is high summer in the southern hemisphere.

So Christmas Eve found us in a traditional asador criollo establishment with suckling pig, cabritos, and beef ribs standing above the fire pit located in the front of the restaurant. Both Kay and I sported gardenia blossoms on our lapels, which we'd been presented by our gentlemen. Flower markets abound on street corners.

A more perfect choice for celebrating the Christmas spirit could not have been found. The menu Navideño contained delicious and exotic entrees of shrimp combined with hearts of palm. The others chose the mixed grill of bife de lomo (rib eyes), while I experienced one of my memorable meals dining on trout topped with hollandaise sauce and almonds. The dessert, fruits with ice cream and liquor was divine – touched by angels. The percentage of butter fat in the ice cream must have been 2000 percent.

Earlier I had walked to St. Martin's Church to celebrate the birth of Christ and to pray for friends and family. The Basilica was decorated entirely with white bouquets and illuminated with white candles creating the perfect Christmas Eve environment.

Friends had provided the contact who made the arrangements for us to travel to the providence of Cordova where he maintains a shooting lodge, and leases properties for dove hunting. Ariel is a polished gentleman with diverse business interests, including his own ranch in Patagonia.

Dove hunting in Argentina is a shotgun enthusiast's dream while their shoulders are still strong. In the guest registry at Santa Ana Lodge, guests noted bags of three, four, and five hundred birds daily during their hunts at Ariel's properties.

The doves are pests to the productive agricultural farms and ranches, as they do not migrate, and raise four hatches of chicks yearly. While visiting the nearby Los Chanares estancia and lodge, we witnessed amounts of birds feeding around watering areas, which were unbelievable to us. My information on the lodge states the property (approximately 150 acres), supports a bird population of 15 million doves.

The property has been greatly improved to support the bird population. Serge (the owner) plants sunflowers (large) every two months around wheat, millet, and corns patches. He has also increased the available ponds on the property, no shooting at water holes or out of trees.

The elegant lodge is entirely furnished by handmade pieces, beds, tables, credenzas, from mesquite wood off the property. Each one is carved with the dove logo of the estancia, and adds a unique flavor and touch to an establishment built for patrons for the special purposes of hunting the doves. People come from all over the world for the experience.

I could easily fill an entire column listing the amenities of La Chanadra alone; we felt privileged to have been able to visit. And I returned to La Paloma with a volume of "Wingshooting," which features the lodge, so I'll be happy to show you its glories

---

★

An Introduction to a Spanish Way of Life

Argentina is an embarrassment of agricultural riches, a land so fertile plus blessed with a mild climate, and its Pampas are watered annually by 40 or more inches of rainfall. It is difficult for us who have spent a lifetime coaching marginal lands into production to comprehend. Fanning out from Buenos Aires in all directions lie the Pampas, alluvial plains with topsoil which reach from depths of 6 (2 meters) to 16 (5 meters) feet.

Unpacking the mules

The pampas humeda supports much of the nation's agriculture, primarily growing soybeans, corn, and wheat in the winter season. Mildness of climate permits harvesting two crops annually, and we witnessed many fields of corn and soybeans growing luxuriously without the benefit of irrigation. In and around the city of Cordoba are many agricultural equipment establishments all stocked with the newest and most innovative pieces of farming technology.

So only until one reaches the pampas seca do you see large establishments of cattle and horses. We drove to one ranch north of Cordoba which housed a feedlot for finishing steers, but all also ran large numbers of cows and calves. Joe and Ariel inspected a set of 450 pound black heifers worth 36 cents market value. Being high summer the bulls (there must have been 200-300) were in the bull pasture; most were Beefmaster, but rarely did we see other herds with Brahma influence. The largest breed of cattle produced in Argentina is Angus or Angus Hereford cross.

The timing of our trip (Christmas holidays) prevented Joe from visiting the Excel beef packing facilities in Buenos Aires. Argentina has a beef export problem due to hoof and mouth disease, but Excel feels this will be abolished in the near future, thus providing an opening to worldwide beef markets for the producers.

The world famous gaucho, Argentina's cowboy, is alive and well. You see them on ranches, riding horses on country roads, or working cattle. Leather goods are one of the country's outstanding products, and shops (talabarteria) are plentiful, and offer all sorts of attractive and serviceable items ranging from polo equipment to gaucho attire.

Joe purchased headstalls, rawhide ropes, horse hobbles, and snaffle bits for use at La Moca and La Paloma. Myself, I chose exquisite shoes, belts, necklaces, key rings, bolos, bracelets, all crafted of leather for friends and family.

The best aspect of shopping in Argentina is the nice rate of exchange for the American money, three pesos to one dollar. So we ate beef (ribeye steaks) for approximately five dollars, and enjoyed world class wines, olive oils, cheeses for a bargain.

From Cordoba we drove through some appealing country and decided the place to which we'd return would be the twin resort towns of Mina Clavero and Villa Cura Brochero. Situated on hillsides above the Panaholina River, these charming towns reminded us of Ruidoso and its resort area. A few days here in December or January would be idyllic.

Arriving in the Cuyo, Argentina's western providence, one finds the desert area has been turned into a lush patchwork of vineyards and olive groves. They are all lined by Lombardy poplars and irrigated with runoff from the Andes snowmelt. Mendoza, the capitol, is the center of the wine industry, and it is pleasurable to tour the local vineyards, which also grow all sorts of fruit and nut orchards. By the roadside we purchased fresh tomatoes (homegrown flavor), beautifully packed olives stuffed with cheese, apricot preserves, walnuts, raisins, and dried tomatoes in olive oil. There were so many attractive choices, I wished for a ship container in which to transport the entire lot to La Paloma.

All of the vineyards and orchards are hand-irrigated, so you can envision the amount of effort involved in growing, harvesting and distilling the wine. I learned the grape vines that are planted for table grapes are pruned to form arbors, while the wines for wine grapes are pruned upwards. We visited a family winery that hand produces 70,000 bottles of wines yearly only for sale to their private customers.

Since our return plane tickets were from Santiago, it was necessary to travel to Chile's capitol. For me, this experience was a once-in-a-lifetime adventure. The highest peak in the Western Hemisphere is the Cerro Aconcagua, 6,960 meters or 22,834 feet, and is situated near the camino de Andes, from Argentina to Chile.

While passing by the mountain, we sighted a train of pack mules numbering 120 or more, so naturally we had to stop for photographs. The teamsters were having hell unpacking the loads, and in order to manage the mules, they would wrap and tie their jackets over the animal's heads. The mules carry supplies to base camps for expeditions attempting to climb the Aconcagua.

Clear water poured from high ravines flowing into the Rio Mendoza, and we stopped for lunch at laguna de los Horcones, a green lake at the mountain's base. Our time in Argentina had been a lovely introduction to its Spanish way of life and the rich productive lands. Joe said if we were 20 years younger, we'd just stay. Vamos a ver.

A Taste of Authentic Cuisine

Dining in Argentina is a large slice of the enjoyment one derives from visiting this rich, productive land. Its citizens consume more beef per person than any other country, so naturally it held great appeal for us Texans.

Upon arriving in Buenos Aires and getting settled in the first residence, we were ready for a real meal. Our hostess directed us down the street to a neighborhood restaurant which richly rewarded our appetites and expectations. My order in a plain sort of unassuming establishment turned out to be one of

Cabrito asado

the most complex and delicious meals of the trip.

Lomo de Florentine con papas, was a culinary masterpiece. A medium rare ribeye wrapped in very thinly sliced ham, was served on a bed of fresh spinach baked with egg, covered with a white cheese and topped with a mild cream sauce then garnished with fried potatoes in the shape of melon balls. Emril would have been much impressed, and I was delighted.

Christmas Eve found the four of us in a true asador criollo dining establishment. Had to consult my Spanish dictionary as to the correct connotation of criollo, as you see it used everywhere, born in Spanish America or traditionally South American as in Creole was the definition.

Las Nazarenas was the name of the restaurant, and the menu explained: "Las Nazarenas are the spurs with which the gauchos dress on festive days. Today you will take part of this feast. Feel as if you were in the country and enjoy the best of Argentine meat."

And enjoy we did. There was an asado grill as you entered the restaurant, and on crosses of steel were entire lenchons (sucking pig), chivitos (young goat), asados (short rib roast), and a vacios (thick beef flank). Inside was another grill tended by a chef in gaucho attire, and it contained a fire of wood coals. The gaucho regulated the meat temperatures by raising and lowering the grill where the meat rested.

Since it was a holiday, only a fixed price menu was being served. For 30 pesos, 10 American dollars, you had a salad course, entree, dessert, coffee, tea, or house wine, plus champagne. Victor John and Joe chose bife chorizo (New York strips), mine was trout with

200

hollandaise and almond sauce, but memory fails on Kay's choice. Needless to say the quality and freshness of the food was first class, the beef excellent, my trout a memorable meal. Almost forgot to note the ice cream dessert with liqueur and fresh fruit was pure decadence, the butterfat content in the ice cream must have been two or three thousand per cent.

Fortunately for us December is high summer south of the equator, so fresh homegrown tasting tomatoes flavored every salad, plus peaches and plums were being sold along the roadsides.

Driving from Cordoba to Mendoza we stopped for lunch at an attractive restaurant, which had cabrito on the crosses out doors.

Empanadas, delicious meat pies, are served at the beginning of each meal. Then we were presented a mixed grill; sweetbreads, calf fries, beef ribs, and cabrito brought to the table on a square, 3-inch deep pan full of hot coals, topped with a grill holding the meats. The cabrito was the most delicious I'd tasted since our visit to Rincon del Viejo.

The taco sauce of Argentina is chimichurric; salt, olive oil, garlic, ground cloves, bay leaf, oregano, wine vinegar, tomatoes, and minced red and green bell peppers, most similar to our pico de gallo, but without the very hot serrano pepper.

The providence of Mendoza is high desert transformed into hugely productive vineyards, olive groves, fruit orchards, all types of vegetable farms, each individual plot bordered by Lombardy poplars for wind protection.

Again we found many individual roadside stands selling beautiful hand-picked olives, stuffed with different cheeses (I chose Roquefort), all flavors of fruit preserves, dried tomatoes in olive oil, jugs of homemade wines, onions packed in vinegar and oil. How I wished to transport one of each back to Crystal, but I remembered the incident in Spain where we purchased all sorts of canned goods, then had to pay $200 extra baggage weight.

Mendoza is the wine capital of Argentina; people travel there from all over the world to add its wines to their collections. Did recognize the bodega of Concha y Toro, available in our markets, and was surprised to learn several French champagne companies process their products in the region.

Crossing the border into Chile, we chose an Alpine restaurant on the edge of a green lake. There Kay and I indulged in fresh salmon, which we learned is one of Chile's largest export items.

Later on the Chilean Pacific coast, we dined superbly on fresh sea bass, choosing from a menu offering toothfish, flatfish, squid, octopus and other unfamiliar sea catches. Our choices were excellent, and accompanied by the real, just fried French fries, which caused us to kick Atkins out the door and indulge ourselves the entire trip.

Shopping after our return home I found creamy avocados from Chile, products from the huge groves we'd seen growing along the Pacific coast. Our world is smaller daily.

San Miguel Ranch

Back in January when hunting season was still in progress in Mexico, we hitched up the Speers' Jeep and headed west of Del Rio for Miguel Chariez's ranch. The weather was cold and windy, the road worsened with each mile, the potholes becoming deeper and wider. After about 75 miles we reached Los Lobos, Miguel's headquarters, located our camp house atop a rocky, windswept hill, unpacked our gear (considerable for two nights), and I turned up the thermostat, grateful to have one.

Our first round in the Jeep took us over a wide, dry arroyo, and back into high country covered with plenty of gamma grass, home to lots of game. We flushed more coveys of blue quail than I've seen in many a year. The area had received more than adequate rainfall throughout 2004, and the cattle were fat, deer in excel-lent condition, lots of jav-elina and doves were at the feeders.

Joe had explained the history of this country, which he had learned from his cattle-buying trips with Miguel. Los Lobos was once part of the huge San Miguel ranch complex owned by George Miers of Del Rio. In the early '50s the San Miguel was expropri-ated by the Mexican govern-

Abandoned schoolhouse and laborers house at San Miguel Ranch

ment for the agrarian land reform movement, leaving Miers only several thousand acres around the headquarters, of the original 700,000 acres he had purchased in 1914.

I was eager to visit the old headquarters, which Joe had described to me. So after two days and nights of hunting we drove about three miles west and rounding a bend, there lay the San Miguel headquarters nestled deep in a low lying area along an arroyo where adequate water was available.

What remains of the buildings give hint of the small village the headquarters comprised.

The main house, white stucco, accented with half-circle arches was large and comfortable and had wonderful porches on both the cast and west frontages. Within the house was a wing for maid's quarters, a large kitchen, living area with an important fireplace, master bedroom wing with fireplace, and blue-tiled bath, a patio with wonderful oven for cooking plus an aviary. Rose bushes were still growing across the front of the house and a high-fenced area for vegetable gardening was close by. A handsome water tower constructed of rock stood in the garden area, as did the foreman's office, a poultry barn, the commissary, and another huge water tank stood above the house area.

Also nearby the main house were two other houses, according to TJ. Jarrett's book, "Kin, Cowboys, Outlaws and Friends," one for the ranch foreman Tom Barksdale, the other for ranch help. A set of horse stables stands within the house complex, as well a set of working pens, complete with a circle of solid posts built to form a bucking arena for Mier's grandson, George Paul. Outside the main house fence stood the rock remains of the original blacksmith shop and garage.

About a half mile distance from the big house across the arroyo are six two-story houses, rock at ground level, wooden second story, where the ranch workers lived. Within this area were also two washhouses, a cookhouse, and on a ridge above, the remains of a rock schoolhouse for the ranch children.

One's mind could envision the numbers of animals and people that would have been involved around the headquarters during its heyday. Jarrett related, "The San Miguel consisted of nearly 700,000 acres, most of it open range. Very few ranches had the complexity of livestock it carried: sheep, goats (meat and hair), cattle, horses, mules, and mountain galisenos (small Mexican horses). Running sometimes between 5,000 and 10,000 brood mares, the ranch sold Cavalry horses to countries in Central and South America as well as Mexico itself."

I was compelled to copy from an old ledger lying open in the ranch office the following list of supplies: 10 sacos de harina mundo (flour), 19 sacos de harina maiz corn 496 kilos (corn meal), 4 sacos de frijol pinto can 410 kilos (pinto beans), 6 sacos of paps (potatoes), 6 cajas de polvo levol (washing soap), 3 sacos de azucar con 50 kilos (sugar), 4 cajas de manteca vegetal (4 cartons of vegetable shortening) and 100 kilos de mi cafe (coffee). I would imagine supplies came once a month by wagon from Acuña to the headquarters, while the ranch most probably supplied its own beef, poultry, pork, mutton, cabrito and fresh vegetables.

Driving away, it was easy to spot Pancho Villa and his horseman on a faraway ledge, and to wonder what it must have been like to see bands of hundreds of mares grazing on the high mesas, and to wish the entire acreage could be intact, the buildings repaired, the animals and the gente returned, so the ranch could spring to life again. What a story lies within those ancient walls, if only Miers and Barksdale were available to relate it to us.

Prepare for Spring

After six weeks of cloudy, misty, chilly, murky, foggy, miserable weather, we South Texans have a remote idea of what living in the British Isles entails. My friend Anne Walston, an American married to a Brit, living near-by Cambridge told me once, "At first living here is an adventure, but now after 17 years the weather is beginning to wear upon me, never any true summer or autumn, just damp, mist, fog, rain, your bones begin to mold ..." So these past weeks I began to identify with Anne, even though I'm living in the tropics.

Burns-Bownds House - ordered from Sears and constructed in 1912, and purchased by Henry and Annalee Burns in 1967

But yesterday and this morning the sun did emerge, and now visions of spring are dancing in our heads, and the Speers are revving up the planters and tractors to be ready for planting corn. At the Chaparral, hail gave the rye and oats a large pounding last Wednesday night, and the wind turned one of the sprinklers topsy-turvy. From the radar reading on the front of the Leader News, looked as if the darkest red square was on top of that area.

One given we are assured, it will be a spring of great glory and many, many wildflowers. So make plans to get out and about and see Texas in full flower.

Trying to get my tomato project off the ground, my friend from Evant recommended this new method: take a large tire, till the ground under and out from the tire, fill the center of the tire with sheep and/or goat manure, make a circle of 4/4 wire around the tire, plant the tomato plants around the wire circle, add an outside circle of wire, only water the plants through the center of the tire filled with manure. The results are supposed to be fantastic. Vamos a ver.

So my antique group saddled up and toured Castroville last week, and sure enough we found the two Sears houses mentioned in the Express-News, And we were fortunate enough to find the owners out and about the yards, so I had a nice interview with both.

A dead ringer for Burns-Bownds house is the A.H. Tondre home at 509 Florence Street. Built in 1912, the house was ordered from Sears Roebuck, it was shipped by rail to LaCoste, and hauled to Castroville by horse and wagon, then assembled by local carpenters Louis Fuos and Sam Etter. The water cistern and other outbuildings were built by A.H. Tondre, his son, Elton Tondre, who lives in the house and has kept it and grounds in pristine condition.

Elton showed me where the back porch on his home had been closed in to accommodate a larger family. And his house has the original pillars, bay windows, fish scale decoration, the original screen doors with spool trim, and dormer windows, and I'd be willing to bet a center living room, such as ours.

Annalee would love the fact the Tondre house has a porch swing, such as we once had at Bownds-Burns, a weather vane, three fireplaces, and an antique iron fence in A-1 condition.

The Nancy and Rick Baes house at 304 Paris has most recently been renovated in wonderful colors. Built in 1911 by Henry Vonflie, a muleskinner, Nancy has spotted some of the house's original light fixtures in old Sears catalogs. Sears not only sold the houses, but everything that went into them. Our house has a marvelous original brass light fixture in the entrance hall, which Horace Mauldin t6ok down for us and transported to Castroville to be rebrassed, this was in 1968.

The Baes home also has an antique wrought iron fence, and an out building that dates to the time of the house. They had made an addition at the back of the house to accommodate more living and working space.

Friend Fanny Hindes reported her in-laws, Leroy and Mazie, had resided in a Sears house in Pearsall where they would move into town from the ranch at Hindes so the children could attend school. And she states the house is still standing, but did not elaborate on its condition.

So feel sure Uvalde may sport some still standing Sears houses, as most probably does Fredericksburg, Kerrville, New Braunfels, and San Marcos – much to investigate.

Our lunch at the La Normandie Restaurant was delicious, and we splurged with the chocolate pound cake enriched with walnuts. Later we toured the Landmark Inn, and peeped in the guest bedrooms, marveled at the watermark on the scale of the gristmill, and decided this would be the perfect setting for a family reunion.

Closed out our visit shopping for quilting fabric at Friends and Fabric, were overwhelmed at the extensive selection. And classes are available for those interested in certain projects. Castroville remains a special place in my heart, memories taking me back to the days when Eunice Rainwater, Ann Munk, and I would meet at Stella Strayhorn's home over Dan's Meat market and sew and quilt to the aroma of sausage being prepared downstairs.

Back to Utopia

As you might imagine, Utopia is one of my favorite places on the planet, so my several trips there the past few weeks have added pleasure and given me an update as to the happenings in the Sabinal canyon.

Driving by, noticed a new building going up on Main Street, a source indicated it will be available office space, provided by the Jack McClain family.

West view of Burns-Bownds House, 1913

Nice to see many plants and materials available for landscaping at the library, and we loved the display of Ninnie Hillis handiwork in the glass case and on the walls. Visited with Lanelle Kellner and Tacie Redden at the San Antonio Rodeo, we were all despondent and complaining about Wille Nelson being a no show for the performance. Later I remembered hearing about Lanelle and Bill being grandparents to twins – congratulations to the families.

And I mulled on the fact that Tacie and Rusty Redden are two of the most congenial, pleasant people, you'll ever hope to meet. And after many (how many?) years of being the proprietors of the Lost Maples Cafe, which just might be a business that at times would try your happy disposition.

But you can count on being cheerfully greeted by Rusty and Tacie anytime at the lost Maples Cafe, and be insured a tasty meal. How can one go wrong with that combination?

So as usually happens in life the time has come, can't delay it any longer. Bownds-Burns house must be leveled, replumbed, rewired, repainted, plus a few other extras to bring it into the 21st century, and to keep out the wasps, skunks, bees, squirrels, mice and other pests which are bound and determined to make their home in, around or under its sheltering boards.

My antique-loving friend sent along an article in the San Antonio Express-News giving information on Sears houses, which were shipped by rail, along with blueprints, boards, kegs of nails, roofing tar and shingles, paint and varnish, and perhaps other building essentials.

I remember hearing Annalee and Robert discuss the fact that Mr. Bownds ordered the plans and materials for our house from Sears.

After reading the article I am more sure than ever we have a Sears original. Reading from the Express article: "Classic proportions of architecture were instilled within those kits," says John Grable, San

Antonio architect. Those elements included large porches, decorative woodwork, and creative interiors that maximized every inch of square footage.

Two Sears homes stand in Castroville, one belonging to the Tondre family. So am going to have to make a trip to that favorite Alsatian town to identify these houses, and to have a visit with the owners.

So sad Annalee and Robert aren't able to provide us the details of the old house's construction, and we weren't listening when they were discussing it among themselves.

Friends and family always go out of their paths to provide a special and heartwarming birthday celebration for me, but this year my husband and his amigo Jim Barden came up with a celebration for Bebe and myself, which provided one of the happiest days ever.

Those two brilliant men made the plans for a birthday lunch at The Laurel Tree, located below Utopia, the brain child and creation of Laurel Waters.

Quoting from the description on the hand-out cards, "The Laurel Tree, a charming Guest Table in a European-style rock building, the Tree offers varied, seasonal cuisine with the freshest ingredients available, many grown in the adjoining garden. Owner Laurel Waters classically trained with a grand diplome in cuisine/pastry/wine from Le Cordon Bleu in Paris, and cooked in three famous restaurants in southern France. The Laurel Tree features not only indoor dining by fireside in winter, but also a garden setting under a venerable oak tree, or patio seating."

The menu for our party offered a choice of bacon-wrapped scallops on a field of greens, or stroganoff of filet mignon over creamy noodles.

The delightful desserts of peach-amaretto-pecan crumble were individually decorated with pansies (edible), and fresh mint. The interior decor is charming country French, and Laurel and mom, Wanda, made us feel happily at home with their welcoming ways.

How fortunate we are to have this special addition to our Utopia community, and do not miss seeing the red poppies when they flower on the restaurant property this spring.

Bebe Barden, Chef Laurel Waters, Dorothy Kinsel and Anne Hargrove

Celebrating Annalee's 90th Birthday Party

Difficult to plan and organize with shingles rattling around your eye and up and down the body, but knew the month of May held Annalee's 90th birthday; she was born in 1915, at Utopia, last of the five Wentworth sisters. Our grandfather Murray comforted his wife, Elizabeth, "Don't cry Lizzie, she has black curly hair like your people (the Fisher clan)."

Our grandmother was so disappointed by the arrival of another girl, she and her sister, Ella Fisher Harper joked of exchanging children. Ted Harper was born a few days after Mama, the third boy in the Rollie Harper family.

And I perceived Mother would still be able to enjoy her family, friends, music, and some desserts so we could celebrate, and both my brothers would be in residence at Utopia on the proper date. So I made a date with Mike Carr of Radio Station KCWM AM 1460 to be at Amistad on May 14, with his band in tow.

Called the cousins and ordered the cakes, fixed the flowers, Laura and I got Annalee all decked out, in red, of course and when the fellow struck up "Happy Birthday," Mama entered dancin' to the music, so celebrate we did.

With Sid and Bub Mauldin by her side, it was easy for Mama to keep time to "Over the Waves," "Redwing," 'Tennessee Waltz," and other favorites she pounded out on the piano in years past. And the festivities closed to the notes of "I'll Fly Away," the old spiritual which has been played on the first fiddles in Texas to the best instruments of present day musicians. A happy time for all of us.

Next day we traveled to Utopia for the dedication of the new piano in the Methodist sanctuary dedicated to Mother, her sister Lucille Wentworth-Matthews, and Mariella Wentworth Mauldin. All three provided music for Sunday school and church services over the years, but Lucille gave many years of her life playing the Hammond organ presented to the church by the Frank Jones family.

And Elinor Feland brought the new piano alive with her rendition of "Arabesque," after Minister Deb Youngblood had delivered the most excellent sermon on Pentecost I had heard in all my many years of Methodism. And naturally, we had a feast, dinner on the grounds, afterwards at the church annex. So it was a weekend of remembrances

back - Madis Keath, Marilyn Harbison, Doris Kruger, Taylor Burns, Joy Davenport, Murray Burns, Anne Hargrove
front - Bub Mauldin, Annalee, Sid Mauldin, 2005

for me, and gratitude for being able to return to worship at the lovely, refurbished church of our forefathers.

And now we are entering June, the season for family reunions, and already I have attended one, the Slover family gathering at Rio Frio, and am making plans to be at the Fisher Family Reunion Grounds on Sunday where we always sing, "Shall We Gather At The River."

The Slover family was treated to a delightful and delicious lunch under "The Big Tree" at Rio which is still in the Slover family. Here Phil and Eva's parents established a general store in their front yard, beneath "The Tree." Their white frame house is still in use by the family, and next door another dwelling serves as a Bed and Breakfast.

Claudia Sanderlin, daughters Eva and Leslie were hostesses for the luncheon colorfully spread beneath the limbs of the magnificent oak. Eva had just graduated Friday evening from Knippa Junior High as class valedictorian, so I was glad to present her a bag of books.

My presence at the Slover spread was due to Mary Jo Smith Burns being a first cousin to Eva senior and Phil. And Larissa Burns Linton, husband Kenny, daughters Trystin and Tessa were among the family members situated in cabins by the river. It occurred to me how pleased Mother and Elsie Slover Smith would be to know their great grand-children were frolicking on the banks of the Frio.

Monday, I attended the services of Joyce Sherrill at Rushing-Estes-Knowles Chapel. The speaker, Rev. Jerry Scott, spoke befittingly on

Memorial Day of Word and Joyce being members of "The Greatest Generation," and the sacrifices they made for country and family.

My favorite Sherrill story is the one Joyce would tell of when Word was county agent, and she would hold Mac on her lap as they traveled to out-of-town livestock shows where Mac competed with his Anxiety 4th Hereford steers.

So this June 7, 2005, it is my hopes you have a family reunion to attend, and a home church to which you are able to return and worship. And lest we forget, let's say a prayer of thanks for "The Greatest Generation" whose sacrifices at home and abroad made these freedoms possible.

A Graduation Gift Worth Reading

Received graduation invitations from some of my favorite young scholars, and was delighted to learn of the marvelous scholastic and athletic achievements they have accomplished during their high school years. Trying to think of appropriate gifts, I hit upon the idea of perhaps filling a gift bag with some of the books I wish I'd had under my hat when I ventured out into the university world.

I, like Larry McMurtry of Archer City, Charlena Chandler of Sheffield and Iraan, and Bessie Whitehead Smith of Blanket, grew up in a day and time in the Lone Star State when books were not easy to come by. Charlena in "On Independence Creek," describes her entrance to public school in Iraan, "The library was also on the third floor, and my first sight of all the books left me in a state of awe. I didn't know there were that many books in the world." Larry in an article I came upon describes himself as "growing up bookless in Archer County."

I myself grew rather "bookless" in Utopia. If it had not been for Annalee's membership in the "Book of the Month" club, and a few volumes in the school library, I would have not had John O'Hara's or John Steinbeck's novels to pass the time during dull periods of answering, "Number Please" at the Utopia Telephone Company.

And even in college I have no memories of being required to delve into classics or recent literature. I do remember being required to read Henry James, "The Ambassadors," which I could never comprehend, and to this day I doubt I could summon the focus to wade through a James novel.

And I pause to question why Annalee, herself being a great and passionate reader (as Aunt Lola declares, "The baby (Mama) was never given any chores, but was allowed to lie upon the bed, eating apples and reading books") did not require us to work our way through certain classics when we were young. But she was a Mother with an easy hand, and gave us much leeway to pursue our own passions, mine being sewing, Taylor's baseball, and Murray's the construction of model airplanes, ships, and cars.

Only until I entered Oliver and Anne Walston's home at Thriplow Farms, Cambridge, England, did I fully realize the extent of my personal ignorance when it came to books. Oliver's entire living room (large) was lined from ceiling (high) to floor with volumes as was the master bedroom and his office, and he had read all those books. He had 'em in his think bank; he referred to them in his articles and books. Graham Greene had passed time as a guest at Thriplow.

I was stunned, I almost wept because I realized if I began at that moment, I could never catch Oliver in his knowledge of the printed word, and that made me sad and insecure. Yes, I had already read thousands of books, but not hundreds of thousands, and no education within any academic walls can provide the one that readers can obtain from books.

So, I wish to suggest to every graduate from Kinder to Master's degrees that the internet, movies, video games, Cliff Notes, television do not have the power to expand your mind as books are able to do. And I wish to suggest some to you, which over the years have provided me great pleasure plus added to my education and improved my judgment.

First I wish to encourage you to find a time daily (preferably) early mornings to study a small portion of the Bible and to commit the exceptional verses to memory. Hey, it's the most quoted book in the literary world.

Second, I wish you'd begin and keep for the rest of your days a daily journal of the events, people, experiences, and quotes that make up your world. It's the record of your life, if you don't do it, who will?

Three, begin your own scrapbooks of letters, cards, photos, postcards, magazine articles, play bills, etc., which you treasure. When the Nueces floods I'm bent on saving my journals and photo albums

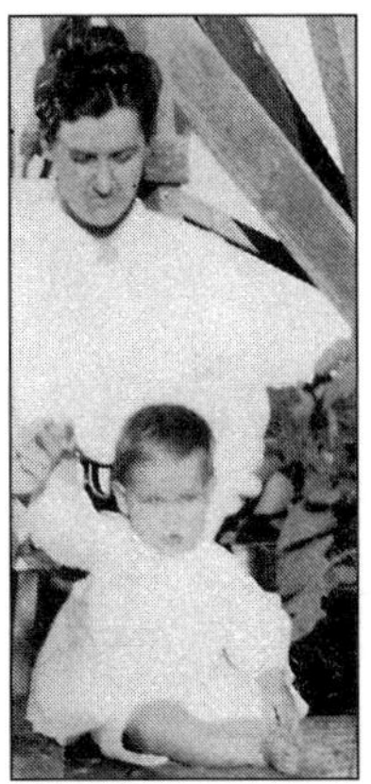

*Edna Payne Burns
and son Henry*

instead of the vacuum cleaner and the silver, because they tell my story. You always hear people remark after a flood or fire, "If only we'd been able to save the photographs."

Four, if you wish to compete in this highly competitive world you'll be one step ahead if you are a reader and comprehend the education that books offer. So, just like Oprah, let me suggest a few titles nobody can afford to miss, we'll call it Anne's List.

Anne's List: "Les Miserables," one of the most readable classics ever, and if you can transfer the lesson Jean Valjean learns to your own life, you'll be a winner; "The Red Badge Of Courage" washes away any misconception of the glories of war; "The Road Less Traveled," Scott Peck's excellent guide to the reality that life truly is difficult, but you can learn to manage the difficulties; "Men Are From Mars, Women Are From Venus," real life is as true as the title, but you can learn from this book how to handle male/female relationships; Harper Lee's marvelous "To Kill A Mockingbird," and of course, "Gone With the Wind" (I've read it four times) is the to die for romance; "The Little Flowers of St. Francis," simple life lessons from that gracious Saint, Willa Cather's "Death Comes For The Archbishop," the first archbishop's life in New Mexico; "Out of Africa," Isak Dienson's interesting life on an African farm; and of course, "The Bible," which I try to read once a year, but now I skip over parts of the Old Testament.

Well that should keep you busy until college begins in August. Congratulations and Best Wishes, Anne.

Hot Weather

Time hangs heavy on my hands these endless July days, heat penetrating every aspect of our lives, and no ticket to cooler climes in sight. So, just as those women in cold climates do in winter when they are snowbound, I'm tackling projects that have been pushed aside until now while sun bound.

Read a magazine article which suggested compiling lists of five favorites so decided to fill in the categories with a few of my choices, you can do the same with your own: favorite movies: "Gone With The

Wind," "Giant," "War and Peace," "Out of Africa," and "Lawrence of Arabia." Heroines: Mother Teresa, Annalee, Dale Evans, My Grandmother Burns, and Dorothy Kinsel. Heroes: Pope John Paul, My Dad, John Wesley, and Ronald Reagan. Books: "The Road Less Traveled," "Les Miserables," "War and Peace," and "Death Comes for the Archbishop."

Rancho La Paloma with new fountain

Favorite foods: guacamole, My Grandmother Burns's fried chicken, homemade tamales, home grown tomatoes, sweet corn on the cob. Places: Santiago de la Compestela, España, Santa Fe, Quien Sabe Ranch, California, Utopia, Victoria, B.C.

This could go on forever with flowers, birds, musicals, houses, museums, golf courses, songs, but the list offers time for reflection on the places you've traveled, delicious food you been served, and the many experiences life has afforded us.

One of my main attractions these 110-degree days is my fountain, which did not just spring up overnight. Last year I traveled to Laredo to purchase the perfect one cut from the stone near Guanajuato, Mexico. It lay on the back patio until 2005 when Oscar Contreras and his helpers journeyed down to add a few touches to La Paloma. It took quite a bit of designing and planning on Oscar's part before the five heavy pieces were upright, with a pool underneath, and water spouting through the center.

Now that the fountain is working daily, it is the main attraction for all sorts of birds along the Nueces. To date I've spotted that rare jewel, the painted bunting, the blue grosbeak, Bullock's and orchard orioles, many rosy finches, the great kiskadee, a vermillion flycatcher, cardinals, pyrrhuloxia, wrens, and many more species bathing, drinking, and delighting in the fountain's splashes. I've discovered birds love to bathe, but the water must be shallow, even the hummers buzz by for a dip.

Sunday, I e-mailed my friend in England to check on their safety after the London bombings. The Walstons live on a farm outside of Cambridge, but maintain a London flat, and have two children living in the city. Anne replied all of her family was safe, but the mental security concerning public transportation had been shaken for English citizens.

The world today is not as safe as in years past for any of us who traveled so freely and easily across its borders.

And on July 2, Trevor Noon arrived in Plano, Texas, a welcome addition to our family circle. Grandfather Taylor was delighted to greet his first grandson, and Annalee would have danced a jig as she favors baby boys. Allison, Doug, and Wesley are happy at home with their new arrival.

Aunt Anne got busy stitching that boy a quilt. An alphabet quilt it happened to be, tied with red buttons, and each square portraying a hungry animal. I amused myself identifying each letter such as S, where a sheep had shoes, snow outside his window, a pot of sunflowers, a sugar bowl, sink, a pot of soup, some suitcases, salt and peppers, shutters, and a stove. This quilt could keep Trevor rather busy learning the alphabet between naps.

Many friends have agreed that the high temperatures we are experiencing are usually reserved for the month of August. Pastures are drying up, corn and milo ready for the combines, and the rivers are dropping. Hope you have a few books and indoor projects for the next month or so; outdoor activities have lost their appeal.

Mexico My Mexico

Picked up my new eyewitness travel guide entitled "Mexico" while tidying my office quarters this morning, and gazed sadly at it while thumbing through the pages; will I ever travel freely through that colorful, magical country, dear to my heart, again?

Because I've yet to view the majestic vistas of the Copper Canyon, shop at the textile markets of Oaxaca, explore the beaches at Ixtapa and Zihuatanejo, eat red snapper in Vera Cruz, or fish for tarpon off Cabo San Lucas I'd planned to have each of these experiences before zipping away to that great mansion in the sky.

But events of the past few weeks have presented a roadblock to my travel ambitions south of the Rio Grande, and now even the Moderno, only 40 miles from our home, is inaccessible to us. Over the months we'd been hearing the rumors, "Not safe to cross the border."

Last November I ignored the warning and Joe's good sense, because I was anxious to reintroduce my Nevada visitor to the riches abounding in Nuevo Laredo's tiendas and markets. The two of us have the sewing, or the fabric bug, and Mexico's fabrics and the folk art constructed with them is in a class of its own.

On Wednesday before Thanksgiving, the two of us were the only gringos on the street or in the market in Nuevo Laredo. In Marti's, my most favorite shop in the entire world, Marti's son Jack offered us a 25-percent discount on any product and proceeded to digress on the sad state of the businesses that depended mostly on American trade.

At Victoria's restaurant Julie and I were the only customers for lunch. It was an odd, almost eerie feeling for the town that is usually bustling with turistas to be so quiet and deserted.

A January visit with our friends the Martinezes confirmed what we have been reading in the paper and seeing on TV: The Texas-Mexican border is experiencing an unprecedented outbreak of violence. Rosina grew up in Nuevo Laredo where her father prospered with his border businesses. Blas is a native of Zapata, crossing the river was daily commerce for him over the years.

But now the Martinezes do not cross the border to dine at their favorite restaurant, El Rincon del Viejo. Instead they have an amigo transport the cabrito to their casa. They no longer feel safe on the Mexican side of the border.

And Rosina's graphic descriptions of the kidnapping of one of their Laredo friends made me know you when travel across the river you are endangering your life. Their amigo's family was presented a demand for $50,000 while the captor was kept bound with duck tape over his eyes for two months until his release could be negotiated.

He was housed in a room with about 60 other prisoners, and treated as a hostage.

Last week we received word of two different people being kidnapped in Villa Acuña and held for ransom until the families could obtain the cash demanded. We're talking 80 miles from Uvalde.

What a sad state of affairs for our neighbors to the South. The economic impact upon the business community is going to be great and create new immigrant problems.

Those of us who have always traveled freely across the Rio Grande and done businesses there must now take into account the risks involved.

Mexico is a marvelous country, one of great diversity, artistry, creative people, beautiful beaches, wonderful colonial cities and natural resources, built from a fascinating ancient culture.

I pray the powers that govern the country will be able to confront the rising violence along the border, and soon, once again, we Americans can safely enjoy its riches.

Days of August

Showers have provided refreshing relief the past two weeks for some, others of us have not been as fortunate, although La Moca received two wonderful rains, 2 inches one week and 3 more the next, but at Crystal the sprinklers are still running. Someone in our family used to remark, "The most lonesome feeling is missing a rain when it's falling on all your friends."

Attended the wedding of Barbara Horton and Curtis Hanna Jr. Barbara is an A&M graduate, and is now working and residing in the Houston area.

New to me was the wedding dance where all married couples are invited to dance, and at intervals the master of ceremonies asks couples who have been married five years to be seated, then 10 years, 20, and the last couple on the floor was Jack and Inez McClain, who have 58 years (think I'm correct) of matrimony behind them.

Barbara sweetly presented her bridal bouquet to Inez, her maternal grandmother, who could probably provide excellent advice for the bride.

Barbara was always one of my outstanding Bible School students, and I was pleased to visit with Jamie Mathis and Amy Bales, also in my classes at Sabinal Methodist, who are now beautiful and bright college students.

While our minister at Crystal, Mark Krause was away attending classes at SW seminary, I decided to attend Carrizo Springs First United Methodist, and felt much at home in the newly remodeled old sanctuary.

It boasted lovely antique stain glass windows, each inscribed with the family name who had presented the window when the building was constructed. Members informed me the building had been 'remodeled a year or so ago to add the inspiring cathedral ceiling, and refinish the rich wooden floors previously covered by carpet.

Elizabeth Kevilus is the pastor at Carrizo and I related to her excellent sermon entitled "The Perfect Storm." Also I had read "The Perfect Storm," and seen the movie, so I could identify with the parallels Elizabeth drew from the story in Matthew when Jesus walked on water out to the fishing boat and calmed the storm.

Carrizo is blessed to have two attractive brick churches First Methodist and First Baptist in the same block, and I also admire the architecture of their Catholic church.

Charlie Wilson

Our churches are life's blood in our small rural communities; they provide learning and stability for our youth, which cannot be found in any other institution and give guidance and comfort to their members.

Later we drove down to visit Charley and Margie Wilson, whose home is located between Carrizo and Asherton.

Charley has been a regular at Southwest Livestock on Thursday for years, and I've recently become friends with Margie, a sweet, competent ranch wife.

Their home boasts many of Charley's hunting trophies – handsome whitetail bucks with long drop tines, and a turkey tom in full strut, but the most impressive is the skin of a seven foot rattler, measuring 11 inches around the middle and sporting 20 or more rattles on its tail. The Wilson's part of the world grows big snakes and this is one of the largest I've witnessed. Out front of the rock ranch house are trees of deer horns, reminding one this country is also the home of huge bucks.

Charley has put together a handsome herd of Charolais and Charolais cross cattle, which I always admire when any come into the Sale. Yellow cattle are some of my favorites and the Wilson's have an outstanding herd, which you might catch a glimpse of traveling, down 83 between Carrizo and Catarina.

Margie told me of the housing shortage in Carrizo due to the addition of Border Patrol inductees at the training center there. Homeland security problems are causing a large rise in new trainees.

So even deep South Texas is feeling the effects of change brought to America by the threat of terrorism. And our amigos to the south are experiencing chaos and killings due to the drug wars in Nuevo Laredo and along the Border.

All of this in a land that people such as Charley and Margie Wilson have known as serene and peaceful, where big rattlers were more of a threat than terrorists. It is difficult to comprehend.

Troubled About the Texas Corridor

July 4th weekend on its way, have a safe and enjoyable time with your family, friends, and pets, at the location of your choosing. Utopia will host its annual fireworks extravaganza again; if you've never attended, pack up and take your children plus food and lawn chairs. It is a beautiful show out under the stars, in one of America's best small towns.

Had some enjoyable experiences in the Canyon this past Sunday, walking into Utopia Methodist I was happy to see Everett Boyce Jr., now pastor at Bandera Methodist, would bring the sermon. Junior and Taylor, Murray, myself, Cathy, and Suzie Boyce grew up together, and it touched my heart to hear the marvelous message our childhood friend delivered in his home church. Junior spoke quickly, quietly, and most convincingly on "Compassion Is the Heart of Christianity." His parents Katherine and Everett Senior were justifiably pleased and proud.

After services Betty and Joy gave me a treat, a trip to lunch at the Lone Star Motorcycle museum and Ace Cafe above Vanderpool. I was aware of the museum, but did not know the proprietors also served food, which is quite different and delicious. Debbie Johncock makes up Aussie (perhaps a touch of English also) meat pies, served in a tasty crust which you may order individually plus salad, or burgers, real French fries, luscious desserts, and after eating, you can marvel at the many motorcycles on display.

Alan Johncock is a native Australian, and a motorcycle enthusiast; he and Debbie have lived in the Canyon for a time, and now are providing a place of interest and respite to travelers in our part of the world. Stop by and give them a visit.

Speaking of our freedoms this July 4th, I have been intending to discuss the "Texas Corridor" in this space. If you are uninformed as I was, here are a few facts from "David Stall@CorridorWatch.org." David founded Corridor Watch while city manager of Columbus, and became concerned about the effect of this mammoth toll highway on towns and citizens.

Quoting him, "Yes, we need rail but don't go out and take thousands and thousands of acres of private land to generate revenue for a foreign corporation just because the state can ride along and take a piece of the profit."

"Gov. Rick Perry unveiled the concept in 2002, calling it the most ambitious transportation plan since the creation of the Interstate Highway system. A Spanish firm Cintra was selected to build the first segment, a 316-mile, $7.2 billion corridor east of I-35 from San Antonio to Dallas, the first leg of a $184 billion project which would eventually lace the state with 4,000 miles of toll roads, up to a quarter of a mile wide.

The plan calls for 10 lanes for vehicles; six rail tracks; and pipelines of oil, natural gas, water, electricity, and telecommunications. One hundred and forty-six acres is allotted per mile, splitting farms, ranches, properties without regards to the landowner's situation. The Trans-Texas makes no provisions for off-ramps, and it gives developers exclusive rights to build gas stations, restaurants, and hotels to service the toll road, so naturally many communities worry that a significant source of their income will dry up, as it diverts revenue from their communities.

Quoting from the South Texas Cattlewomen's Newsletter. "Mr. Dan Byfield covered the Trans Texas Corridor issue. He says get used to it; it is coming. The important part we play now as citizens is to work on controlling what is done is our areas. He pointed out that an unusual power was given the highway department in this bill. They are able to file on your property and on the 91st day the property is theirs. You could probably not get a court date to fight them anyway."

So we the citizens of Texas are facing "1984" in the form of a mega corridor cutting through the heart of our beautiful, fertile state. This is every farmer, rancher, naturalist, hunter, fisherman, environmentalist and hometown lovin' citizen's worst nightmare. The thought of such an asphalt monster makes me want to fight, and despair. Private property is going to be taken in order to produce revenue for politicians and developers to reap profits in the name of progress. In order to learn more of this massive

threat to Texas go to David Stall CoffidorWatch.org"
<infocenter@corridorwatch.org.

Monday I attended the services at Emmanuel Lutheran for long-time friend Woodrow Ede. Dear Woodrow, how many lives and families did he touch during his lifetime of keeping our business books, and calculating our tax returns? Many, according to the size of the crowd who gathered to pay him tribute.

A quiet, pleasant, capable man, but one not even the IRS could intimidate, Woodrow provided for Mac stable, competent help and advice for our business for many years. I was surprised, but proud to learn he held the rank of Ensign in the US Naval Air Corp. It made me admire Woodrow and his family when three of his children returned to Knippa to join his accounting firm. How many families do you know that can work well enough together to establish and maintain a successful business?

And it causes me to chuckle when I think of a remark a friend made concerning Woodrow's pleasant demeanor, "No matter how large the bottom number on you tax return, Woodrow just smiles when he presents it to YOU."

Local Writers Gather in Uvalde This Weekend

The weekend of April 15 and 16 has been designated as the Writers Palaver gathering in Uvalde, and there is much local material to digest and discuss. Here at the ranch we have been busy keeping abreast with all the new volumes of writing penned by friends in and around the local area.

Last fall Frank Miller Jr. was kind enough to call and discuss a column I'd written, and he took his book to the sale for Joe and me to enjoy. Entitled "Growing Up a Cowboy," Frank, aided by his daughter Beverly Meyer, put together photographs and remembrances of growing up on ranches along the Double Mountain fork of the Brazos and other parts of West Texas where pulling a living out of the ground took dedication and fortitude.

Frank does an excellent job of relating how closely his dad, Frank Miller Sr., and his uncle, Clyde Miller worked together over the years.

The two of them were expert horsemen and judges of horseflesh, and I loved the fact that Frank named every horse pictured or mentioned in his stories.

He speaks of his parents, siblings, aunts, uncles, grandparents, and cousins with true warmth and affection, weaving their lives into a design blessed by the good sense of pulling together instead against each other, a feat not accomplished by many families when property is concerned.

Joe Hargrove, Milton Harper, and Jimmy Speer at the Chapparrel Ranch, Zavala County.

Joe told me he had a visit with Frank a week or so ago, and he had received excellent reports regarding his health problems. Write us some more horse stories, Frank; we need a replacement for Red Stoner.

After our viaje to the San Miguel ranch, I was driven to pursue more information about the hacienda in its heyday. Knew our friend T.J. Jarret born and raised out in the Devil's River country, was a member of the Miers family, and had indeed produced a book himself, entitled "Kin, Cowboys, Outlaws, and Friends." So I telephoned Judy and T.J. and they promptly sent me some copies of the book, which has provided great enjoyment not only for Joe and me, but many friends as well.

T.J.'s grandfather was Bob Miers of Sonora and Del Rio, brother of Mr. George Miers, proprietor of the San Miguel Ranch near "The Sleeping Lady" mountain in Coahuila, Mexico. The Miers brothers were members of the settlers of the Sonora, Devil's River, Juno, Pandale, Comstock, Pecos River and Del Rio area.

The photos of T.J.'s parents, Violet Victoria Miers Jarrett and Edward Jarrett, project the energy and attractiveness of two people capable of dealing with whatever ranch life in Val Verde and Sutton counties could hand them.

Loved the photo of the group of the youngsters on horseback, gathered at Noble and Topsy Taylor's arena to polish their roping skills, included are "Pap" Altizer, Benton Wardlaw, Cody Wardlaw, Bill Cau-

222

thorn, T.J. Jarrett, Jim Cauthorn and Hadley Wardlaw. Kay Cauthorn captured my sentiments when we were discussing the book, "It sounds like T.J.," was her comment.

T.J., I wish you'd expound on the Mexico experiences and ranches, and more of your own life experiences; you did a bang-up job with this volume.

And Judy Jarrett has assembled a delightful tale of "Billy the Kid"– a sancho, or orphan, angora she inherited to raise on a bottle. Perfect for children, Judy chronicles Billy's idyllic life at the ranch and the love and affection he maintains for his adopted parents. The photographs are vivid and special, especially the one capturing Billy in spectacular leaps and jumps, which only kid goats can execute.

Dean Anderson of Rocksprings promised me a volume of his "A Century of Rodeo" when it came off the press, and, sure enough, this past Thursday he made good on his pledge. What a huge effort of interviews, contacts and stories Dean has compiled in a large edition featuring hundreds of rodeo performers, producers, horse people and ranchers.

Here I find the story of our dear friend Milton Harper, who has traded cattle with Joe and Mac for many, many years. Milton joined the Marines at age 17, and took part in the invasions of the Marshall Islands, Saipan, Trinidad and Iwo Jima.

Today he still attends the Thursday sales at Southwest Livestock, quoting Milton, "You have to love the cow business to stay as there are many long days and always the uncertainty of the market. Of all the classes of cattle I bought over the years, I loved to buy packer and stocker cows the most."

Other names familiar to all of us in Dean's biographies are Buddy Groff, runner-up for world-champion calf roper in 1954 and 1956; Wilton Crider, who produced Crider's rodeos at Hunt, Texas, from 1946 to 1966; Jim Bob Altizer, everybody's hero, world-champion calf roper in 1959 and 1967; "Hogg Jones," always a figure at the Utopia rodeos; and Phil Lyne, one of the South Texas cowboys who made rodeo history.

And also Toots Mansfield, four-time world-champion calf roper; George Paul from Del Rio, for whom the Super-Bull event is named; Vernon West, a student of "Pap" Altizer, Ray Wharton, 1956 world-champion calf roper; and hundreds of others you will recognize and remember.

And now leaving the hard work and rodeoing behind and on to the fun we lived, recounted by Tommy Allen in his volume "The Honky-Tonk Trail."

Friend Tommy Allen from Carizo presented me his informative book Thursday. Being new to the Nueces River tropics, I was ignorant of Tommy and brother Johnny's musical accomplishments. Had I been aware I'd have made a date for their music to be in the air at Joe's birthday gathering.

In his book Tommy has compiled the history of country music as it began in Texas honkytonks and progressed on to the Nashville stage and recording studios. Annalee would love this as she was always a fan of Lefty Frizzell.

Quoting Tommy, "In the spring of 1949 Lefty Frizzell drove from Artesia, N.M., to Big Spring, Texas, taking a job at "The Ace of Clubs." Lefty would be discovered in 1950 by a jukebox operator who liked his style and the song, "I Love You a Thousand Ways," which the singer wrote.

In the section dealing with the '50s Tommy stated, "In this small town of Crystal City I was visiting with the local sheriff, and he remarked about my playing music, 'It's a shame you don't play Spanish music.'

"Why?" I asked. His reply, 'Crystal has one bank, two lumber yards, two cafes, five churches, and 53 cantinas.' In later years I realized the music being played in most Mexican American honkytonks was the forerunner of Tejano-Conjunto music."

And Tommy makes a bow to our amigo, Johnny Rodriguez, a million-dollar singer from Sabinal with a huge talent and equally as large a heart. Johnny made Suzanne Woodley Vanham's party a time we shall all remember.

Thanks for the memories, Tommy, and now, do you play "Faded Love?" It's my favorite.

Fat Steers And Filaree in Pecos

"Pecos?" I'd teased Joe, "Surely you didn't send a set of steers out to that desert country; what would they eat?" And we'd discussed how perhaps he'd hit it lucky and this just might be the year the desert would flower and the steers would flourish.

So came time to drive out and check the cattle, as soon delivery time will be on the calendar. Early one morning we drove out of the Paloma and turned west on Highway 90, my hopes were high as to seeing wildflowers in bloom, and I was not disappointed.

Years ago I had seen the downy paintbrushes blooming when we visited the Cauthorns at their Juno ranch. Still have the pitaya cactus Bill dug for me, every year it rewards me with its bright fuschia blooms enough, on the other side of Del Rio the mossy pink blooms began to appear on the roadsides. And they had plenty of competition with many varieties of yellow wildflowers, which flourish in limestone soils. My "Wildflowers in Texas" book stated, "As with other paintbrushes, this plant is semi parasitic to other plants, and grows on dry rocky, gravelly or sandy soils." The roadsides were literally yellow from Uvalde to Alpine with every variety of wildflower in that color range still flourishing in late April. Woolly paper flowers were along the roads as well as in pastures, many yellow Mexican hats danced in the wind, lots of golden asters, and recognized the Simpson resinweed, about which "Wildflowers" noted, "both the Indian and the children of early settlers used the resin as a chewing gum."

Huajillo all along my route was covered with its white ball blooms, and in low places retama waved its bright yellow branches. And as always for the Mother's Day season, yuccas were sending up their sturdy, white bell-shaped blossoms.

Mac used to present me with a bouquet of yucca blooms every Mother's Day, but one year we ended up celebrating the day in the emergency room. Mac's knives were always sharpened to a razor's edge, and it slipped while he was flower gathering. It took 12 stitches to close the wound on his wrist.

Between Dryden and Sanderson a bevy of buzzards covered the highway, and as we passed I was shocked to see a large puma, killed by a passing vehicle. Never have had the privilege of seeing a panther in the wild, and sort of wished this one were still roaming the high places.

Delighted to stop at the bookstore at Marathon, found several titles which needed to be added to our library; I chose "Mexicolor," "Milagros, A Book of Miracles," Bob Wade's "Cowgirls," and John Graves "Myself and Strangers." Joe's selections included. "The Old Gringo," "The Big Ranch Country," "Halff of Texas, Rancher of the Old West," and "Bosque Bonito, Violent Times Along the

Borderland During the Mexican Revolution."

Also picked up some cards, especially love this one of Hallie Stillwell and her daughter, Dadie, if you haven't read Hallie's memories, "I'll Gather My Geese," you should avail yourself of a copy.

Hoped to pass the night at Fort Davis, but not possible. When we learned there were no rooms in town, heading north we followed along the picturesque Limpia Creek, lined with tremendous old cottonwoods. On the road leading through the red rock formations we crossed "Wild Rose Pass"

*Hallie Stillwell and
daughter Dadie*

where the ground was covered with white-eyed phlox, the exact variety that grows on Clayton Hill between Utopia and Sabinal.

About 5 p.m. we pulled into the motel in Pecos, and since hours of daylight were still available, decided to drive on out to the ranch and have a look at the steers.

Northwest of Pecos approximately 10-15 miles was the ranch: flat, sandy country, which would be productive farmland if you could get water to it. Driving into the water lot we found a few sleek, fat, very fat steers, wow, what if they had all done this well?

Ambling over the pastures we found sets of 10 or 12 steers, all in excellent condition, weighing perhaps 750-800 pounds. The more cattle we saw, the happier we became. Perhaps this really had been the year for desert pasture. The filaree covered the pastures, almost knee high to the cattle in low places, and lots of the plants still had plenty of green in them.

After more than an hour we became convinced, "Hey, it's really true, these steers are fat," and it's fun when things go right, because in the cattle business they are more prone to go wrong. Next morning heading back home through Fort Stockton, Ozona and Sonora, we were still traveling a trail of yellow flowers.

In Sonora I was impressed with the admirable job the city has done planting Spanish Oak trees over the town, why don't more Hill Country towns pursue this beautification? The Nueces River was a gorgeous green when we crossed; recent rains had fallen around Rocksprings.

My mistake was not bringing some of those filaree plants to Crystal and seeing how happy they'd be in Zavala County.

★

Traveling South Texas

Does this photo of the winner of the 2004 Los Cazadores contest near Pearsall whet your hunter's appetite for big bucks? This magnificent animal was bagged on the La Ceniza ranch in Zavala County by Russell Gordy from Houston. The deer, which was entered in the high fence division and scored 246 5/8 points, would be the mountaintop experience for anyone who loves hunting whitetails.

Summer Sundays can be long and boring if you tire of TV and terrifically high temperatures, so I traveled over to Pearsall this past Sunday to investigate my friends the Machens' new business, Los Cazadores located on Interstate 35. Barbara and Gary have long been involved in high fencing their Frio Town ranch, and raising deer with huge horns.

Last season they purchased the Los Cazadores hunting contest from Darwin Avant at Cotulla, and constructed an attractive hunting headquarters where hunters can weigh, score, enter the contest, and place their big bucks in cold storage. Also available are all sorts of hunting feeders, supplies, and even gifts for the wives who wait. The building is beautifully decorated with outstanding trophy heads of whitetails, plus exotic game.

Russell Gordy was the winner in the 2004 Los Cazadores contest

Now they are constructing a processing plant, which will be ready for the 2005-2006 season, and will offer five different venison sausage recipes, and also prime beef. The venison and beef will be packed through a Cryovac process to ensure freshness.

Also under construction with an eye toward being open for the 2005-2006 season is the Los

Cazadores Steak House adjacent to the Hunting Headquarters. Amiga Suse Groves will manage the attractive restaurant, which will be decorated, naturally, with trophy whitetails. Being as Barbara and Gary and Suze are all excellent Brush Country cooks; the cuisine will be suited to South Texas tastes.

I was impressed and pleased with the effort, thought, and taste the Machens and their partners have put into such an attractive yet functional facility, which people will enjoy visiting even if they are not dedicated hunters. And now with the addition of the steakhouse, everyone will be able to experience delicious meals while trading a few hunting tales. Drive down to Pearsall and visit with Gary, Barbara, or Jack Becker, the general manager; you'll enjoy the trip. My purpose in visiting Pearsall was twofold, as I had planned to attend their First United Methodist Church ever since I had learned Stan Troy was appointed minister. Sure enough, as I entered there was Stan and an amigo strumming their guitars and singing spirituals. It was invigorating to hear him deliver an inspiring sermon, and to see Krista, whom I had first known as a small child, now grown into a young lady with a peaches and cream complexion. Vicki was in the pulpit down the road at Dilley, and Anna had accompanied her for the morning, Stan informed me. All of us at Sabinal Methodist remember Stan and Vicki as the perfect pastoral couple who began their ministry at our church. It was most gratifying for me to see what a true man of God Stan has become while still sporting his boots and guitar. Now, my next Sunday outing shall be to First Methodist at Dilley to hear Vicki deliver a sermon. The Troys are dedicated Christians, and I like to think we got them off to nice start during their time in Sabinal.

End of Summer - Hopefully

Last week my basket I had transported to the Shackelfords was returned to us full of apples and peaches, which Kenny had grown himself. "Never return a basket empty," Kenny said he had always heard, and for us that was a rewarding maxim.

Because this morning I baked two peach cobblers with the freestones, handed one to our amigo Milton Harper, who is recovering from chemo and radiation, and kept the other for whoever is passing through the kitchen at La Paloma. My cobbler recipe is quick, tried many times over and easy, easy.

Will share it with you: 3/4 cup flour, pinch of salt, 2 tsp. baking powder, 2 cups sugar, use 1 cup to pour over the sliced peaches, and the other cup to mix in the batter, 3/4 cup milk (same as the flour), 1 stick butter (melted), and 2 cups fresh, sliced, peeled peaches.

Melt the butter in a small skillet; peel your peaches into your baking pan. Mix your batter: flour, salt, baking powder, milk, and 1 cup sugar. Pour the batter over the sliced peaches, pour the second cup of sugar over the peaches, and last pour the melted butter over the entire mixture. Bake at 325 for an hour.

Our trip to the Shackelford's comfortable home was a treat for me, as I passed much time in the Frio Canyon during my teen-age years. In those days I pined for handsome Stanley Shackelford to ask me to dance at Garner, and shared many laughs with good natured Jerry, but did not truly know Kenny as he was of Murray's vintage. Annalee and the Shackelford boy's Mother were friends, and I remember Mama explaining to me that Rocille was a Tampke by birth, and related to the Utopia Tampkes.

Kenny and Nita have constructed a lovely brick home on the site of his grandfather George Tampke's home, nestled under some stately oak and pecans close to the banks of the Frio. It is a birder's paradise, and I was envious when Nita reported they have three painted buntings at one time plus an indigo bunting. Here I can only boast one painted fellow coming to the fountain.

We dined at Vinny's and enjoyed delightful Italian food.

I joked with Nita when we were growing up in the Hill Country none of us knew where Italy and France were, and now we have an Italian restaurant in Leakey, and a French restaurant in Utopia. The world has grown much smaller or perhaps it is the outside world has discovered our Hill Country and is changing it rapidly.

Took Dick Kinzer's advice and cut back my tomato plants and sprayed them with a fungicide, and they are putting on new branches. Our tomato cage construction worked quite nicely, and only yesterday, July 31, did I serve our last homegrown tomato.

Hopefully we'll harvest more this fall if I keep up the fertilization program.

Pulled up all the pinto bean plants straggling up the garden fence, dispatched all but three of the squash plants, and got rid of the cucumbers completely. How many cucumbers can two people eat? Was amused that most of the people I shared the white patty pan squash with did not know what it was, or how to cook it. Annalee always called it "Depression Squash" as she claimed they ate bushels of it during the dark days when money was not to be had.

Here at Crystal we need a slow, soaking rain, as we missed the 3 inches that fell at La Moca and around Knippa last week. The cotton is heavy with white bolls, and the sesame continues to grow and flower; they are interesting plants. Joe reported the bees were working the blooms. I'm expecting an increase in the bird population here after the sesame harvest.

If it ever cools off, I'll plant some Kentucky Wonders to run up the fence and perhaps some leaf lettuce and Swiss Chard. Everything grows wonderfully in this rich Winter Garden soil, but you are responsible for getting the water to it. It is a pleasure to garden here. I remember my efforts at La Loma were usually disappointing, but this alluvial loam rewards a farmer or gardener with amazing yields.

Soon, I hope we'll kiss summer and high temperatures goodbye, and begin to enjoy the wonderful days of autumn, my favorite time in the brush country.

Santa Fe Soothes With Climate, Culture

Dorothy Kinsel and Betty Leighton at Fenn Gallery Gardens

Time had slipped away, and, over 10 years had passed since my last stay in Santa Fe, so I was somewhat prepared for the aspect of change when my amigas and I returned to sample cooler temperatures and some peeks at art and opera. Yes, the plaza and the four-story buildings were the same, thanks to the foresight of founding fathers who had the good sense to draw up a city ordinance preserving the unique atmosphere of the "city unusual."

But the simple, easy-going ambiance of a small, western trading, post has exploded into a world-class art center where people have chosen to retire or build a second home among the pinons and sage. I mused as to how long they could produce enough water flow to service the influx. Homes of million dollar value are just standard along the roadsides leading to Taos, Teseque and Lamy, and the new residents must have lots of dollars to spend looking-at the prices of paintings and sculpture.

For us the best treat was the lovely, cool, mountain air, a charming view of the Sangre de Cristo mountains from our hotel, and the invigorating atmosphere of art being produced and displayed all over the adobe city and its surroundings. The evening of the opera the moon rose up over the dramatic outdoor facility and cast a lovely illumination over the proceedings, and a cool mountain breeze caused us to reach for our wraps.

First we headed for the portal of the Governor's Palace to scope out the offerings of Native American handcrafted jewelry; look first, buy later is our motto. It is always a joy to me to visit with these talented, industrious people who labor nightly to produce exceptional, fairly priced adornments for the tourist trade.

When I did make my purchases from Rama Chavez of the Santa Domingo Pueblo, she was especially warm and we had a lovely conservation. I learned her children were working and learning the jewelry trade also, which made her exceptionally happy, as she is anxious for their family traditions to continue. The pieces I chose were of the lovely, bright blue turquoise stone imported from Arizona; the pieces handcrafted by the native people are genuine turquoise.

Later I wandered up the streets to the O'Keefe museum, which is new to the city since my last stay. Built with funds furnished by Anne and Charles Marion of the Four Sixes Ranch at Guthrie, Texas, the building is adobe in keeping with city standards. An exhibit of flower paintings by Andy Warhol and O'Keefe was in progress, and I chose Georgia's "White Calico Rose" and "Red Cannas" as my two favorites.

Loved this quote from the woman who came West and made New Mexico her own, "Color is one of the great things in the world that makes life worth living for me, and I have come to think of my efforts to create an equivalent with paint – color for the world as I see it."

Naturally a visit to the former Fenn Gallery, now Nedra Matteuci's, was on our agenda. Inside I chose Clark Huling's small burro for my favorite, but with the price tag at $35,000, it is still sitting in the gallery.

Outside in the enchanting garden we wandered among huge sculptures. Dan Ostermiller's "Rearing Elephant" poured water into the pool through its trunk, Glenna Goodacre's Native American's "Basket Dance" features three Indian Maids, and Ostermiller's large hen, "Penny" were all standouts.

Lunch at Rosalea's Pink Adobe was delightful, and we indulged in the favorite chicken salad, garnished with pimento, hard-boiled eggs, parsley and olives. But a small, quick shower forced us indoors, where we passed the time remembering the many delightful meals with friends and family we have enjoyed in this quaint restaurant.

Still have my small copy of "Cooking with a Silver Spoon" produced by Rosalea in 1956; quoting from the author, "Having come from New Orleans via San Antonio, it is quite natural that my inclinations and tastes in food are Creole. And Santa Fe where I've lived for many years, afforded the most compatible of backgrounds for this type of food.

"Santa Fe is a focal of racial meetings. And in addition to the Anglo-American, Spanish, and Indian cultures, it attracts a colony of anthropologists, artists, and writers, far out of proportion to its size. These also contribute through educated tastes and lives of diverse experience – an influence, a conflict in terms of cooking."

Shall always remember the Girard Exhibit at San Antonio, Hemisfair, so we journeyed out to the city's edge where a wonderful complex of museums has sprung up, including the Folk Art Museum, which houses the Girard collection. There are also the Wheelwright Museum of the American Indian, which exhibits Native American art, The Native American Museum, which displays artifacts of that culture, and the newest is the Spanish American Collection.

In his worldwide travels, Alexander Girard collected thousands of pieces of original folk art, and subsequently the collection found a permanent home in Santa Fe. A whimsical delight of handcrafted toys, figures, trains, buildings, furniture, animals, plants, nativities - whatever the human mind could conceive, is grouped together to form home scenes, villages, festivals, weddings, funerals, you name it. My special favorite is the Mexican village constructed of hundreds of clay pieces, topped by an exotic church, all depicting scenes from Mexican life.

"Tutto il mondo e paese," "The whole world is a hometown," a quote from Girard, applies to the settings created with his folk pieces. A visual fantasy, which enchants both children and adults; try not to miss this museum when you visit Santa Fe.

We noted the plaque in the courtyard of our hotel on the Old Santa Fe Trail, commemorating the U.S. Calvary led by General Stephen Watts Kearny taking possession of New Mexico for the United States on Aug. 18, 1846, almost 200 years before the time of our visit. General Kearny's descendants, Clinton and Cresson, lived for several years in the Sabinal Canyon on the old Bob Harper and Haby ranches.

Leaving Santa Fe I sort of felt the same as artist Gislea Loeffler had described in a framed note I found of hers in Fenn Gallery, "Dear Evelyn, Are you better? It is beautiful weather here like heaven - and my so much glamour! Don't people ever get down to earth? No. The houses, the trees, the shop windows, it all looks like the movies."

Trip East Reveals Cultural Surprises

The invitation was the most exquisite mailing we had received, fine ivory parchment, edged in gold, scalloped and completed with a small wooden dowel decorated with tiny bells.

It proclaimed: Sara weds Ahmed. Mr. & Mrs. Sulennan Malik request the pleasure of your company at the wedding of their daughter Sara with Ahmed, Insha Allah on Saturday 3, September, 2005, reception of Barat, 7 p.m., dinner, 8:30 p.m., Hyatt Regency, Philadelphia, PA.

A first to receive a special invite to a Pakistani Muslim wedding - how interesting, but I dismissed the thought of Joe traveling thousands of miles, and set the invitation aside.

But Malik kept persistently calling Joe insisting the wedding would not be complete with his presence. So one evening, I received the news, "Make some reservations, we're attending the wedding in Philadelphia." Well, Wow! Okay.

Some background information on Malik and Joe's business relationship: Malik owns and operates a packing house in New Jersey and is one of Joe's best customers for mutton goats. The ethnic trade in and around the cities of Trenton N.J., New York City, Philadelphia and the entire cast coast requires a large amount of cabrito and Southwest Livestock is happy to supply it.

So packed my best; don't own a sari, and no time to run out and purchase one, so what was in the closet would have to do. Booked reservations fortunately, as we were traveling on Labor Day weekend, and early Friday a.m. we dashed to catch a plane.

Bride Sara and groom Ahmed with members of the wedding party

Had never visited Philadelphia, but friends informed me it was an interesting and attractive city. Our hotel was situated right on the banks of the Delaware River, overlooking an anchored tall ship (one powered by sailing masts), a naval destroyer, and a retired cruise ship. The Delaware is a mighty river at that point, and I had much more respect for Washington's crew who rowed him across it, remember the famous painting, "Washington Crossing the Delaware?"

First evening we were invited to Malik's home for a Rasme-JHina of Sara. To this minute I have no clue as to the meaning of the above phrase, but I took it to suggest the welcoming of Ahmed's family by Sara's family to the Malik home.

It was quite a spectacular, driving up to the spacious home in the New Jersey countryside, ropes of golden and green lights formed a passageway ending in an arch decorated with lights and fresh flowers under which all the guests passed. I whispered to Joe that I must try harder with the outside lighting display at La Paloma this holiday season.

Then we were led to a huge decorated tent for the guests, the centerpiece inside was an elevated platform on which sat a golden swing backed by richly decorated curtains.

This was the setting for the bride and groom and as the evening progressed the couple seated themselves on the swing and the women guests passed by, they kissed the bride, congratulated the groom, and then dropped $100 bills into a golden basket placed near the bride.

Next we dined on all sorts of Indian dishes, cabrito loaded with strange spices, chick peas seasoned with curry, a sweet sort of pudding similar to oatmeal, potato salad such as we serve, filets of fried fish, filets of fried chicken, these were cooked on the spot, a tortilla or pita type bread made by hand then placed on a hot griddle by the helpers, and all sorts of sweet concoctions made from dates, raisins, coconut, almonds, and sweetened milk.

After everyone had eaten sufficiently, the real party began (remember no liquor served) as the men began to enter into the festivities, and dance, and toss real bills of money into the air around the bride and groom. At intervals, someone would scoop up the bills and then the dancing and singing (there was a band) would begin all over again.

At 1:30 p.m., somewhat past our usual bedtime, we caught a ride into the city with a compatible couple, both born in Pakistan.

He was a CPA who had been in the States about 25 years, and his lovely wife, Tami, a registered nurse, mother of four, was 18 years younger than her husband, who had come to the States as the bride of an arranged marriage. She described to me in vivid detail the agony of loneliness she experienced, being separated from her family, and not knowing anyone in America.

Next morning we made an early visit to the Reading Terminal Market in the Center City of Philadelphia. I wanted to taste one of each type of food available, which would have probably taken the entire day. From Lancaster County the Dutch Eating Place caught my eye, as an Amish girl was producing pancakes larger than dinner plates on a hot griddle. The cakes could be topped with fresh homemade butter, and an assortment of many types of honey, syrup, or homemade jams and jellies. I wished for Jamie Woodley and Dan Kinsel, both lovers of pancakes.

Kauffmann's Lancaster County Produce enticed me with its array of seasonal fruits and produce, Amish crafts, jams, and fruit preserves. Joe was busy checking out L. Halteman Family's Country Foods, an attractive display of home raised ducks, geese, beef, pork, and farm produce. Mr. Halteman told Joe he worked at the local cattle auction on market day. I noticed the price of the appealing rib eyes was $11.90 per pound, in line with the same pricing I found at our local grocery earlier in the week.

After staring at all the wonderfully fresh foods, a great idea struck Joe. "Why don't we rent a car and drive out to Lancaster,

County, I was told it is perhaps only an hour and a half drive from here." Soon we were driving west along toll way Interstate 76 toward the Amish country we had always read about, but never experienced.

Arriving at our destination, I needed to dash into Wal-Mart, and were we ever surprised to find a separate parking space for the horse-drawn buggies the Amish use as their main mode of transportation.

Sure enough driving along the back roads we found the huge barns and silage storage of the Amish farmers, also many dairies home to Holstein cows, two story homes near the barnyards, all in immaculate condition.

The main activity in early September was hand harvesting their corn crop using wagons drawn by teams of either mules or draft horses.

Morgan type horses drew all of the buggies we encountered on the highway; there were many horses and large red mules in the pastures.

Aloud I wondered how long the Amish could continue to bind their children to such an intensive work ethic and strict lifestyle. It is easy to see the suburbs encroaching upon their land; new expensive homes springing up everywhere, probably their farmland is worth thousands of dollars an acre.

Without the Amish where would Philadelphia and surrounding metropolitan areas get their wonderfully fresh food and produce? Are cities going to swallow up the entire earth?

For lunch we stopped at an Amish style restaurant, and ordered the family meal which consisted of three meats: fried chicken, roast beef, and stuffed chicken breast, mashed potatoes, a coleslaw, green salad, noodles, melted butter for noodles, fruit jam, gravy, green peas with carrots, and buttermilk style pie. You could taste the freshness of the chicken, the noodles were homemade, and the gravy delicious. Much too much food for the two of us, but we gave it our best shot at eating most of everything.

I pined for a stop at an Amish quilt shop, but time was of the essence, and we were uncertain as to our return route. But Lady Luck was with us, and we did not make a single wrong turn, passing by Villanova University, and through Bryn Mawr, both of which I'd always read, but did not know their locations.

Back to the hotel, and time to attend the wedding, which was being held in the hotel ballroom. I was the only one not wearing a sari, and tons of REAL 24 karat gold jewelry, but it was so fun to watch the fashion parade. All the saris were pure silk, embroidered in either gold or silver thread, and laden with beaded embellishments. The gal who won my prize as "Best Dressed" was a member of the groom's family from Pakistan, and her jewelry consisted of a gold mesh worn over her head and attached to her golden shoulder length earrings. Her gown was of brown gold tones, covered entirely with golden embroidery and rich beading. We could not converse, but I took her photo, which seemed to please her mightily.

Again we were treated to a huge feast, the centerpiece being a whole mutton goat (did it originate in Texas?), and all of the dishes of the night before plus more American foods, potato salad, pasta salad, all sorts of rice, and many, many sweets.

The bride and groom again took their places on golden chairs, and the entire evening was taken up with the guests passing by and offering their best wishes, and kisses and all of us being photographed and videoed from every possible angle.

The ballroom was decorated with huge tall arrangements of red roses and white, carnations. Almost forget to mention the groom wore a gold lamé turban, an ivory silk jacket embodied in gold, silk slim trousers to match the jacket, and ivory silk slippers whose toes turned up in an elaborate circle.

The bride also wore ivory-silk with gold embroidery; in fact their garments looked as if they were cut from the same cloth, could be as I learned from a guest the groom's family is in the textile exporting business.

Finally at 1:30 a.m. we turned into pumpkins, while the festivities were still going strong, but we had a plane to catch for Texas at 9 a.m., and did not wish to miss it.

The flight gave me ample time to ponder the fact we had seen the world of "Plain and Simple" and the lavish weddings customs from halfway around the world. Cultures were interesting, the Pakistanis especially warm and welcoming to us, Joe summed it up perfectly with the remark, "People are all the same inside regardless of the color of their skin."

God Bless Our Troops, Our Library, and Willie Nelson

Cool air blew into our area of the world, and some people actually received rain before its arrival, but down here at Crystal, rain is a commodity that is hard to come by. Actually I was in the perfect setting when the first norther of the season burst upon us, and it was chilly. We were at Concan awaiting the arrival of Willie Nelson when some of our group began to wish they had brought their jackets. Purchasing some long sleeve T-shirts with Willie emblazoned across the front solved the problem. Being a Hill Country gal, I was prepared with a jacket.

Sitting outdoors and listening to Willie by the Frio River was about as close to heaven as us Hill Country natives can hope to come. And accompanying him was Sister Bobbie on the piano and, boy, can that girl pound it out, she's got music in her bones. Then add the harmonica player, Mickey Raphael, plus the drummers and Willie on the guitar and vocals and you've got a special sound.

Willie and Bobbie were born in Abbott, Texas; their parents were rural farmers. After serving in the Air Force, he began his singing career in Texas honky tonks. After he made the move to Nashville, Nelson began playing bass in Ray Price's band, the Cherokee Cowboys. But it was as a songwriter that he made his reputation, beginning with "Funny How Time Slips Away," and "Night Life," and then the huge hits, "Hello Walls" for Faron Young, and "Crazy" for Patsy Cline. So when Willie struck up "Blue Eyes Crying in the Rain," it was special as Annalee played that tune daily.

He is a unique figure in modern music, clearly one of the most influential of all Country writers and singers. His songs reflect American popular culture drawn from the traditions of Folk, Blues, Standards, Honky-Tonk, and Western Swing, truly a Texas Original. And he puts on a an excellent show, never talking except to respond, "thank you very much," and Thursday night he played non stop for over an hour and a half, providing pure pleasure for the crowd.

Was pleased to become a member of El Progresso, and the first meeting was interesting and informative. Nancy Balzen brought us up to date on the financial standing of the library, and the facts were impressive. The first year the new building has been in service 109,000 patrons have been served, and the use of the new building has seen

Felicia Reyes at Rancho de la Loma, 1979

the following increases: 58 percent new patrons, 71 percent in Hispanic patrons, 70 percent use of Spanish language that teach English for Spanish speakers, 17 percent more children have checked out books, and 287 percent use of local history/genealogy material. These are no small numbers providing information and a perfect setting for residents of Uvalde county, plus tourists and residents in near by counties.

And yes, financial concerns have arisen, a $40,000 shortfall due to the move from a 5,000 square-foot building to 35,000 square-foot building, new federal law requiring 15 feet of fresh air must come in at capacity per capita at all times, more clientele (new patrons up 58 percent), certain state guidelines for operating libraries, group health insurance for a small group, no funding increase from the city in four years, and utilities.

Wisely the library board has chosen to reduce the book budget by 45 percent, reduce library hours, chose a block of time to reduce energy consumption, retain part-time help and reduce the hours of the high school student, thereby reducing the payroll somewhat.

Here's how you can help: volunteer, donations and memorials, support fundraisers, share the facts, and be positive and encouraging. The marvelous building is a credit to our community and a special gift to its reading citizens, and their children. It is a jewel in the center of Uvalde, one we have much reason to proud about. El Progresso and its members ask you to join us in providing support for our marvelous library and the facilities it provides.

In Sabinal Saturday evening, I attended the Wedding of Felica Reyes and Allen Edward. The evening could not have been more perfect. The weather, and backyard setting was sparkling with thousand of white lights strung along the fence, and through the trees. Felica still has the same charm as when I photographed her years ago at La Loma. Her parents and I are proud of her accomplishments as an RN in pediatrics. She and Allen will reside in Houston; I requested to have my photograph made with the bride – congratulations and best wishes to the happy couple.

At Sacred Heart Church Sunday morning, area members of the military were honored, and it struck a cord in my heart to see how very young these people are who have voluntarily placed themselves in harm's way. In San Antonio a young man behind me in the coffee line ordered a mocha freeze, and I gladly paid the price for him. He was most appreciative, and when I thanked him for his service to our country, he positively replied, "It's my job ma'am, and I'm proud to perform it."

As this war in Iraq drags on, we need to never forget the sacrifice our people in uniform are making for America.